THE MODERN NATIONS IN
HISTORICAL PERSPECTIVE

ROBIN W. WINKS, *General Editor*

The volumes in this series deal with individual nations or groups of closely related nations throughout the world, summarizing the chief historical trends and influences that have contributed to each nation's present-day character, problems, and behavior. Recent data are incorporated with established historical background to achieve a fresh synthesis and original interpretation.

STANLEY WOLPERT, the author of this volume, is well-known for his novel on the assassination of Mahatma Gandhi, *Nine Hours to Rama*. He has also written *Tilak and Gokhale: Revolution and Reform in the Making of Modern India*, for which he was awarded the American Historical Association's Watamull Prize in Indian History. Dr. Wolpert, a graduate of The City College of New York and the University of Pennsylvania, has spent several years in India. He was a Social Science Research Council Research Fellow and a Ford Foundation Overseas Training and Research Fellow, and is now Associate Professor of History at the University of California, Los Angeles.

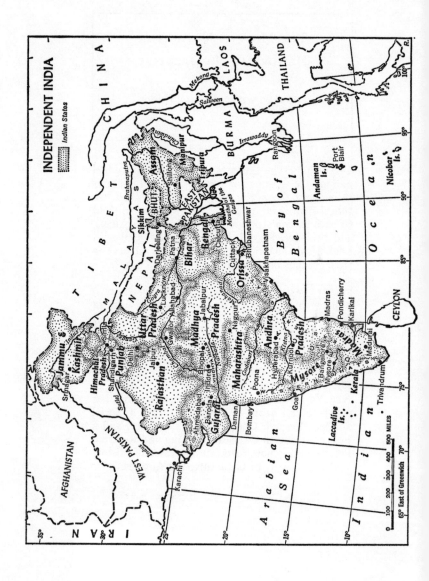

INDEPENDENT INDIA

Indian States

INDIA

STANLEY WOLPERT

Prentice-Hall, Inc.
Englewood Cliffs, New Jersey

Current printing (last digit):

11 10 9 8 7 6 5 4

P 45693, C 45694.

For
Daniel and Adam

India, the second most populous nation of Asia, contains many cultures. No more plural society presents itself to the sociologist, no more complex a course from distant past to immediate present has plagued the chronicler, and no more rich a civilization seals the lips and halts the pen of the historian who would attempt to relate its story. To the American in a polarized world, India is a land of incalculable importance. To the European, where Indian scholarship long has been well established, only China presented similar intellectual variety and challenge. To the British, India was the jewel of the Empire, just as today India is the single most important member, after the United Kingdom, of that unique experiment in historical continuity, the Commonwealth of Nations. India is a land of superlatives both now and historically.

There are, of course, many short histories of India; but few attempt to do what Stanley Wolpert does so well here. This book is frankly present-minded, written from the belief that history may serve a present as well as a past purpose. In this extended essay Professor Wolpert outlines the nature of the major dilemmas now confronting India and shows how these crises arose from the long and entangled Indian (and European) past. He has emphasized broad trends; he has examined the major stages by which the Indian people have moved to their present world position; and he has developed conceptually what is virtually a case study in the emergence of the so-called new nations. The success of this effort is attested to by the fact that we may so readily see from this book: that India scarcely is a "new nation," for its national roots reach far into a legend-laden past. Thus, the present essay is an implicit and thoughtful inquiry into the problem of nationhood and nationalism in an international age.

Robin W. Winks
Series Editor

CONTENTS

ONE India Today   1
Land and People, 2; Government and Politics,
8; Society and Economy, 17; Education, 22;
External Affairs, 24

TWO The Hindu Heritage   30
Pre-Aryan, 30; Aryan, 32; Upanishadic Revolt,
33; Buddhist and Jain Revolt, 34; Hinduism,
35; Hindu Polity, 40; Hindu Society, 42; The
Arts, 44

THREE The Impact of Islam   47
Islam, 47; Islam and Hinduism, 49; Muslim Ad-
ministration During the Sultanate, 54; Mughal
Rule, 56

FOUR British Conquest and Rule   64
Portuguese Power in Asia, 64; Dutch and Brit-
ish Power in the Indies, 66; British Merchants
in India, 68; Anglo-French Rivalry, 72; The
British in Bengal, 75; Consolidation of the British Raj, 84; Reform and Renaissance, 87; The
War of 1857-1858, 93

FIVE Crown Raj, Nationalism, and Partition   101
Crown Raj and the Legacy of 1857, 101; Indian
Nationalism—the First Phase, 109; Nonco-
operation, Independence, and Partition, 128

SIX   The Nehru Era   148

      Suggested Readings   165

      Index   171

      Maps
      Independent India   *Frontispiece*
      India Under the British Raj   100

INDIA

ONE

INDIA TODAY

The death of India's first prime minister, Jawaharlal Nehru, on May 27, 1964 ended an era of independent India's history. To many Americans the names Nehru and India had become almost synonymous, and some feared the demise of the one meant destruction for the other. Yet in its first year of independent rule, on January 30, 1948, India had survived a far more violent shock, the assassination of its saintly "Father" (*Bapu*), Mahatma Gandhi. Nehru's passing was historically most significant, not because of the challenge it posed to India's capacity to survive as a nation, but rather because it marked the final transfer of power within India from British-oriented to indigenous rule.

The image of Lal Bahadur Shastri appeared so much less familiar to Western eyes than had that of Nehru precisely because it was so much more thoroughly Indian. As had so often happened throughout Indian history, the "new" was more a reassertion of the past than any bold affirmation of faith in the present or future. Paradoxically enough, for all the sound and fury of planned economic development and Western-style reform, tradition plays a more potent part in Indian life and society today than it did at the dawn of independence in 1947. Perhaps the ultimate secret of India's unique capacity to endure has been the remarkable ability of many Indian institutions to retain their essential nature despite seemingly fundamental changes. At any rate, in no other nation today (China included) does the past weigh so heavily upon the present.

Modern India, like the timeless cosmic essence (*Brahman*) of Vedantic philosophy, seems a montage of fragments drawn from various epochs of antiquity and ideas borrowed in remote and recent ages from abroad. A cart that rolls through modern Bombay on pneumatic rubber tires is still drawn by a dewlapped brahmi bullock, which looks as though it might have posed for one of the Harappan seal carvings etched by Indus Valley artists more than 4,000 years ago. The cart is driven by a *dhoti*-clad, loose-turbaned peasant, whose dress, manner, and mental attitudes would seem to exclude him from the "modern" world. The genius of Indian civilization has always been syncretic, its primary powers those of absorption and retention. New ideas, like new invaders, while tolerated and often assimilated, have never totally displaced the old. Much like China, India has long proved herself capable of captivating her captors. Because it is recent, the British role in Indian history has loomed disproportionately large in historical studies during the past century. Given time perhaps it will appear but the latest of many "interludes" of foreign rule over India, releasing vigorous new forces, but forces no doubt already within Indian society; transmuting rather than transforming the basic pattern of Indian life and thought.

When viewing the current Indian scene from the broadest perspective four problems emerge as most important: internally, the conquest of poverty, and retention of national unity; internationally, defense of the northern frontier against China, and settlement of the Kashmir dispute with Pakistan. All four of these unpleasant legacies of Indian history are intimately associated with the geographical facts of Indian life.

Land and People

India is often described as a rich land with poor people, or, in other words; an "underdeveloped" and "overpopulated" nation. Some 450 million Indians (as of 1964) seek sustenance on barely more than one and a quarter million square miles of land; thus, India's population density is roughly six times that of America. Yet unlike America India lacks the industrial resources and agricultural capacity to employ her population properly or to feed it adequately. Although about 70 per cent of India's total population labors at agriculture alone, devoting three-quarters of India's arable land entirely to food grain production, India requires massive grain imports to avoid widespread famine. From 1959-64 America shipped India seventeen million tons of grain, and in 1964 India urgently requested another twenty million tons for the ensuing five-year period. The average Indian diet remains considerably below the daily calorific minimum (2,400) prescribed for sustaining proper health by the Food and Agriculture Organization of the United Nations. The life expectancy of the average Indian infant at birth is little more than forty years, or less than two-thirds that of his American contemporary.

Statistics alone, however, offer scant insight into the reality of Indian poverty, which can (mercifully enough) hardly be understood from the vantage point of the affluent. Most Indians have never known how it feels to go to bed at night without a gnawing pang of hunger. Not least among the sins of malnutrition, of course, is how vulnerable it leaves the body to disease of all kinds, especially India's foremost present-day cause of death, tuberculosis.

Though India supports most of its population poorly, the fact that she does manage to sustain the world's second (after China) largest national population, and has supported civilized life almost (with the sole exception of Mesopotamia) as long as any region of the world, amply attests to the salubrious quality of her natural location and lush endowment. Suspended funnel-like south of the Himalayas and Hindu Khush in central Asia, the Indian subcontinent (since 1947 shared by India and Pakistan) is protected from the freezing air of Siberia by the world's highest natural wall. Thanks to the snowclad peaks of this wall the subcontinent receives the bounty of three ever-flowing great river systems: the Indus; the Yamuna-Ganga; and the Brahmaputra. Were it not for these snow-fed rivers, in fact, the fertile heartland of India and Pakistan, the northern sedimentary plain (from west to east) of the "five rivers" (Punjab) would not even exist. Little wonder, then, that Indians have for thousands of years worshipped the river Ganga as their "Mother," and that just as all Muslims yearn to make a pilgrimage to Mecca at least once in a lifetime, every Hindu longs to purify himself with a bath in the sacred waters of the Ganga. So rich is the rice-bearing soil of India's irrigated northern plain that two and in some places three, crops are raised annually, helping support population densities of between 500 and 1,000 per square mile throughout Uttar Pradesh, Bihar, and West Bengal. Such prolific production is also possible in this region because between June and September the monsoon rain adds anywhere from forty to one hundred inches of water to the soil.

Traces of the earliest fully developed urban civilization in India (dating back to about 2500 B.C.) were found in the Indus region of what is now West Pakistan, but it was in the Yamuna-Ganga plain that the Aryan forebearers of North India's present population consolidated their conquest over the pre-Aryans (or Harappan peoples) between 1500-500 B.C. These Indo-Aryan tribes were offshoots of the great Indo-European linguistic family, whose dispersion from their presumed *Urheim* in what is now southern Russia somewhere around 2000 B.C. was of such cataclysmic significance to world history. Thanks to the Aryan conquest, Indians and Americans (as well as all other English, Germanic, and Greco-Latin speaking peoples) are linguistically and ethnically related. Thanks also to the Aryan conquest, northern India acquired its "great tradition" of Sanskritized culture with its many branches of Indo-Aryan languages and literatures, including India's "national" language, Hindi. Uttar Pradesh State, the central and most populous region of the Yamuna-Ganga plain, birthplace of India's first two prime ministers and the home of nearly eighty million Indians today (the vast majority of whom speak Hindi), reflects, as a modern center of prestige and power, the predominance this region enjoyed 3,000 years ago. From this hub Aryan culture radiated throughout the subcontinent; today ten major Aryan languages are spoken in India as the "mother tongues" of some two-thirds[1] of the total population.

Most of India has been far less favorably endowed with water than the rich northern plain. Dividing the Indus from the Yamuna-Ganga valleys is the barren Thar Desert and rugged Aravalli range of Rajasthan. Bleached by a merciless sun, colored only intermittently by droves of wild peacocks, the tints of peasant saris even more brilliant than those lustrous silks of Banaras, and tales of conflict and chivalry barely matched by Arthurean lore, Rajasthan is the dry extreme of the sub-tropical subcontinent. Yet almost everywhere else in India as well, heat, enervating and unremitting, is man's most powerful natural adversary. The impact of heat on Indian philosophy and history can hardly be exaggerated. The philosophic ideal of the Indian is the attainment of mental equipoise, a mood of calm or peace (*shanta-rasa*). Any one who has lived a few months under India's sun can appreciate the practical value of a behavioral ethic enjoining quiescence. Their different political systems no doubt have something to do with India's inability to match China's recent rate of economic growth, but difference in latitude is perhaps a still more important factor. Between March and July, or whenever the monsoon "breaks," much of central India (Madhya Pradesh as well as Rajasthan and parts of Maharashtra) becomes a climatically hostile land of blistering, parched soil.

[1] A total of 239 million out of a population of 356.87 million, according to the 1951 Census.

The Vindhya-Satpura mountains pose a rugged divide between the northern plains and southern (peninsula) India, ranging from the west coast below the great mill city of Ahmadabad (capitol of Gujarat) across most of India in an easterly direction. These mountains blend into the most primative tribal region of eastern India, the still heavily wooded, thinly populated Chota Nagpur plateau. The tribal peoples residing in isolated and remote pockets of Chota Nagpur are believed to be descendents of the subcontinent's earliest occupants. The many languages spoken by these tribal peoples belong to the Munda linguistic family, which is found in Southeast Asia, indicating migration from the East, perhaps originally from southern China. Nonlinguistic evidence seems to support the belief that India's first inhabitants were "Austro-Asiatics" who came overland through Burma, possibly as much as 100,000 years ago. Many other tribal peoples living in the mountains and jungles of northern and eastern India are more clearly related both ethnically and linguistically to their Burmese, Chinese, and Tibetan neighbors, speaking a variety of Tibeto-Chinese languages.

Peninsular India, south of the great Vindhya-Satpura-Chota Nagpur divide, is geologically India's oldest region. There are no snow-fed rivers here, and southern India's peasantry relies almost wholly on the monsoon which blows from the southwest, bringing moisture from the Indian Ocean during the "rains" of June through September. If the monsoon comes "on time," that is to say soon after the soil has been turned up and seed planted, the crop is fine and the year ahead will be a good one. Should the monsoon start too early, however, or a few weeks late, the effect upon millions of Indian peasant families can be disastrous, ranging from serious financial loss to starvation. Almost half of India receives under forty inches of rainfall annually. Huge multipurpose hydoelectric schemes like southern India's Tungabhadra Project are designed to store and make better use of rain when it falls, but much of India's food supply will long continue to depend on all too fickle monsoons. Only the Malabar and Konkani coasts, peninsular India's narrow western littorals, receive more rain than they can use (over eighty inches), thanks to the Western Ghats which rise sharply to some 3,000 feet barely forty miles from the Arabian Sea. With its high rainfall, coconut palms, pepper, rice, and lagoons, the Malabar State of Kerala supports an average population density of 1,000 per square mile. Little more than a hundred miles to the north and east of Kerala, however, the neighboring states of Mysore and Andhra barely sustain one-fifth that density.

The four southernmost states of Peninsular India (Mysore, Andhra, Kerala, and Madras) are all predominantly Dravidian language areas, reflecting once again the persistant vitality of presumably pre-Aryan cultures. There is good reason to believe that the present-day Dravidians of southern India are descended from the people whose monumental urban civilization in the Indus Valley was conquered by Aryan invaders somewhere between 2300 and 1500 B.C. We know quite a bit about the highly sophisticated, technologically advanced culture of these Indus Valley dwellers thanks to the elaborate drainage systems, building foundations, skeletal remains, potsherds, and other artifacts excavated at many Indus sites. Unfortunately, however, we still can't read the pictographic script on Harappan seals, and have no other written documents to help more positively identify the precocious authors of this remarkable civilization. The early Aryans, on the other hand, have left copious "written" (transmitted and preserved for centuries in spoken form) records of their society, though practically no archaeological remains. These Aryan "books" (the Vedas) are primarily religious works, yet they provide much illuminating historical information, including references to fierce battles against "dark-skinned" enemies, who were found in fortified cities and conquered. Though many of the pre-Aryans of the Indus Valley were thus overwhelmed by Aryan tribesmen, other peoples fled southward across the Vindhyas. For many centuries the Aryans were content to consolidate their grip over the fertile northern plain, expanding initially from west to east rather than southward, since just beyond the low Aravelli divide they discovered the Yamuna-Ganga doab, which came to be called Arya-Varta (Land of the Aryans). Their dark-skinned captives were enslaved, and later only grudgingly accommodated within the fourfold social class (Varna) system of Aryan society as humble servants (Shudras). The three higher classes had been brought to India as the basic structure of Aryan tribal society, led by warriors (Kshatriyas) and priests (Brahmans) who ruled the pastoral-agricultural commoners (Vaishyas) composing the bulk of each tribe. Gradually (during the next millennium at least) these loose and often changing class categories evolved into the more rigidly enforced and generally accepted major strata of the Hindu caste system.

Protected by the Vindhya-Satpura divide, Dravidian culture flourished in virtual isolation from Aryan contact and control. Hindu epic literature, especially the Sanskrit epic, *Ramayana,* indicates that some northern kings early attempted to overcome the greatest natural barrier to Indian unification and tried to subdue the vigorous "demon kingdoms" of the south. Not before about 269-236 B.C., however, was any even temporary unification of northern and southern India achieved. In the first millennium of the Christian era, moreover, Dravidian empires emerged, often wealthier and more powerful than the dominant kingdoms and empires of the invasion-racked north. Tamil, the classical Dravidian language, produced its own epic, court, and dramatic literature to rival that of classical Sanskrit. Small wonder, then, if many Dravidian-speaking people today retain a strong sense of cultural separatism, chafing at the attempted imposition of Hindi as India's sole "national" language, resenting what is sometimes spoken of in southern India as "U.P. (Uttar Pradesh) imperialism." Extremists have even formed a political party (the Dravida Munnetra Kazhagam—DMK) advocating the creation of a separate nation, Dravidistan, posing what is potentially the most dangerous, if not as yet serious, challenge to India's political integrity.

The region of geographic as well as cultural transition between northern and southern India, a plateau called the Deccan, includes most of the modern state of Maharashtra. Marathi, the language of this region, is descended from Sanskrit, and is as closely related to Hindi as French is to Spanish. However, most Maharashtrians, particularly the non-Brahman majority, appear more intimately linked ethnically to the Dravidian south than the Aryan north.

Many waves of post-Aryan invaders from Central Asia and the Middle East contributed their share to the ethnic, linguistic, and religious jungle of Indian society, making the country more pluralistic in every respect than any other on earth except, perhaps, Indonesia. To some extent a caste system emerged in India as the social defense mechanism of peoples who feared the threat of their cultural identity posed by proximity to so many diverse ways of life. Within India today there are more than 2,000 communities, or "castes" whose religious "laws" prohibit intermarriage, interdining, and in some cases all physical and even visual integration. Naturally, in modern India's "secular state" observance of these Hindu religious restrictions varies considerably between urban and rural areas, and among members of the same caste with differing amounts of and exposure to Western ideas. If the Hindu caste system may be seen as an extremely conservative response to the reality of multicultural coexistence, however, Hinduism's philosophical tolerance and latitudinarianism may be recognized as the reverse side of the same historical imperative. "Live and let live" might indeed almost suffice as a general definition of Hinduism.

Government and Politics

Modern India is an independent republic, a union of states, and the world's largest political democracy. Independence from British rule was attained on August 15, 1947, while the constitution that created the Republic of India has been in effect since January 26, 1950. When she became a republic in 1950, India chose to remain within the Commonwealth of Nations. This unprecedented development was a tribute to both British and Indian statesmanship. It also reflected India's political maturity and her government's recognition of the importance of cooperation as well as independence in the modern world. This has remained India's position, and though Prime Minister Shastri was prevented by doctors' orders from attending the conference of British Commonwealth prime ministers in London in July, 1964, India was represented by two other ministers, for as Shastri stated, "there is an underlying link which holds members together and makes the Commonwealth an association which can help to further world peace and friendship amongst nations."

India's government, like its land and people, is a remarkable synthesis of East and West, old and new. In form and in practice it is more generally traditional, uniquely Indian. In this wide-spread dichotomy between form and actual practice India probably resembles Japan more than any other nation. The form of India's government is a syncretism of the British, American, French, and Weimar Republic constitutions. Naturally enough, British influence predominates; the country is ruled by a prime minister and his cabinet, which serves in and is collectively responsible to a lower house (Lok Sabba, or House of the People). In the British tradition, the prime minister and his cabinet are members of the majority party, though India has never yet had an officially recognized "opposition" party.

This party, whose leaders have ruled India since independence, is the Congress Party. It is the post-1947 political heir of the Indian National Congress, founded in 1885 and thereafter the foremost organization in India's national struggle. Lal Bahadur Shastri, unanimously elected prime minister by the 537 Congress members of both houses of Parliament in June of 1964, joined Congress in 1921 at the age of seventeen, and remained loyal to the party ever since. Barely known outside India till Nehru's death, Shastri's reputation within Congress grew steadily after 1935, when he became general secretary of the Uttar-Pradesh Congress, thanks to his organizational talent and singular capacity for hard, unglamorous political work. Elected a member of this state's Assembly from 1937-39, and parliamentary secretary to his province's chief minister in 1946, Shastri was made minister of police and transport of Uttar-Pradesh in 1947, a portfolio he retained for about five years. During the 1951-52 election he was called to Delhi to serve as Nehru's leading campaign lieutenant, and again proved his value as a party organizer. In 1952 he entered the cabinet as minister for transport and railways, and during the next decade held a variety of ministerial posts. His respected and moderating role in the Party explains his selection as prime minister. Immediately after Shastri was elected, Congress President Kumaraswami Kamaraj asserted that India would be ruled by "a collective leadership, a collective approach, and collective action."

This shift from what at times seemed to be one-man rule during Nehru's lifetime to something more closely resembling national management by an administrative board of equals clearly reflects the gap in personality, power, and ability between Nehru and his successors. How long it would be before another Nehru, or Gandhi, emerged —someone able to win the affection and allegiance, to spark the imagination, of so vast and varied a population as India's—is impossible to predict.

Shastri initially attempted to serve as his own minister of external affairs, following the precedent established by British viceregal rule and Nehru. The burden of work involved, however, soon forced him to appoint a cabinet member solely responsible for implementing India's foreign policy, and in July, 1964 Swaran Singh became India's first full-time minister of external affairs. A devout member of the Sikh community, Swaran Singh in turban and beard strikingly illustrated to the outside world both the regional and religious diversity within India and his government's determination to secure a unified secular nation by overcoming divisive traditional barriers. Born in the Punjab in 1907, Singh (meaning "Lion," the surname given to all sikhs since the seventeenth century) was trained as a lawyer and physicist before entering politics. He served on his state's cabinet after independence, and since 1952 in the central government in various ministerial posts. Unlike Shastri, who had never been outside India when he became prime minister, Singh had traveled widely before taking command of external affairs. Even more important training for his new post, however, was his protracted experience in negotiations with Pakistan.

India's cabinet has since independence included at least one representative of the most important social and religious communities or "depressed "minorities, including the "untouchables" (since 1935 called "scheduled castes"), Muslims, Sikhs, and women. Most famous among representatives of the latter is Nehru's daughter, Mrs. Indira Gandhi, minister for information and broadcasting in the first Shastri cabinet, an elected member of the Upper House, and former president of the Congress Party.

In India's bicameral legislature, the relative powers of upper (*Rajya Sabha*) and lower (*Lok Sabha*) houses follow the British, rather than American, prototype. All money bills initiate in the lower house, which includes some 500 members elected by universal adult suffrage to represent territorial constituencies of from 500,000 to 750,000 population. The upper house is only half as large, with twelve of its 250 members appointed by the president for distinguished attainment in the arts and sciences, the others elected by representatives of the sixteen state Assemblies. As in Britain, the upper house is powerless against the majority will of the lower house, but India's lower house itself is merely a formal replica of the House of Commons. Few Indian M.P.s wield the authority or assert to its letter the constitutional power that is theoretically theirs. The paternalistic and hierarchical character of the Indian family, caste, and village community is found everywhere in public and political life. Gandhi was revered by his followers as "Father" (*Bapu*), and Nehru as "Uncle" (*Chacha*); Shastri's surname means "Teacher." Position and age, if no longer mere family status, command far more deference within India's lower house than they do in either the American Congress or the British Commons. Few of India's back-benchers possess the initiative, courage, or self-confidence to seriously challenge cabinet authority. Most M.P.s lack the financial resources to retain close contact with their constituents while residing in Delhi. Even members with personal fortunes, however, are prevented by inadequate and overburdened travel and communications facilities from sustaining the sort of rapid, continuous, intimate dialogue with their constituents that is so important an aspect of British and American democracy.

The Indian head of state is a president, elected for five years by members of both houses and the elected representatives of the state Assemblies. As in France before De Gaulle, the president seemed to be intended to have a purely ceremonial, or at least non-political, role. During Nehru's era as prime minister, for most of which Rajendra Prasad was president, this was in fact the case. Nor did the power balance between president and premier change in 1962, when Dr. Sarvepalli Radhakrishnan was elected the nation's second president. An eminent philosopher and scholar, Dr. Radhakrishnan's elevation to head of state was everywhere hailed as the fulfillment of Plato's ideal of a philosopher turned king, but Nehru ruled on. Two years after Radhakrishnan's election, however, the president of India for the first time was obliged to appoint an interim prime minister, and the nation suddenly became conscious of the powers its constitution had actually vested in this office. Though ordinarily obliged to administer India's government with the "aid and advice" of the prime minister and his council (cabinet), India's head of state is constitutionally armed with the most far-reaching "emergency powers" entrusted to an executive by any of the world's parliamentary democracies. For example, he may issue a Proclamation of Emergency if "satisfied that there is imminent danger" of war or threat of "internal disturbance," which would in effect suspend the constitution for two months, abrogating all individual civil and state's rights, and could then procede, free of parliamentary, press, or public criticism, to take whatever measures he deemed essential for maintaining national security. The President is also empowered to administer any state government directly upon recommendation from the state governor. Thanks to this latter provision, the Indian constitution, while creating a federal form of government (union of states), is in fact unitary in emergency, if not entirely in "spirit." [2] An elected vice-president presides over the upper house. Dr. Zakir Hussain, the nation's foremost Muslim educator and a former governor of Bihar, was elected vice-president in 1962, succeeding Dr. Radhakrishnan.

India's unitary judicial system evolved out of the legal establishment of British-ruled India, though in emulation of the American system, the Supreme Court of India has assumed powers of judicial review, thereby enforcing a non-British "check" upon Parliament. The most clearly American-inspired feature of India's constitution

[2] See Norman D. Palmer, *The Indian Political System* (Boston: Houghton Mifflin Company, 1961), pp. 94-98.

is its third section on "fundamental rights." A wide range of civil rights is guaranteed in non-"emergency" times, including those of "equality of opportunity in matters of public employment" and "prohibition of discrimination on grounds of religion, race, caste, sex or place of birth." Freedom of speech and expression are protected subject to unfortunately elastic legislative limitation "in the interests of . . . security . . . public order, decency or morality." The government's freely employed censorship and book-banning policy has aroused articulate criticism from some of the most respected leaders of opposition parties. Though habeas corpus is usually guaranteed, independent India has retained the "preventive detention" statute (introduced during British rule and generally attacked by Indian Nationalist leaders) under which any person may be arrested and detained in custody for an indefinite period without being informed of the specific charges against him and without access to legal counsel.

The governments of the sixteen states of the Indian Union are miniature models of the central government. In ordinary times states have control over such matters as public order, police, local government, public health and sanitation, education, and agriculture. They share responsibility with the central government, moreover, for a wide variety of things ranging from criminal law and procedure to economic and social planning. For strategic, historic, and political reasons, the degree of actual autonomy enjoyed by the states varies greatly. For example, Nagaland, India's youngest state, born on December 1, 1963, can hardly be equated in terms of political experience with Madras, whose capital city has been an important administrative and political center since the seventeenth century.

All states are subdivided into districts and subdistricts administered by collectors and district magistrates and their assistants appointed from "above." At present, moreover, a parallel three-tiered system of local government has emerged from "below," called *panchayati raj* (meaning "rule of the *panchayats*," or "councils of five"). Inaugurated in 1959 in Rajasthan, this radical attempt at stimulating rural interest in self-government has deep roots in tradition, harking back to pre-Christian times when India's villages were governed by elected councils of five members. Indian Nationalists long argued that village *panchayats* were islands of democracy, surviving centuries of superimposed monarchical and autocratic rule throughout India's long history only to be submerged in recent times by British rule. (Actually, what records we have of these councils show that they consisted of the most powerful, conservative, wealthy, and indeed respected leaders of the hierarchical and conservative Indian rural society.) Restoration of *panchayats* became a "directive principle" of state policy after independence. By 1964 practically all of the states had been divided into *zila parishads* (district councils), consisting of *panchayat samitis* (councils of *panchayat* leaders), which in turn embraced the *gram panchayats* (village councils) of their regions. Members of each tier were elected by the membership of the tier below, the lowest by adult members of the village. The Planning Commission noted that the chief purpose of this policy is "to involve all the people in the rural areas to work for their own development." The political implications of the new rural democracy may prove even more important than its impact on economic inertia. Some astute observers[3] of the political scene suspect with good reason that the advent of *panchayati raj* may cause a transfer of political initiative from urban to rural India.

With the possible exception of China, India is not only the world's largest bureaucracy, but its oldest. We know that from the fourth century B.C., if not earlier, imperial India was always administered with the aid of a vast and powerful army of civil servants, clerks, tax-collectors, and spies. British rule merely added some Western variants to what had long been an Indian institution. Although proliferation of bureaucratic personnel often only increases confusion, most perceptive students of India's administrative system agree with Dean Appleby's conclusion[4] that India needs a larger, rather than smaller, bureaucratic machine. Members of the small élite corps of the Indian Administrative Service are more overburdened today than even their notoriously hard-working predecessors of the British Indian

[3] Hugh Tinker, "Tradition and Experiment in Forms of Government," in *Politics and Society in India,* ed. C. H. Philips (London: George Allen & Unwin, Ltd., 1963), pp. 155-186. Also see Hugh Tinker, "The Village in the Framework of Development," in *Administration and Economic Development in India,* eds. Ralph Braibanti and Joseph J. Spengler (Durham: Duke University Press, 1963), pp. 94-133; and in the same volume, Richard L. Park, "Administrative Co-ordination and Economic Development in the Districts of India," pp. 134-151.

[4] Paul H. Appleby, *Re-examination of India's Administrative System with Special Reference to Administration of Government's Industrial and Commercial Enterprises* (New Delhi: Cabinet Secretariat, Government of India Press, 1956).

Civil Service were. To compound the difficulties there is what one might call a psycho-cultural[5] reluctance among many Indian officials, even at the highest levels, to make rapid decisions or take initiative leading to immediate action. Yet, though shortage of "action-minded" leadership is one of India's most serious bureaucratic problems, the government leans much more heavily upon its official administrative leg than on the still frail limb of its elected parliamentary leadership.

Though the Congress Party dominates, four other national parties continue to compete vigorously with Congress for the support of the world's largest electorate (some 216 million in 1962 general elections). Two of these parties, the Communist and Socialist, provide leftwing alternatives; the other two, the *Swatantra* (Freedom) and *Bharatiya Jan Sangh* (Indian People's Party) offer rightwing alternatives. In addition, there are at least seventeen minor political parties, which have varying regional power and state representation and even some members in Lok Sabha (the DMK won seven seats in 1962). In the three general elections held between 1951 and 1962, Congress won a substantial plurality (never quite a majority) of all votes cast, and it has kept approximately three-quarters of the total membership of the lower house (361 out of 494 elected members in May 1962). Congress also dominates the state Assemblies, winning some 1,800 seats in 1962 out of a total of 2,930. All state chief ministers as well as the prime minister belong to Congress. Congress power and popularity are rooted in India's Nationalist movement and in the strength of personalities like Tilak and Gokhale, Gandhi and Nehru. Congress, moreover, is the modern political manifestation of India's passion for synthesis. It is all things to all factions. On the spectrum of modern Indian politics, Congress not only commands the center, but probes boldly to both left and right in its multifaceted appeal for mass electoral support.

At present, though the challenge to Congress from the left musters more lower house membership than that from the right, the latter seems potentially at least the stronger. As long as Communism continues to pose so real an international threat to India, the Indian Communist Party will make no serious political gains. Early in 1962 the Communist Party was, with twenty-nine representatives, the second largest on the national scene; by late fall most of its real in-

[5] See G. Morris Carstairs, *The Twice-Born* (Bloomington: Indiana University Press, 1961), especially p. 106.

fluence was crushed like Himalayan snow under the heels of the invading Chinese army. The Moscow-Peking split was another, almost equally mortal blow to the party.

The merger of Socialist parties, which created the *Samyukta* (United) Socialist Party in the summer of 1964, gave what appeared to be a new lease on life to the fragmented, ineffectual Socialist alternative to the "socialist" Congress. Though the new party could claim only eighteen representatives at its inception, it hoped to gain significantly in the 1967 elections, but early in 1965 the experiment in Socialist unity collapsed over a heated leadership struggle.

The major parties to the right of Congress are both of recent vintage: the *Swatantra* Party was founded in 1959, the *Jan Sangh* in 1951. They have at times united against Congress in electing some of each other's members to Parliament, but in basic approach and outlook the two are in fact eons apart. *Swatantra* is in policy, as in name, the Indian party of "freedom," especially economic free enterprise, rural as well as urban. Fathered by Rajagopalachari, India's foremost elder statesman, and backed by Tata, the Ford of Indian industrial history, the *Swatantra* Party might have been expected to win more than eighteen seats in the lower house in 1962. Perhaps its modest achievement to date shows how politically poor a slogan "laissez-faire" has become in India. *Swatantra* leaders have concentrated their efforts on India's largest segment of small capitalists, the land-owning peasantry, posing as the champions of the "free peasant" against Congress "threats" of "tampering with the sacred constitution" and each tiller's "fundamental right" to his land. In *Lok Sabha*, party leader Masani is probably the most vigorous defender of individual freedom and parliamentary democracy. Standing on a platform so familiar and attractive to most of us in America, the *Swatantra* Party seems somewhat exotic to most Indians and has as yet failed to win mass support.

Potentially the most powerful opposition to Congress today comes from the extreme right in Hindu society, represented politically by many parties, strongest of which is the *Jan Sangh*. Founded on a program of reuniting India and Pakistan under Hindu rule, this party represents religious revivalism in modern Indian politics. It appeals powerfully to the passions of millions of Hindus who suffered personal privation and loss of property or family members as a direct result of partition in 1947. By stressing the Hindu "nationalism" embodied in India's cultural heritage, and promising to work for a revival of Bharatiya culture, the *Sangh* pretends to be the only national party truly concerned with the welfare of India's Hindu majority. In attacking Congress "secularism" as a policy of "Muslim appeasement," it openly proclaimed what many Indians, including Gandhi's Brahman assassin, secretly believed. Posing as a purely "Indian" party (it even prefers the old Sanskrit name, *Bharat*, to the "foreign" name *India*, derived from the name of the Indus river, now in Pakistan) the *Sangh* has won the allegiance of narrow nationalists, who find everything "Western" impure or harmful to India. In a nation where more than half the population is still totally illiterate and devoutly Hindu, the potential mass appeal of "communal" parties like the *Jan Sangh* cannot be exaggerated. The fourteen members of the party elected to *Lok Sabha* in 1962, represent more than a quadrupling of representative power in the first decade of the party's existence, and when considered together with the some 120 seats held in the state Assemblies indicate the swiftly accelerating success of its appeal. Like that of ultra-patriotic parties the world over, however, this party's greatest power probably lies hidden in the untallied extremist influence it exerts over moderate and responsible leaders, especially in the field of foreign affairs. A major reason for Indian intransigence toward Pakistan over Kashmir, for example, is the unspoken threat to India's Muslim minority posed by Hindu communal extremists should any settlement lead to India's loss of the Vale.

Though Indian democracy has developed with the experience gained from three general election campaigns, it remains more of a unique byproduct of Indian history and culture than an exact imitation of the British or American system. The constitutional grant of universal adult suffrage, while a noble affirmation of faith in democratic principles, could not by itself transform Indian society overnight. Caste, with all of its built-in loyalties, obligations, limitations, and antipathies, remains the most vital "political" reality of contemporary Indian life.[6] Nor has enfranchisement quite brought equality of status to India's sexes. Literacy, moreover, though perhaps no valid requirement for voting, would be a most useful attribute for any member of a democratic society, if only because it would allow him to communicate directly with his political representatives at his convenience rather than at theirs. Many other factors, including those tech-

[6] See Morris E. Opler, "Factors of Tradition and Change in a Local Election in Rural India," in *Leadership and Political Institutions in India*, eds. Richard L. Park and Irene Tinker (Princeton: Princeton University Press, 1959), pp. 142 ff.

nological handicaps common to any underdeveloped economy, help
to severely limit the functioning of democracy as we know it in India.

Society and Economy

More than 80 per cent of all Indians are Hindus. The structure of
Hindu society, based upon the joint family unit generally located
within an agricultural village, is at once fragmented and unified by
the caste system. Though officially committed to the secular, democratic state, India is perhaps the world's most religious society, ordered
upon the basic principle of inequality.

Universal enfranchisement, state-supported education, economic
development, and increasing urbanization all continue to erode the
walls of caste distinction, yet with respect to general social mobility
Indian society remains the most conservative in our modern world.
At least seven out of every ten Hindus are born in villages to caste
communities whose relative position in the hierarchy of Indian society has long been established. The occupation, social status, marital
partner-pool, and circle of friends and dining comrades available to
these children is determined at birth, and will in all important respects remain the same as those available to the parents. The son of
a Brahman will be educated as a Brahman, and though his father
may be a cook in a great household rather than a priest (all Hindus
readily accept food from the hands of a Brahman), he will learn the
prayers required for every important occasion, and may, if blessed
with no better paying work, become a rural schoolteacher. The son
of a sweeper will probably never see the inside of a school except when
it is empty of all but dust, yet even if he should attend several classes
a few minutes each day for a few months or years, he will rarely rise
to an occupation in which he may stand erect.

Each caste has its own governing board (*panchayat*) of elders, who
serve as arbiters of social behavior, and mete out regularly prescribed
punishments to members who fail to abide by the traditional rules of
proper conduct. The ultimate and still most potent weapon with
which the *panchayat* retains its grip over the free citizens of a secular
state is the terrible threat of ostracism. An "outcaste" may, of course,
make his way to a large city and possibly find work in a factory or
shop, yet an individual cut loose from the moorings of his caste world
will find it almost impossible to marry or settle down to normal family life, and has no cushion of social support when he is ill or old. In
Indian society caste and family provide at least the rudimentary bene-

fits of medical care, unemployment insurance, and social security, none of which the "Socialist" government can as yet afford. More than material comfort, however, is provided by the caste fraternity, which offers every person, no matter how lowly his status in society, a brotherhood to guide, assist, and accompany him in whatever he may do throughout life. Perhaps the more miserable a man's material status is, the more valuable the company of others equally miserable becomes.

The "joint" Hindu family retains its traditional patriarchal and patrilocal character. Ruled by an autocratic *paterfamilias*, whose hearth becomes home for his sons' wives and children, the Hindu household is run on the principle of shared income, labor, and space. Privacy is almost unknown in India, and though the search for employment obliges many young couples to move off after marriage, most newlyweds prefer to live with the groom's family. The new bride comes under her mother-in-law's stern guidance, and many contemporary Indian dramas depict the tyrannical mother-in-law in even less flattering terms than are familiar in America. The Indian woman's role is one of subservience to fathers, husbands, and sons. Here too, of course, practice often conflicts with theory; nonetheless, even now far fewer women than men receive any formal education, and at the last census (1961) little more than one-third as many females (12.8 per cent) as males (33.9 per cent) were considered literate. The incredibly backward state of village women is further indicated by the fact that some five million female voters were disqualified at the second general elections for refusing to state their own names when asked by official registrars, modestly identifying themselves only as so-and-so's wife, daughter, or mother. Since 1955 the law has forbidden the marriage of girls under fifteen, yet most village girls continue to be married at the onset of puberty, assuming full responsibilities as housewives and mothers when their American counterparts would still be attending elementary or high school. For more than a century enlightened Indian social reformers have recognized the plight of Indian females as one of the most crucial and urgent problems of Indian society, and at least in one respect as a key to Indian weakness. So long as the mothers of the next generation remain uneducated, timid, and physically frail, their children will inevitably suffer in what are probably the most important and impressionable years of their lives.

Beyond the pale of respectable Hindu society is a "fifth" great class, those whom Gandhi called "the children of God" (*harijans*), but who were known to most other people as "untouchables." The lowest of the low, they are the menials who do the jobs no respectable person would take, and the landless who till other men's soil. More than sixty million of them continue to cling desperately to the lowest rung on the ladder of Indian life, for though the "practice in any form" of "untouchability" has been abolished by the constitution, the continued existence of untouchables remains the most grim, intractable reality of India today. The problem, no doubt, is ethnic, religious, and social in origin. Its persistence at present, however, mainly reflects India's marginal economy and the dimensions of Indian poverty.

Modern India's most immediate internal problem is securing sufficient food to feed its vast population. The hunger marches, demonstrations, and riots that shook India's major cities in the summer of 1964 brought together all parties of the left and right in opposition to government tardiness with respect to "hoarders and blackmarketeers." The cry of "Give us rice and oil or give up office!" rang through the streets of Calcutta, and tens of thousands demonstrated in Delhi, Bombay, and Ahmadabad.

After more than a decade of planned national effort to "raise more food," the age-old spectre of famine continues to haunt India. Below the surface of material resources and factors of climate noted above lurk aspects of religious belief and cultural habits of mind less easy to fit onto an economic balance. Hindu worship of the cow, and widespread belief in the doctrine of nonviolence to living creatures (*ahimsa*), have conspired to convert most Hindus to vegetarianism, leaving a cattle population of roughly half the number of India's human population to compete with the latter for what little food is available from the soil alone. Instead of providing much needed protein for Indian diets, moreover, cattle serve as an economic drain, since millions are supported in their old age by state funds used to build and maintain special facilities for keeping them.

The roots of Indian hunger lie deep in the soil of rural relationships, however, penetrating to some of the very well-springs of Indian culture and psychology. It was once assumed that all the Indian peasant needed was more fertilizer, water, and farm machinery, better seed, and a bit of instruction to resolve the problem of food scarcity. Thanks to Kusum Nair's painstaking research and brilliant study,[7]

[7] Kusum Nair, *Blossoms in the Dust. The Human Element in Indian Development* (London: Duckworth, 1961).

however, we can no longer think in terms of such relatively simple solutions. Great dams may place more water at the disposal of peasants, but if a religious taboo or negative cultural attitude toward irrigation is strong enough no community development worker can make the landowner drink. The same is true of material incentive, of course; it is most difficult for westerners to understand why anyone (especially if he happens to hover on the brink of starvation) would care nothing about improving his material position, or would be willing to work only toward attaining a very slight increase in income, and no more. Yet entire communities of Indian cultivators share these hostile attitudes toward progress, valuing leisure above income, and meditation above physical occupation. Then too, peasants are so hopelessly indebted to village money-lenders that they know all too well where any additional earnings must go. Another incentive-crushing factor is the fluctuating market price paid to a peasant for his grain; a bumper crop brings the scale down. Rural cooperative societies and government subsidies have in some measure reduced the inequitable impact of good crops, but unfortunately these co-ops and subsidies generally help those who need support least.

Some of the most respected students[8] of rural India's economy feel that the basic reason for the continuing frustration of Indian agricultural development lies in the actual frustration of land reform efforts, despite the plethora of land reform legislation enacted by independent India. In many parts of northern India, the abolition of *zamindars* (great landowners), much like the deposition of *maharajas* (many of whom now represent areas over which they once reigned), has been a matter of form rather than fact. Laws designed to remove the burden of unproductive middlemen and absentee landlords have instead often served to transform peasant-tenants into landless laborers working for the same middlemen, who now claim legal immunity as cultivators. As long as the problems of sub-infeudation, holdings of uneconomic size, fragmentation, and disguised unemployment on the land continue it is difficult to imagine any dramatic rise in total grain output, at least not enough to offset the annual population growth. India's villages remain the strongholds of traditional Hindu society, and village Headmen as well as other members of the *panchayats* are usually the leading landowners, and often money-lenders, of the areas

[8] Daniel Thorner, "Economic Development," in *India, Pakistan, Ceylon*, ed. W. Norman Brown (Philadelphia: University of Pennsylvania Press, 1960), rev. ed., pp. 36-38.

over which they preside. The village accountant (*patwari*) is in the employ of these leaders, and will himself more often than not be a landowner. It is easy enough to prescribe, as the CPI for example does, agrarian social revolution to revivify India's rural economy, yet the very "classes" it would eliminate are those whom all other Hindus look to for leadership, and whose lives in many cases epitomize the aspirations of the masses.

Increasing unemployment, despite protracted planned economic effort, is another dismal indicator of Indian poverty and underdevelopment. The third Five-year Plan was embarked upon in 1961 with an officially estimated "backlog" of nine million unemployed workers (unofficial estimates of rural underemployment run as high as 100 million), and seventeen million young men and women are expected to enter the labor market by 1966. At best the Planning Commission aspired to hold the unemployment line, and our own most qualified expert on Indian planning, Wilfred Malenbaum, saw "little hope" of any diminution of unemployment by 1966.[9] Millions among those for whom there remains no prospect of work have attended college. Their education has seemingly qualified them for nothing but articulating their economic grievances, igniting others by the passion of personal indignation, and forming a readymade cadre of leaders for any extremist attack upon government. The Planning Commission, which functions almost as an alternate Indian "cabinet" under the chairmanship of the prime minister, knows how urgent the problem of unemployment is, and hopes to reduce its dimensions through more and more labor-using projects like road building and reforestation and soil conservation work. Unlike China, India is of course committed to democratic government and development, and remains a predominantly (over 80 per cent) private enterprise economy; she cannot therefore reallocate resources (especially manpower) with authoritarian facility.

Industrially, India is one of the world's ten most advanced nations. Producing some 3.5 million tons of steel ingots and 2.2 million tons of finished steel in 1961, India "planned" to turn out 9.2 and 6.8 million tons of each respectively by 1966, when hopefully the mills at Bhilai, Durgapur, and Rourkela would be fully operative and the plant at Bokharo at least partly productive. At the start of the third Plan India extracted some 54.6 million tons of coal, aiming for an

[9] Wilfred Malenbaum, *Prospects for Indian Development* (New York: Free Press of Glencoe, 1962).

annual rate of 97 million tons by 1966. Though electric power capacity was merely 5.7 million kilowatts in 1961, there were hopes that it would rise to 12.7 million in 1966. India's strongest industry at present, as in the past, is textile production, and in 1961 more than 5.1 billion yards of cotton cloth were made in Indian mills. Textile exports are India's best source of the foreign exchange desperately needed to pay for indusrtial imports and help service the more than $1 billion foreign debt. The annual value of all Indian exports was little more than $1 billion in 1961, however, leaving India still very much dependent upon foreign aid for the achievement of its Plan targets. Thanks to the international "Aid-to-India Club," of which the United States is leading contributor, India's third Plan had by mid-1964 been pledged almost $4.5 billion of the total $5.4 billion required through mid-1966. Estimates for expenditure (about $40 billion) during the fourth Plan period (1966-71) were almost twice the size of total investment in the third, but India's master planners hoped that by so intensified an economic commitment, the nation's economy may emerge from the trough of continued dependency on others, to attain a level of self-generating industrial "take-off."

Education

To help attain both rapid economic development and government by democracy, India has made one of her "directive principles" the provision of free and compulsory education for all children through the age of fourteen. The original target date was set at 1960, but with only 20 per cent of the children aged eleven to fourteen, and barely over 60 per cent of those between six and eleven, enrolled in schools at that time, more realistic goals were adopted. The third Plan's target was to provide free education for some three-quarters of all children in the six to eleven age group by 1966, which would mean teaching approximately fifty million students, a staggering task for even the most developed economy. Over one-third of a million more teachers would have to be trained than were available in 1961, and almost 50 per cent more schools would have to be constructed and equipped. India spent about $600 million on education in 1959-60; she would have to find at least twice that amount to meet her educational aspirations for 1966. So much for the sheer quantitative problem involved. The quality of Indian education is by and large poor, suffering for a variety of reasons, not the least of which is lack of funds. Teachers are notoriously ill-paid, textbooks are almost nonexistent, plant and equipment are inadequate at every level, a weakness most seriously felt, however, at technical and scientific institutions of learning. The mixed blessing of British rule is perhaps nowhere more apparent than at the level of higher education in modern India. Thanks to more than a century of instruction through the medium of English, India's educated élite the country over enjoy at least one language in common, and have direct access to the world's most advanced scientific knowledge and information. However, the British university system, with its predominantly humanistic curriculum, is an excellent institution for training British imperial civil servants, but hardly adequate to meet the needs of an independent, underdeveloped nation. So many college graduates remain unemployed mostly because they have been superficially trained as nineteenth-century English gentlemen. India's colleges reflect in magnified form the worst features of British higher education, enjoying none of this system's greatest assets. Britain's mass-attendance lectures and standard examinations have not permanently impaired the intellectual initiative and creative capacity of most British students because the low student-tutor ratio has always provided the essential stimulus of mentally invigorating tutorials. The student-teacher ratio in India not only excludes tutorials, but makes it almost impossible for instructors with heavy lecture loads to so much as learn the names of all their students. Students whose comprehension of English is imperfect, moreover, often find it difficult to follow lectures read rapidly with an Oxford intonation. Attendance at lectures falls as the year progresses. More importance is given to the examinations alone, especially to memorizing answers to those questions asked on previous examinations, many of which are printed for mass sale and used as primers by most students during the last week or two of the school year. With so much stress placed upon examinations, it is hardly surprising that students who fail often become morbidly depressed or ill, while those who pass all too quickly forget what they burned so much midnight oil to commit hastily to memory. Not all Indian higher education is a pale imitation of the British method, however; the grow of Nationalism spurred some experiments in "national education." Closely connected with the over-all problem of education in India is the language controversy, one of the more critical issues of the Nehru era which remains as yet unresolved.

External Affairs

India's most crucial foreign problem is the threat of renewed attack from its northern neighbor, China. The Sino-Indian dispute over their Himalayan boundary is in fact a conflict of potentially global proportions, and it has forced India to abandon its "nonalignment" foreign policy in everything but name. The 2,640-mile-long border stretches over mostly remote terrain in the high Himalayas, much of which has never been properly surveyed or demarcated. The eastern end of the border has, India believes, been settled by the McMahon Line, drawn primarily on the highest watershed principle between India's North-East Frontier Agency (NEFA) and Tibet and agreed upon by plenipotentiaries of Great Britain, the Republic of China, and Tibet at Simla in July, 1914. The Chinese government never ratified the "Convention," however, and Nationalist as well as Communist Chinese maps have persistently claimed some 32,000 square miles of India's NEFA. On the western end of the border, in the Kashmir region of Ladakh, some 15,000 more miles of almost barren land are jointly claimed by Asia's conflicting giants. China's "cartographic aggression" against India acquired menacing potential in 1950 after military units of the People's Republic moved into Lhasa, dramatically enforcing China's claim to sovereignty over Tibet. Contested violations of the Indian border began four years later, ironically enough with the supposed dawn of an era of Sino-Indian "brotherhood." Adding substance to their claim to the Aksai Chin desert of Ladakh, the Chinese constructed a road about one hundred miles long across the barren plateau connecting Sinkiang province with Tibet. On October 21, 1959, when an Indian police patrol advanced toward this road, Chinese troops killed nine Indians and captured the others. Less than two months earlier (August 25, 1959), Chinese forces had overpowered India's NEFA outpost at Longju. All opposition parties but the CPI called in *Lok Sabha* for military retaliation. Nehru, only too conscious of the inadequacy of his northern defenses, counseled calm, and invited Chou En-lai to Delhi for "border talks" early in 1960. Diplomacy resolved nothing, however, and the Chinese continued to advance by intermittent probes in the disputed sectors, which included several outposts in northern Uttar Pradesh, especially around Bara Hoti. By the summer of 1962 Nehru considered the situation intolerable and insisted that "all our territories" be taken back from Chinese "aggressors." The Indian army was ordered to enforce this demand, and by September 8, 1962 had moved into most of the Indian-claimed area of Ladakh. It proved no match, however, for Chinese forces, which outnumbered Indian troops in the region by some three to one and were better armed and trained. In October-November of 1962 massive Chinese attacks pushed more than one hundred miles into Indian territory, overwhelming inadequate Indian defenses all along the line, even where resistance was as bold as that of Major Shaitan Singh's 114 soldiers of the Kumaon Regiment, who fought to the last man at Rezang La in Ladakh. The war stopped as unexpectedly as it had begun when, on November 21 of the same year, the Chinese announced their unilateral cease-fire and withdrawal to the line they had held in November of 1959. American and British military aid, urgently requested by Nehru, had already begun to bolster Indian defenses, while the outraged Indian nation responded with a surge of unity unmatched since the more ardent hours of the "freedom struggle" against British rule.

As the Sino-Indian war of 1962 not only shattered the foundation stone of India's foreign policy, but threatened to destroy entirely the tenuous web of Afro-Asian unity woven at Bandung, six Afro-Asian peacemakers[10] met at Colombo, Ceylon, in December 1962 to seek a basis for settling the border problem. They proposed that Chinese troops withdraw twelve and one-half miles from their November 1959 position in Ladakh, leaving a neutral zone to be jointly controlled by Sino-Indian civilian posts; and that the McMahon line be accepted as the NEFA boundary, subject only to minor adjustments. The principles of peaceful coexistence and nonaggression were, moreover, to be reaffirmed by both parties prior to direct negotiations for peaceful resolution of the dispute. By mid-1964 India had accepted the Colombo formula in its entirety, while China claimed to balk only at Indian partnership in the control of Ladakh's neutral zone. The latter point was one on which India seemed flexible, and negotiated agreement might, therefore, appear within easy reach. Militarily, however, the situation became more explosive, the Chinese buildup along the border continuing unabated, while Indian defenses were toughened by joint American and British aircraft units and Defense Minister Chavan's top-priority program for raising and fully equipping six army mountain divisions. Since the 1962 "emergency," India's National Cadet Corps (NCC) more than doubled; some 900,000 NCC "Rifles" were being trained at India's colleges and universities less than a year

[10] Burma, Cambodia, Ceylon, Ghana, Indonesia, United Arab Republic.

later. Meanwhile within China the cartographic "war" continued to expand, an ominous portent perhaps of long-range strategy. As to the dispute itself, most Western observers would agree with Lamb[11] that China has legitimate claim to a fair portion of Ladakh and other small tracts along the entire border, though India's sovereignty over the vast majority of contested mileage is indisputably established by treaty and precedent.

If the Chinese threat helped Indians to view the "challenge" of Pakistan more realistically, it also served to complicate and intensify the dispute over Kashmir, still the foremost problems between India and Pakistan. The sources of this dispute run deep, involving questions of Indian history as basic as the nature of Hindu-Muslim communal conflict and whether or not the British pursued a conscious policy of "divide and rule." The controversy that brought India and Pakistan to war in their first year of independence, however, was most immediately a struggle between the heirs of partitioned British India for control over the largest and most beautiful of the 562 princely states to acknowledge British "paramountcy" in 1947. Bordering Tibet and China, and separated from Russia only by a narrow strip of Afghanistan, Kashmir had a strategic value that intensified the ardor of both claimants. Controlling the headwaters of the Indus, Jhelum, Chenab, and Ravi Rivers, moreover, Kashmir commands four of the five major waterways of West Pakistan, which adds a vitally significant economic aspect to this many-sided dispute.

More than three-fourths of Kashmir's population is avowedly Muslim, and no one doubted where Kashmir would have gone had a plebiscite been held in August of 1947. Maharaja Hari Singh, however, and the Hindu minority, which ruled the state in his service, naturally preferred accession to India, though only as the lesser of evil choices; the maharaja's first choice was independent statehood, and the role he envisioned for Kashmir seems to have been that of the Switzerland of Asia. By postponing accession to either India or Pakistan, Hari Singh hoped perhaps to win his way, but on October 22, 1947, Muslim "tribesmen" of the northwest frontier, aided by units of the Pakistan Army, advanced toward Srinagar, the state's summer capital in the lovely Vale. On October 26 the maharaja decided to accede to India. The next morning Indian troops were flown from Delhi to Srinagar, starting a major airlift operation which turned the

[11] Alastair Lamb, *The China-India Border. The Origins of the Disputed Boundaries, Chatam House Essays.* (London: Oxford University Press, 1964).

tide of battle, and has placed the southern and eastern two-thirds of Kashmir firmly within the Indian Union. At the end of 1947 India brought charges of "aggression" against Pakistan before the United Nations Security Council, initiating an international debate over Kashmir in which Pakistan has maintained that India's army "invaded" Kashmir to help enforce "Hindu tyranny" over the Muslim majority. Taking its stand on the high ground of self-determination, Pakistan urged that a U.N.-directed plebiscite be held in Kashmir, a position Nehru agreed to in 1948. A cease-fire was accepted on January 1, 1949, and the larger, wealthier portion of the state has been integrated into the Indian Union, the remaining portion adhering to Pakistan as *Azad* ("free") Kashmir. No plebiscite has been held, and like Korea, Kashmir is in fact divided into two states today. Since 1957, when the State of Jammu and Kashmir officially became "an integral part" of the Indian Union, India stopped accepting the plebiscite formula, even in principle. India charged that while Pakistan "preaches democracy" in Kashmir, "she does not permit even a vestige of democracy in her own territory," [12] and that Pakistan's claim to Kashmir "on the basis of its Muslim majority" was "a vicious communal approach repugnant to the entire spirit animating our national struggle for independence." [13] Pakistan in response insisted that India "willfully dishonored" [14] commitments to help carry out the plebiscite, while Pakistan stood ready to accept the verdict of "any impartial third-party" on how a plebiscite should be arranged and conducted.

As the international dispute grew more acerbic, the political situation within Indian Kashmir deteriorated. In mid-1963 Bakshi Ghulam Mohammed, the state's prime minister and political strong-man since 1953, was told to resign under the "Kamaraj Plan," but when his successor turned out to be Kwaja Shamsuddin, the Bakshi's leading lieutenant, popular hopes of promised reform in administration disappeared. Then late in December 1963 the Prophet's hair disappeared from Srinagar's Hazratbal mosque, serving almost as the signal for mass rioting in the summer capital. The sacred relic was recovered in

[12] Mahomedali Chagla, India's Ambassador, speaking at the United Nations Security Council, May 7, 1964.

[13] Prime Minister Nehru, before both houses of India's Parliment, August 13, 1963.

[14] Zulfikar Ali Bhutto's statement to the United Nations General Assembly, September 30, 1963, as reported by Arnold Lubasch, *New York Times*, International Edition, October 1, 1963.

less than two weeks, but the communal passions released by its brief
loss spread with terrifying speed from Kashmir to East Pakistan more
than 1,000 miles away, where Muslims were so incensed by the theft
that they killed Hindu neighbors, driving thousands of others from
East Pakistan in mortal terror to West Bengal. There, especially in
the metropolis of Calcutta, tales of atrocities against Pakistani Hindus inflamed the Hindu majority to "retaliatory" attacks upon inno-
cent Muslims, many of whom fled in despair to East Pakistan, where
the fires of hate were fanned by fresh news of terror. So it went for
the worst part of three months; official accounts of those killed in
Calcutta alone numbered in the hundreds, while unofficial estimates
of lives lost on both sides of the border were in the thousands. In
Pakistan, the irate press called for a *jihad* (holy war) to "liberate"
Kashmir, while K. H. Khurshid, president of the Azad Kashmir government, insisted that his army was ready to take action against the
Indian "occupation."

Within Indian Kashmir the immediate results of the rioting that
followed the theft of the sacred hair were the replacement of Shamsuddin by Ghulam Mohammed Sadiq as prime minister in February,
and Sadiq's release from jail of his old political comrade, Shaikh Mohammed Abdullah, on April 8, 1964. Abdullah, the "Lion of Kashmir," had been prime minister of the state's "emergency" administration from 1948-53, when he was deposed and arrested by his assistant
and successor as premier, Bakshi Ghulam. Jailed for five years without
charges, Abdullah was freed in 1958 for four months, only to be rearrested and finally charged with seditious conspiracy in 1962. His
release in 1964 was "unfettered," and all charges against him were
withdrawn unconditionally. Delhi appeared to feel that Abdullah
alone could restore harmony to Kashmiri politics, and it was clear
from the reception awaiting him in Srinagar that "The Lion" had
lost none of his popular power. Nor, it seemed, had a decade behind
bars tamed his independent spirit. Abdullah made it quite clear
to the world at large that the Kashmir dispute was one matter from
which Kashmiris themselves could not be excluded. On the eve of
Nehru's death, Abdullah's personal mediation had arranged for a
meeting between the Indian prime minister and President Ayub Khan
of Pakistan, which he would have attended also. At the Commonwealth Conference in July 1964, Ayub Khan accepted an invitation
from Shastri to discuss Kashmir and other outstanding differences,
but before such a summit conference could be arranged, Abdullah was

rearrested by the Government of India in May 1965, and held in Ootacamund in Madras state. A non-violent civil disobedience campaign was then launched in Srinagar, demanding freedom for the Shaikh, and a plebiscite for Kashmir. The Kashmir conflict thus reverted to the stalemate reached after six rounds of ministerial level talks between December 1962 and May 1963, when Swaran Singh and Z. A. Bhutto had been forced to report that "no agreement could be reached on the settlement of the Kashmir dispute." [15] Recently Pakistan's president warned, "so long as the dispute over Kashmir continues, India-Pakistan tension will continue to mount, immobilizing the bulk of the Indian and Pakistan armies in a senseless confrontation." [16]

Faced with the challenge of China, India most urgently requires the assurance of peace along her other borders, as well as the internal order possible only through communal harmony. China has already taken advantage of the Kashmir controversy to drive deeper the wedge of discord between India and Pakistan, supporting the latter wholeheartedly, and settling by treaty in 1964 the Sino-Pakistan boundary. India doubly resented that settlement, since with it Pakistan gave China some 2,000 square miles of Kashmir land that India claims. Clearly Kashmir remains the key to many of modern India's most critical problems. Why then has its solution proved so elusive? Some of the reasons are almost as old as Indian history itself.

[15] From the Joint Communiqué issued in New Delhi, May 16, 1963.
[16] Mohammed Ayub Khan, "The Pakistan-American Alliance, Stresses and Strains," *Foreign Affairs* (January 1964), p. 208.

TWO

THE HINDU HERITAGE

Indian history may be subdivided most simply into Hindu, Muslim, British, and national epochs. The sequence is chronological and cumulative, the title of each period indicating its guiding spirit or directing force, rather than its exclusive character.

The first was the longest period of Indian history. It too was a historical compound, for the Hindu religion as we now know it emerged only shortly after the start of the Christian era. Major ingredients of Hinduism, however, may be traced back to the pre-Aryan splendor of Mohenjo-daro and Harappa, twin "capitals" of what appears to have been India's first imperial state, which flourished over 4,000 years ago.

Pre-Aryan

The Indus Valley (or Harappan) civilization, the major sites of which lay along the Indus river and coastlines of Gujarat and Makran,[1] was a highly sophisticated, technologically advanced urban and commercial society. Though the sturdy bricks of Harappa provided underpinning for more than one hundred miles of British railway track laid in the Punjab in 1856, the ancient city itself was not unearthed until 1921. Since then archaeologists have continued digging for Indus Valley remains, shedding light on a civilization as precocious as its contemporary in Mesopotamia. Traces of several primitive cultures have been discovered near the capital cities, indicating that a gradual process of evolution led to the complex society of Harappa, which lasted from about 2500-1700 B.C. The fine kiln-burned bricks of standard measurement, elaborate sewerage and plumbing systems, painted wheel-made pottery, metal statuary, and magnificent glyptic art of the Harappan civilization have long evoked universal acclaim.

[1] George F. Dales, "Harappan Outposts on the Makran Coast," *Antiquity* (1962), XXXVI, pp. 86-92.

The grid-plan according to which the major Indus cities were laid out, and the uniform shapes and sizes of many commodities found at sites hundreds of miles from one another, attest to highly centralized administrative authority. Though no great "temple" has as yet been located, one may well have existed directly under the Buddhist shrine still standing above Mohenjo-daro, for immediately adjacent to that sacred ground lies the great "bath," a huge hypocaustically heated tank of brick, much like the water tanks found to this day beside Hindu temples all over India. Ritual ablution, a vital part of daily Hindu worship, may date from the pre-Aryan days of Harappa. Indeed, the extreme conservatism that dictated the rebuilding (after floods perhaps) of city after city on precisely the same spot would seem to indicate belief in the sacrosanctity of these sites. Traditional Hinduism has always included a sacred geography of *Bharat* (India), and belief in the divinity of a proper *raja* (king).

From artifacts found at pre-Aryan sites we can infer that both mother-goddess and phallic worship were popular, just as they are among Hindus today. We also know that certain vegetation, especially the pipal tree, was sacred to pre-Aryan man, as it remains sacred to Hindus and Buddhists. The tree depicted on Harappan seals is of the same type as that under which Gautama became the Buddha almost two millennia later. The symbolic intertwining of human and vegetative growth, so popular a theme of Hindu art and literature, is depicted on Harappan seals; this theme has perhaps become most widely apparent through the association, daily refreshed, of Jawaharlal Nehru and a rose. Animal worship, moreover, was probably a part of pre-Aryan faith, though the bull, rather than the cow, seems to have played the predominant role during this period. Even geometric designs, like the swastika, which retain symbolic sanctity for Hindus, were used, no doubt for much the same mysterious reasons, by the pre-Aryans of Harappa.

Like their successors throughout Indian history, the Harappans were cotton-spinners and rice eaters. They were probably the first people to domesticate fowl. (Much to its nutritional loss, India long neglected this ingenious discovery, but recently many Indian farmers have been taught the value of raising chickens by Peace Corps volunteers.) The Harappans were a sea-faring, commercially enterprising people, whose trade contacts extended well into Central Asia and south almost to the tip of peninsular India, west to Sumeria, and east to the Bay of Bengal. The glorious civilization they developed came to a violent end [2] at about the time when the Aryan invaders entered India over the northwest passes.

Aryan

Aryan[3] civilization was socially far more primitive than the pre-Aryan world it conquered somewhere around 1500 B.C. Primarily pastoral and nomadic, the Aryans seem to have introduced horses to India and also to have enjoyed military advantages other than cavalry over their predecessors, wielding hafted axes and possibly still more formidable weapons. For the almost 1,000 years following the Aryan invasions, our primary sources of Indian history are the four "revealed" books, or Vedas, of the Aryan canon, the Rig, Yajur, Sama, and Atharva Vedas, and the voluminous didactic commentaries compiled on each of them, known generally as the Brahmanas. The latter, as their name indicates, exalt the role of Brahman priests in the ritual ceremonies and sacrifices prescribed by the Vedas. Indeed the Brahman was regarded as even more powerful than the gods during the late Aryan age (c. 1000-700 B.C.), and the religion of that period is known as Brahmanism rather than Hinduism. Contributing their canon and sacred language (Sanskrit) to Hinduism, the Aryans, as noted before, also brought the three higher classes of Brahman, Kshatriya, and Vaishya to Indian society, and helped make the cow sacred by using kine as their unit of currency. The religion of the Rig Veda, earliest tome of the Aryan canon, is based upon a naïve and optimistic world outlook, and the Vedic pantheon, like that of other Indo-Europeans including the Greeks and Romans, consisted primarily of deified natural phenomena. Aryan worship centered around sacrificial offerings of food, wine, and wealth to the gods through the intermediary god of Fire (Agni), in return for which man sought long life, healthy sons, and prosperity. Indra, the warrior god, who often led the pantheon (though elders like Varuna were at times hailed as his senior), reflected the robust qualities and world outlook of early Aryan man: lusty, youthful, fearless, all-conquering. Certainly little of the

[2] See Robert L. Raikes, "End of the Ancient Cities of the Indus," *American Anthropologist* (April 1964), 66, 2, pp. 284-299.

[3] See W. Norman Brown, *The United States and India and Pakistan* (Cambridge: Harvard University Press, 1963), rev. ed., pp. 31ff; and by the same author, "Religion and Philosophy of Indian Origin," in *India, Pakistan, Ceylon*, ed. W. Norman Brown (Philadelphia: University of Pennsylvania Press, 1960), pp. 93ff. For a longer statement on Hinduism, see A. L. Basham, *The Wonder That Was India* (London: Sidgwick and Jackson, 1954), pp. 137ff. and 297ff.

pessimism or world-weary resignation and search for release so typical of Hinduism can be found in the more than 1,000 hymns of the *Rig Veda*. Orthodox Hindus naturally insist that every aspect of Hinduism has its seed in Vedic revelation, but the Hindu heritage emerges in fact as a distinct synthesis of Aryan and pre-Aryan beliefs, with the latter perhaps the more potent.

While the Aryans spread east and south, expanding upon and consolidating their conquest, the primitive tribal communities evolved into princely states many of which, as the epic *Mahabharata* recounts, struggled for control over *Arya-varta* (Land of the Aryans). As more peoples were brought under Aryan dominance sub-castes proliferated and caste differences gradually rigidified. At the same time, Brahmans compiled increasingly elaborate works of Vedic exegesis, and by making the execution of the sacrifice the most important aspect of religion, elevated themselves to positions of primacy in the universe. Two reactions against Brahmanic formalism and pretensions, one orthodox and one heterodox, began around 700 B.C.

Upanishadic Revolt

The orthodox revolt against Brahmanic dogmatism was eloquently and profoundly expressed in the final segment of Vedic revelation, the philosophically speculative *Upanishads*. Some 108 of these lyric treatises have been preserved, ranging in length from under one hundred lines to more than as many pages. The *Upanishads* were concerned less with ritual than with salvation. They looked beyond the name and form of prayer and sacrifice to the ultimate purpose of life, to the nature of reality, man, and God. Upanishadic thought developed as a dialogue of ceaseless enquiry, rather than a doctrinaire statement issued by hieratic authority. Its authorship is generally presumed to be more Kshatriya than Brahmanic, and it is the ideological as well as chronological link between Brahmanism and Hinduism. Rejecting polytheism as an imperfect appreciation of reality, and sacrifice as but an aid to the attainment of ultimate insight, Upanishadic speculation centered around the equation of an individual's soul (*atman*), or "real" self, with the Universal Essence (*Brahman*). Man's goal was no longer to propitiate the gods, or the priests, but rather to try truly to understand the mystic meaning of *Tat tvam asi* (thou art That One). Such understanding alone would bring the salvation, not of achievement, but of release. For by now the end purpose of Indian life was no longer to fulfill the ambitions of optimism, but to escape the shackles of material suffering. In the process of spreading across most of the Yamana-Ganga plain, to Bihar and Bengal, Aryan thought had reversed its perspective, the cheerful conquerors were conquered by what appears to have been a predominant strain of pre-Aryan pessimism. Protracted warfare and basic social change marking the transition from tribal communities to imperial states seem to have stimulated the reappraisal of values, and unprecedented fermentation of philosophic thought.

Like Protestantism, Upanishadic Brahmanism turned radically from good works alone and the indispensability of priestly mediation to advocate a direct mystic approach to *Brahman*, which could be facilitated by moral action, devotion to the personality of some god, or ascetic practices. Explanations of the proper use of these various aids to salvation were later developed by separate schools of classical Hindu philosophy, while the central theme of Upanishadic monism itself became the primary concern of classical *Vedanta*, meaning literally "end of the *Vedas*," the name by which the *Upanishads* in general are also sometimes remembered. Upanishadic thinkers attempted to reconcile a universally transcendent yet individually immanent principle with the world as we know it through the concept of *maya* (illusion). They found all familiar shapes and forms but illusory impressions seen by eyes dimmed with veils of ignorance. The true "Seer" could pierce those veils to the one Reality, *Atman* or *Brahman*. This path to release was an intellectually rigorous struggle in which only an élite minority could ever hope to succeed.

Buddhist and Jain Revolt

In the sixth century B.C. Buddhism and Jainism appeared in the same region of northern India as the heterodox side of this revolt against Brahmanism. Siddharta Gautama (c. 560-480 B.C.), the Buddha, and Vardhamana Mahavira (c. 540-468 B.C.), founder of Jainism, both princes of ancient Bihar (Magadha), were reared in a world of sudden change and impending chaos in some respects surprisingly like our own. Abandoning the pleasures of palace life as young men, they became mendicant wanderers in the forests of Magadha, where they met many other ascetics searching as ardently for more meaningful answers to life's perennial problems. Mahavira and Gautama rejected entirely the authority of the *Vedas* and vigorously repudiated the pious claims of the priesthood, and each weaned many adherents from Brahmanism. The "middle path" to salvation expounded by the Buddha, and that of extreme asceticism taught by Mahavira both profoundly affected Indian thought and the evolution of Hinduism. Though Buddhism was welcomed more warmly in eastern and southeastern Asia than in India, the Buddha himself was subsequently brought within Hinduism's fold, as an incarnation of Vishnu. Jainism, while remaining theoretically aloof from Hinduism, has in fact become so closely identified with it as to appear now a variety of the latter rather than a separate religion. Fasting and non-violence to living beings (*ahimsa*), for example, two of the foremost doctrines of Jainism, have become significant features of Hinduism, and were religiously adhered to by Gandhi throughout his mature life. Hinduism in good measure arose out of the Buddist-Jain threat to Brahmanical dominance. In their pristine forms, however, both philosophies were far too austere and intellectual to exert mass appeal, though after the dawn of the Christian era Buddhism changed radically, and in its spacious "Greater Vehicle" (*Mahayana*) promised to convey all of mankind to "the happy land" of eternal bliss. Brahmans recognized then that if their doctrine was to retain broad-based support it could stay neither a narrow exaltation of the sacrifice, nor a lofty philosophic promise of salvation for the few. The "lesser traditions" of pre-Aryan village faith were brought within the mantle of the great Sanskritic tradition. The Hindu "way of life" in its numerous ever-changing varieties emerged.

Hinduism

Underlying every aspect of Hindu doctrine and action is the concept of cosmic law or religious order, *Dharma*, from which each individual derives his unique duty (*dharma*), varying with his caste and "stage of life" (*ashrama*). Hinduism has in this way been able to accommodate as wide a range of difference in behavior as the variety of ethnic origins, linguistic allegiances, and castes found in Indian society. In essence, and to perfected vision, *Dharma*, like *Brahman*, would be the One. In everyday life, however, it assumed many forms.

Traditionally, a Brahman's *dharma* was to preserve and transmit the sacred law, teach others the paths of righteousness, and warn men against the pitfalls of perdition. A Kshatriya's *dharma*, on the other hand, was to fight, to defend his people, and to rule them wisely with the aid and advice of his Brahman chief minister. Others were born to serve, labor in the field or factory, dance for the gods, convert stones into sacred art, build towering temples, or toil extracting gold for still others to fashion into bangles and rings, worn as part of their *dharma* by Hindu women. No one calling himself a Hindu lived outside this very special "rule of law," for *dharma* applied to the lowliest of the low as well as the pantheon of gods. Codes[4] compiled from the sixth century B.C. onward helped order the daily life of India's people for more than two thousand years before the British arrived to impose their own "rule of law." Few distortions of history have been as gross as the popular nineteenth-century British conception of "civilized" Englishmen introducing law to "barbaric" India.

Just as there were four major classes in traditional Hindu society, each with its special *dharma*, so too there were four stages within each man's life. An individual's sacred duty varied as he passed from one stage to the next. The first stage began after a young man belonging to one of the three higher classes underwent his Hindu initiation ceremony, or "second birth," at which he was invested with the sacred thread, thereafter worn over his naked torso. (Thanks to this ceremony and the thread symbol, "twice-born" Hindus, otherwise divided by caste, acquired a sense of unity which served to facilitate the growth of nationalism in recent times.) The young man of from eight to twelve years of age would then begin the first stage of celibate studenthood (*brahmacharin*), leaving home to reside with a *guru* (teacher), from whom he imbibed the sacred lore. This stage usually lasted twelve years, though the most devout chose never to abandon it. Toward the end of his life, Gandhi often spoke of himself as *brahmacharin*, considering the vow of celibacy one of the most important he ever made.

The second stage, that of the householder (*grihasta*), began with marriage and was associated with worldly cares, passions, and problems, which now became the good Hindu's *dharma*. The supposed dichotomy between "Eastern spiritualism" and "Western materialism" is not valid; feasting is as important an element of Hindu life as fasting. Hindu tradition neglects none of the needs of the flesh; sacred textbooks on passion and material matters were written contemporaneously with those on religious law, and no doubt studied as avidly. The Hindu heritage united the sumptuous and erotic with asceticism and prolonged celibacy, while Hindus served God alone at one stage of life, Caesar throughout the next.

After seeing his grandson, the householder might embark upon the

---

[4] The most famous, *Manava Dharmashastra* (The Code of Manu), was written between *c.* 200 B.C. and A.D. 200.

third stage, that of forest-dweller (*vanaprastha*). Few Hindus actually ever left the second stage, and the final two stages may have been added to the traditional pattern of Hindu life as a Brahmanic attempt to win over or lure back to Hinduism without proselytizing those who were avidly meditating in northern India's forests. The forest-dweller's *dharma* was to concentrate upon how to sever the bonds of material life and personal attachment to friends and family in prep-aration for the final stage, that of mendicant wanderer (*sannyasi* or *bhikshu*). Here, stripped of everything transient, the Hindu could finish his life a solitary soul, obliged to beg even for daily nourish-ment. The ultimate goal was total release, not simply from society, but still more important, from the imperative of rebirth and the snares of selfish action. Belief in the cyclical nature of life became axiomatic to Hinduism at much the same time as pessimism per-meated indigenous Indian philosophy. The pessimistic premise un-derlying Theravada Buddhism, Jainism, and Hinduism might indeed have its roots in pre-Aryan India; at any rate it was clearly apparent by the sixth century B.C. Considering the continuing floods, famine, and pestilence that plagued India, it is not surprising that pessimism first appeared in full-blown philosophical form on Indian soil.

With the doctrine of transmigration and the pessimistic goal of escaping rebirth, which was viewed as punishment rather than re-ward, there emerged another characteristic tenet of Hinduism, the "law of *karma* (action)." According to karmic "law," a man's lot in life resulted from his actions in past lives. All human action was seen as the planting of seeds, each of which would bear fruit in some future action, good or evil, depending on the seed's nature. This ingenious rationalization of inequality helps explain why such a heirarchical society remained so stable. Untouchables believed that they alone, through wickedness in past existences, were responsible for their status, and if they did not meekly accept the role in society to which evil *karma* had reduced them at this particular birth, they would lose the privilege of humanity entirely, and in their next incarnation might find themselves insects. At the same time Brahmans found justi-fication for their social privilege in the law of *karma*.

Yet was not life itself, even on the best of terms, inextricably bound up with pain and suffering, with sickness, old age, and death? The reason was *karma*, acquired because of ignorance (*avidya*). Man suffered because of his inability to appreciate phenomenal illusion and the transience of existence. The wise man, therefore, aspired to release (*moksha*) or, in Buddhist terms, to the "blowing out" of existence (*nirvana*). If past action determined a man's present condition, obviously present behavior would dictate his future; to make that future impossible he had to stop doing things that "bore fruit." Thus, eliminating *karma* became the goal of all Hindus who considered themselves potentially worthy of salvation. Many sought to reduce *karma* to a minimum by yoga practices and ascetic withdrawal from society. Meditation, fasting, breath control, and single-pointed concentration were all designed to diminish karmic input, but the body's unconscious acts and needs continued to frustrate the best of ascetics, and so some even fasted themselves to death.

Much as such quiescence appealed to Indian seekers and has remained a significant aspect of the Hindu heritage, however, an activist alternative proved far more popular. This was expounded in "The New Testament" of Hinduism, the *Bhagavad Gita* (Song of the Blessed One), a devotional poem describing a dialogue between the warrior Arjuna and his charioteer, Krishna, avatar of Lord Vishnu.

Shattered by the prospect of having to face his own relatives and friends on the field of battle, Arjuna dropped his weapons and sat despondent as the trumpets sounded their call to battle. Krishna thereupon bolstered his companion's spirits by explaining the indestructibility of man's true self (*atman*), and the illusory nature of those beings about whom Arjuna seemed so concerned. The Blessed One explained that as a Kshatriya Arjuna's dharma was to fight, and that if he did so in the proper spirit of "disinterested action" (*karma-yoga*), he would not only be performing his highest duty, but the very karma thus generated would be consumed in "the fire of knowledge." According to this poem, man could attain release while remaining attached to life and the necessity to act so long as his actions were devoid of self-interest, passion, desire, pleasure, or pain. The true karma-yoga would do everything solely from knowledge of his duty; to him "gain and loss, victory and defeat," [5] clods, stones, and gems were all alike. This belief was expounded most elaborately by Bal Gangadhar Tilak[6] in recent times, and became the generally accepted "philosophy" of Indian revolutionaries throughout the Nationalist struggle. Even murder, if performed for "disinterested" or "higher"

[5] The most accurate translation is Franklin Edgerton, *The Bhagavad Gita* (Cambridge: Harvard University Press, 1946), Vol. I.

[6] Bal Gangadhar Tilak, *Srimad Bhagavadgita Rahasya*, trans. by B. S. Sukthankar (Poona: R. B. Tilak, 1935, 1936), 2 vols.

motives such as "patriotic duty," would, they believed, bring no bad karma to its practitioners.

Though Tilak insisted that the path of karma-yoga was the central teaching of Gita, that work also propounded another means to salvation, one that proved even more important since it attracted the majority of Hindus. That method was devotion (bhakti) to Vishnu, or one of his ten divine forms. "No devotee of Mine is lost," [7] promised Krishna, and that promise specifically included those who had committed much evil and were of base origin as well as "Women, men of the artisan caste, and serfs too." From about A.D. 200 onward, devotional theism became the distinguishing feature of the Hindu faith, and most Hindus to the present consider themselves devotees either of Vishnu or Shiva, and their respective consorts, emanations, and children. Without bhakti Hinduism could never have held so vast a following. Most sectarian Hindus aspire to the bliss of residing in the heaven of the divinity whom they worship with daily offerings (puja). The majority of Hindus primarily worship the mother goddess in one of her numerous forms (Devi, Kali, Lakshmi, ect.), for the female divinity is believed to possess more cosmic creative power (shakti) than her consort. The many forms of Vishnu and the large family of Shiva are evidences of Hinduism's absorption of pre-Aryan religious cults as Aryan rule spread.

At its least sophisticated level, Hinduism sanctions the worship of stones, vegetative growth, water, and animals, especially the cow. The Hindu pantheon emerged as the world's largest, and Hindu temples have come to be adorned with images of the gods, to whom offerings of flowers and food, music and dance are regularly presented. Unlike Muslims and Christians, Hindus ordinarily worship alone, though holidays would be celebrated by all members of a community together. Recently, however, public festivals such as that annually held in honor of the birth of Shiva's son, the elephant-headed Ganesh, have acquired considerable popularity.

Spanning the doctrinal range from atheism to pantheism, Hinduism is probably the world's most tolerant faith. Anyone born a Hindu remained one so long as he adhered sufficiently to the rules of his caste. A Hindu's "good standing" was traditionally determined more by whom he married and with whom he ate than by what he believed or to whom he prayed, indicating at least the all-encompassing character of this unique way of life, if not its singular wisdom as well.

[7] Edgerton, op, cit., p. 95, stanza 31.

Hindu Polity

The traditional Hindu state was a divinely ordained monarchy. Though the ideal of a Hindu "Universal Emperor" (*Cakravartin*) emerged shortly after the advent of Buddhism as the temporal aspiration of most Hindu *rajas* (kings), before the later part of the Muslim epoch we know of only two periods of unified imperial rule. Alexander's invasion of India (326-5 B.C.) stimulated the first era of its unification; in its wake Chandragupta Maurya was able to bring the many petty kingdoms of the Gangetic plain under the mantle of his Mauryan Dynasty (324-184 B.C.). Mauryan power spread from northern to southern India in the reign of Chandragupta's remarkable grandson, Ashoka (reigned 269-232 B.C.). A convert to nonviolent Buddhism after his bloody conquest of Kalinga (Orissa), Ashoka was one of the most humane monarchs of world history, becoming the first great emperor to make peace his foremost aim. We know of his protracted efforts to teach the *dharma* of love to his subjects thanks to numerous inscriptions he had carved on rocks and sandstone pillars strategically situated around his realm. Ashoka's example inspired many succeeding monarchs, and Jawaharlal Nehru, who called him "unique" among the captains of history, often acknowledged his personal debt to this ancient ruler. The Mauryan dynasty survived Ashoka by almost half a century. Some four centuries of disintegration followed, during which northern India was racked by a series of Greco-Bactrian and Central Asian invasions, while the South broke away from Magadhan control. The second era of political unification, under the Gupta dynasty (A.D. 320–c.500), was the classical age of Hindu India, a time of unmatched artistic splendor as well as imperial grandeur. Once again northern India paid allegiance to a single monarch, while parts of the South were briefly brought under the umbrella of Chandra Gupta II (375-415). During this period the Hindu state reached its pinnacle of wealth and power, and Hindu culture carved out an empire for itself in Southeast Asia.

Our knowledge of ancient Hindu polity was greatly augumented in 1905 with the discovery in southern India of a detailed "textbook of material matters," the *Arthashastra*, presumably written by Chandragupta's Brahman minister, Kautilya. Some of the information contained in this manual of political science and economy is supported by a variety of different sources, including the *Vedas*, the epic *Mahabharata*, and the corpus of Hindu legal literature known collectively as *Dharmashastra*. The Ashokan inscriptions and accounts of early foreign visitors to India all help to depict, in general outline at least, the administrative structure of India's traditional state.

According to Hindu political theory a *raja* was needed to defend the faith against invaders, and also to keep his subjects in order by inflicting punishment upon those who strayed from the path of duty, a necessary power given traditional India's pessimistic view of human nature. A monarch's rule was, therefore, autocratic and the state he administered totalitarian. Nonetheless, the *raja*, himself subordinate to religious law, was enjoined daily to "worship aged Brahmans," act impartially, and avoid the snares of sensual pleasures. Since his highest duty was to protect his people, the *raja* who failed to do so because of unrighteous behavior would "sink into hell." (The political implications of unrighteous action signifying a monarch's loss of divine favor were drawn by Tilak during the Nationalist movement as religious justification for overthrowing the British *Raj*.)[8] The *raja*, or, as his power expanded, *maharaja* (great king), ruled with the advice of a council of ministers, traditionally composed of eight members. Below the ministerial level was a vast and powerful bureaucracy, including an army of tax-collectors, clerks, and spies. The empire was divided, then as in later epochs, into provinces, districts and sub-districts, at the administrative base of which were innumerable villages. The peasant bulk of the population supplied the primary support for this large, expensive machine of state; a substantial share (generally one-fourth) of the harvest was collected by the king's men in return for "protection" against invasion. Cattle and trees were taxed as well as crops, and merchants had to pay a tax of about one-tenth the value of most items of import and export.

Most traditional sources write of the *raja* as the "owner" of all land within his domain, though from Mauryan times onward a difference was made between "crown lands" near the capital, and the remaining territory, which was given to royal favorites or local rulers under quasi-feudal conditions. Royal "tax-farmers" had to either pay a fixed sum annually to the central treasury, or raise a minimum force of cavalry and infantry to aid in defending the realm.

The ancient Indian state had a more thoroughly "socialized" economy than does modern India, with all mines under direct central con-

[8] Stanley A. Wolpert, *Tilak and Gokhale: Revolution and Reform in the Making of Modern India* (Berkeley and Los Angeles: University of California Press, 1962), pp. 204-206.

trol, and forced labor exacted from most of the population, including city artisans, who were expected to work one day a month for the king. The government executed ambitious public works projects, including the completion of the Grand Trunk road along the Ganga plain, which in Mauryan times was reported to have extended more than a thousand miles. We know of several impressive irrigation schemes as well, including large dams built before the Christian era; thus, modern India's Five Year Plans may be as much a part of Indian tradition as the administrative bureaucracy.

The *Arthashastra* elaborated a doctrine of power politics called the *Mandala* (circle) theory, a comprehensive scheme of international relations according to which the state was surrounded by eleven circles of neighboring states. Closest to the "conqueror's" central circle was "the enemy," and in the ring beyond that "the friend," after which came "the friend of the enemy" and "the friend's friend" in classic Machiavellian style. The two outermost circles were occupied by "the intermediary" and "the neutral." (We might draw contemporary parallels in India's strained relations with her immediate neighbors, Pakistan and China, and the "neutralist" role she has played toward the conflicts of more remote states like America and Russia.) Of six policies elucidated by Kautilya concerning interstate relations, four dealt with methods of preparing for war, one with peace or "alliance," and one with "neutrality." Ashoka's policy of nonviolence was clearly an exception; for traditional India's princes conflict and conquest constituted both a sacred obligation and fact of everyday life. The state maintained imposing armies, including that unique branch of natural heavy armament, the elephant corps.

Hindu Society

Traditional Indian society knew of no separation between sacred and secular life; the Hindu faith embraced all facets of existence. Caste determined social status; within each family the individual's role was dictated by sex and age. Only men were traditionally deemed worthy of learning the *Vedas,* and though the female principle of power (*shakti*) enjoyed celestial exaltation, women on earth were subordinate.

According to *Dharmashastra* independence "ruined" women who, like children, slaves, and pupils, required constant adult male supervision and strict control. A Hindu wife was taught to view her husband as little less than a deity. Manu wrote that the wife who obeyed her husband would "for that reason alone" be exalted in heaven. Till marriage, of course, a girl's master was her father, and after her husband's death the mother came under the protection of her eldest son. The ultimate test of a woman's devotion was her willingness to follow her husband onto the funeral pyre, and a wife who preferred immolation to widowhood was distinguished by the title of "true one" or *sati*. Sanskrit poetry and literature hailed the *sati* as the noblest example of female perfection, though the practice of widow-burning did not become widespread until after the Muslim epoch. Nineteen-century British reformers viewed this custom less romantically, noting that most of the widows had to be tied down to the pyre and cried out plaintively for release once the flames approached them. In some respects, perhaps, the widow was hardly to be more envied than the *sati*. Obliged to shave her head and cease wearing jewels, flowers, and bright colored clothes, she was confined by tradition to a life of perpetual mourning, attending no festivity, hearing no music, meeting no company. Naturally, she could not remarry; widow remarriage in India has been legal for only little more than a century.

Hindu marriages were generally—and still are—arranged by parents with the advice of Brahman astrologers. Traditionally bride and groom could not see each other before the wedding; they certainly were never to be alone together. Love, it was believed, would develop after marriage; far more important than personal preferences or physical attraction were caste and family background, as well as horoscopic compatability. The best age for women to marry was at puberty, and after the Muslim epoch infant male as well as female marriage became the Hindu rule, especially among the higher castes. Hindu ritual stressed the importance of male progeny for performance of prayer ceremonies required to assist the souls of departed parents in their search for salvation. Coupled with the precariousness of life in India's trying environment, this religious duty of sons helps to explain why marriage ages were progressively reduced. Even in the later nineteenth century Brahman castes advocated the marriage of boys of fourteen to girls of ten or twelve.

While monogamy was the norm, polygamy was common among wealthier Hindus throughout Indian history. Polyandry was known at least in epic times, and matriarchal succession still survives in parts of the extreme South. Traditional Hindu law made no provision for divorce, and until quite recent times men could initiate action against their wives, never the reverse. Prostitution was common in ancient

India, to judge from numerous literary references to courtesans and their accomplishments. The practice of leaving poor girls to be reared in Hindu temples as "Slaves of the God" antedates the dawn of the Christian era. Many of these temple-slaves, though primarily prostitutes, became fine dancers and artists.

Caste regulations prescribed the daily ritual of every member of Hindu society, as well as dictating relations among all members of that society. In most villages traditions of reciprocal obligation sustained community life. Peasants shared their yield among village artisans and craftsmen, who in turn served peasant families on a "retainer" basis. The British, bringing with them the economic forces of a world market, did much to revolutionize the traditional pattern of ancient India's socio-economic life. But the strength and longevity of the caste, joint family, and reciprocal obligation systems amply testify to the breadth and enduring power of the Hindu way of life.

The Arts

During the Guptan era (A.D. 320-c. 500) Hindu India enjoyed its golden age of artistic as well as political glory. Kalidasa, the Shakespeare of Sanskrit drama, who probably flourished at the court of Chandra-Gupta II in the early fifth century, immortalized in his plays the classical traditions, goals, and aspirations of Hindu society. Brilliant portrayals of classical Indian life are found in tantalizing fragments of fresco in the caves of Ajanta. The luxury and splendor of Hindu court life, as depicted by anonymous Indian artists, attest to the high level of sophistication and material attainment in ancient India, and indicate why so many covetous Central Asian neighbors were tempted to invade, plunder, and ultimately conquer this increasingly alluring and affluently decadent civilization. In Guptan times the Hindu temple began to evolve as the finest architectural monument to Hinduism; the plastic microcosm of the pantheon completely covering it in provocatively full-fleshed form reflected the continuing coexistence in Indian history of spiritual and material motifs. Shortly after the Guptan age, the apogee in cave temple artistry was attained at Ellora with the magnificent Kailasanatha (Mount Kailasa was Shiva's mythical abode) carved out of a mountain, and recognized as one of the wonders of the world of art.

Classical Hindu music and the dance, recently revived in India and widely acclaimed abroad, flourished under Guptan patronage. As in every other facet of Hindu life, religion was both spur and guide to artistic genius. Shiva is most popularly depicted in sculpture as "Lord of the Dance," whose cosmic gyrations at the dawn of time were supposed to have helped initiate the "game of life." The governing precepts of dance and drama both were recorded in a Sanskrit textbook before the Guptan era, which explained all the hand-gestures and emotions of the classical school of Hindu dance, each with its particular message and symbolic meaning. The songs described in this book were related to devotional Hinduism, and from these evolved the classical pattern of Indian music. The traditional Indian scale was heptatonic, and the improvisational character of Indian classical music is surprisingly modern.

In science and technology ancient India was very advanced, often ingeniously precocious. Mathematics and medicine were both highly developed by the Guptan era. We have Sanskrit literary references to place notation and the use of the Indian discovery of zero dating from the dawn of the sixth century, and inscriptions based on the decimal system from before the end of the seventh. The Arabs referred to mathematics as "the Indian art," and brought decimal notation to the West after learning it in India's Sind, which they conquered in 712; what we call "Arabic" numerals are in fact Indian. By the second century of the Christian era, Indian medicine had its first textbook and two centuries later a work on surgery was compiled; both indicate a fully evolved and refined system of healing, far in advance of contemporary developments elsewhere. Indian technological skill and craftsmanship from the dawn of the Harappan age have long been a source of amazement and universal admiration. Eminent scholars of medieval science and technology like Lynn White have recently shown that Western civilization's debt to Indian inspiration has been far more extensive than earlier imagined, including not only the "Indian invention" of the big-toe stirrup, but the infusion of ideas like the concept of perpetual motion, which "not only helped European engineers to generalize their concept of mechanical power, but also provoked a process of thinking by analogy that profoundly influenced Western scientific views." [9] In metallurgy, Guptan India was probably the world's leader, as the rustless iron pillar of Meharauli alone should prove, having maintained its unblemished surface after far more than a thousand years of monsoonal assaults.

The variety and excellence of Guptan India's agriculture and industry evoked comment from numerous foreign visitors (mostly Chi-

[9] Lynn White, Jr., "Tibet, India, and Malaya as Sources of Western Medieval Technology," *The American Historical Review* (April 1960), LXV, 3, pp. 515-526. The quotation is from p. 526.

nese). The silk textile industries of Bengal and Banaras were universally envied, their products sought by all who saw them. The cotton cloth of Mathura must have helped dressed not only the inhabitants of northern India, but peoples of Africa and Southeast Asia as well, even as Indian cotton textiles continue to do today. Like China, ancient India was an exporter of produce, a world center of desirable commodities, which could be purchased only for gold and specie. Included in the ransom demanded of Rome by Alaric in 410 were several thousand pounds of Indian pepper. The drain of Roman gold paid for Indian jewels, indigo, and spices became so alarming after the reign of Nero (A.D. 54-68) that gold exports to India were prohibited by imperial decree. Yet the unbalanced trade persisted. Guptan India was the workshop of the world. The cities, temples, indeed the very fields of Hindu India at the peak of its power seemed to glisten with golden allure. Covetous eyes watched from beyond the Hindu Khush. Central Asian armies waited for the decay of unified power.

Shortly after the middle of the fifth century (c. 465) the Hun invasions began. By the mid-sixth century the Guptan line had vanished. An era of warring states followed, and centralized rule gave way to a patchwork quilt of princely provinces. Strong monarchs like Harsha Vardhana (ruled 606-647) tried to revive the unity at least of northern India, but no subsequent Hindu dynasty managed to regain Guptan glory.

The forces that brought an end to the Hindu epoch came from the West. The Arabs in Sind were but an advance guard of that new and militant faith of Islam, whose dynamic impetus transformed the map of the Middle East and North Africa in the seventh century. Hindu India in the "Age of Imperial Kanauj" [10] survived, politically divided against itself, until the end of the tenth century. As a new millennium started, the second wave of Islamic invasions began, and with them dawned India's Muslim epoch.

[10] The title of Vol. IV of the multivolume *The History and Culture of the Indian People*, ed. R. C. Majumdar and A. D. Pusalkar (Bombay: Bharatiya Vidya Bhavan, 1955).

THREE

THE IMPACT OF ISLAM

The Turko-Afghans of Ghazni brought the sword of Islam to India in the eleventh century, beginning the Muslim epoch of Indian history. The impact of Islam upon Hindu civilization, and the importance of the Muslim legacy to subsequent South Asian history were as great as the effect of the earlier Aryan and later British invasions. For more than two centuries Muslim raiders, secure in their home bases beyond the Hindu Khush and Sulaiman mountains, probed intermittently at the outposts of Hindu power. They early incorporated the Indus Valley region of what is now West Pakistan into the Islamic world. After 1206, when the Delhi Sultanate was founded, Muslim expansion continued for three more centuries under a series of Turko-Afghan dynasties entrenched in the very heart of northern India. The final phase of Muslim power began with the founding of the Mughal Empire in 1526. Under the aegis of the great Mughals Islam conquered all of India, reaching its peak of power by 1700. Nominally, Mughal rule endured until the last emperor was deposed in 1857. By then, however, British rule had in fact become paramount, and actually the Muslim epoch barely extended beyond the middle of the eighteenth century. The birth of Pakistan in 1947 amply proved, nonetheless, Islam's persisting vitality in India throughout the British epoch. Recent Indian history would be incomprehensible without some understanding of Islam and how it differed from Hinduism, and of those areas in which syncretisms were effected as well as others in which antipathy was fundamental.

Islam

Like Hinduism, Islam[1] ("submission") is a religious faith, whose precepts guide every aspect of its adherents' lives. The Koran, con-

[1] The best brief statements on the nature of Islam and its impact on India are H. A. R. Gibb, *Mohammedanism. An Historical Survey* (New York: The

taining the revelation of Allah to His last Prophet, Muhammed (570-632), has served as the fountainhead of Muslim thought and action since A.D. 622. The personal practices of the Prophet, compiled as sacred tradition, offered further guidance to his devout followers, though less than thirty years after Muhammad's death the Muslim world was divided into orthodox (*sunni*) and unorthodox (*shi'a*) sects. The *shi'a* in turn were fragmented, primarily on the basis of differing interpretations of the unorthodox concept of the *imam* (divine messenger) and the precise number of *imams* promised to the world. Soon after Islam assaulted India, moreover, several schools of mysticism (*Sufism*) appeared which, while still within the fold of orthodoxy, posed by their advocacy of direct union between man and God a formidable challenge to Islam's orthodox establishment. In many respects Sufism seemed so closely akin to devotional (*bhakti*) Hinduism that its teachers had singular success in winning converts. By the Mughal era, however, orthodox interpreters of Islamic doctrine in India came to fear that perhaps the process of conversion was backfiring. *Sufism* and *bhakti* Hinduism did, in fact, evolve into several syncretistic religious sects of great importance to Indian history.

By the time Islam reached India it had expanded much beyond the basic doctrines of the Koran, yet these remained fundamental to the faith. The single most important Islamic doctrine is transcendent monotheism, and in the final analysis the test of a Muslim is his willingness to submit to the credo, "There is but one God, and Muhammad is the Prophet of God." The true Muslim would, of course, prove his piety in other ways as well, especially by performing the daily prayers, which should if possible be uttered in company with other devotees. This congregational aspect of Islam strikingly illustrated the unified brotherhood of the Muslim world under God. Unless illness inhibits him, a good Muslim prays five times daily, facing and kneeling in the direction of Mecca. The most important weekly prayer is at noon on Friday, when mosques throughout India are fullest, and thousands of worshippers may be seen bowing as one man in time with their leader. If the playing fields of Eton were a training ground for Britain's imperial expansion, the mosques of Islam may equally

New American Library, 1953), second edition; and P. Hardy, "Islam in Medieval India," in *Sources of Indian Tradition*, compiled by Wm. Theodore de Bary, Stephen Hay, Royal Weiler, and Andrew Yarrow (New York: Columbia University Press, 1958), pp. 367-528.

have prepared Muslims for the group action that brought about Muslim victories in many battles.

Almost as important as prayer in uniting the Islamic brotherhood are such ritual acts of piety as the month-long fast of *Ramadan* (the ninth lunar month), and the pilgrimage to Mecca, which every member of the faith should undertake at least once in his lifetime. The giving of alms is also enjoined as a religious obligation, and serves as the most important single tax levied on the Muslim community.

Though Allah is often described in the Koran as "compassionate," "loving," and "merciful," the faithful who submit to His will are expected to wage "holy war" (*Jihad*) against non-Muslims in order to convince them of the wisdom of submission to Allah's commands. This divinely revealed advocacy of militant conversion helps account for the zealous fury with which Islam swept down upon Hindu India in the first centuries of conquest. To the Turks of Ghazni and their successors India was first and foremost the "abode of war" (*Dar-al-harb*), which they diligently labored to convert into an "abode of the faithful" (*Dar-al-Islam*) by periodic and merciless plunder and pillage. In Muslim eyes, Hindu India's greatest temples were abominations to all-seeing Allah, and hence fair game for desecration. Impelled as they were by such divine fervor, the messengers of Allah were able to succeed against imposing numerical odds in conquering a subcontinent and converting many of its millions to their monotheistic faith.

Islam and Hinduism

The aspects of doctrinal incompatibility between Hinduism and Islam are more glaringly apparent than their areas of similarity. With its prolific pantheon Hinduism presented a more striking contrast to Islamic monotheism than any other religion of the world. The Hindu caste system, moreover, was as basically undemocratic as the Islamic brotherhood was (at least in theory, under Allah) democratic. While most Hindus considered idol-worship and the presentation of devotional offerings to icons central to their faith, Muslims viewed all such attempts by imperfect man to depict God's perfection as sacrilegious. Whereas one reason for Hinduism's longevity has been its toleration of difference and capacity to absorb what it could not defeat, the success of Islam has in good measure resulted from unflinching self-righteousness and militant proselytizing. The cow, sacred to Hindu dogma, was for Muslims merely a source of human nourishment or an instrument of sacrifice. Music, used by Hindus in festive worship, seemed to Muslim ears a cacophonic insult diabolically designed to disturb Allah. Superficially at least, coexistence among the adherents of two such diverse world outlooks seemed impossible. Insistence upon this irreconcilability became, indeed, the central thesis of the British Indian Muslims who called for the creation of Pakistan.

Nonetheless, in some respects these "civilizations" were quite compatible, as the length of their intimate association alone proved. We must remember, moreover, that when Islam left its Arabic homeland, it was "still in a fluid state," [2] new enough to absorb many ideas and practices from the distant regions it conquered.

Nor was Islamic orthodoxy itself by any means as monolithic as it might appear. Hardly two centuries after the *Hijra*, for example, at least three "orthodox" legal codes, variously interpreting the Koran and prophetic tradition had become widely accepted. The concept of *ijma* (consensus among learned leaders of the Muslim community) soon acquired the status of prophetic infallibility, adding an avenue of innovation and flexibility to Islamic doctrine. Even individuals, if specially respected for theological perception, had the right of individual interpretation of dogma. Finally, local custom served to transmute sacred law through the medium of recorded and preserved "briefs" drafted by eminent legal advisers (*muftis*) in the various sultanates. While on the one hand, therefore, "the truth of Islam" was "indivisible" and "immutable," [3] human understanding of that truth varied considerably in adequacy, such variation reflecting in part the historical variety of Islam's many sultanates. Hindus, for example, originally considered "infidels" by the Muslim world, should have been offered only the alternatives of submission or death, yet they were quickly elevated by the Arabs of Sind to the status of "protected tributaries" and left to practice their own religion as long as they paid their taxes.

The overriding necessity of fashioning formulas allowing Hindus and Muslims to live and let live was perhaps the most powerful reason for the continuing doctrinal accommodation that characterized the epoch of Muslim rule in India. A small minority of Turks and Afghans made Delhi the capital of a new sultanate in 1206, and that kingdom could not hope to endure long without Hindu assistance.

[2] Gibb, *op. cit.*, p. 85.
[3] G. E. von Grunebaum, "Problems of Muslim Nationalism," in *Islam and the West*, ed. Richard N. Frye (The Hague: Mouton & Co., 1957), p. 13.

Even before the founding of the sultanate we know of "unconverted" Hindu warriors employed in the service of Muslims. Hindus were more essential still in the civilian ranks of administration, especially those bureaus of state concerned with the collection of revenue. War and plunder remained endemic throughout the first century of the sultanate, and official Muslim chronicles of the era are replete with reports of temples destroyed and "infidels sent to hell," [4] yet the preaching of *sufi* saints had at the same time begun building ideological bridges designed to unite the embattled civilizations.

Muslim mystics spread a devotional message of salvation across the heartland of northern India in the early decades of the Delhi Sultanate. The greatest of these, men like Nizam-ud-din Awliya (1238-1325), won with their piety and love the "submission" of countless Hindus whom the sword of terror had failed to convert. Ascetic practices much like *yoga* were advocated as aids in effecting such union, moreover, as was the guidance of a spiritual preceptor, whose role sounded to Hindus exactly like that of the *guru*. Echoing the central tenets of Vedanta and the *Gita*, Sufism singled out "true knowledge" derived from faith rather than works as the highroad to eternal bliss. Small wonder if many Vaishnavite Hindus found the words of such "divinely intoxicated" teachers of Islam no different from the popular devotionalism of their own faith, yet more alluring by far for socio-economic as well as political reasons. Simultaneously, Hindu saints like Ramananda (fourteenth century) and Chaitanya (1486-1533) roamed the land seeking to end defections from Hinduism's ranks with their unalloyed doctrines of love for God and the single family of mankind. The primary ethical tenet of Islamic social democracy thus found its echo in the hearts of Hindu mystics, who rose above all barriers of caste and even succeeded in winning the allegiance of Muslims.

Many who listened to the preaching of these remarkable advocates of Islamic *sufi* and Hindu *bhakti* must have wondered what, if anything, differentiated these two great religions. Some even decided that no essential differences existed, and that the names given to both religions and their respective divinities served only to confuse. Poet saints like Kabir (1440-1518) thus founded syncretic sects of their

---

[4] See extracts from Minhaju-s Siraj's *Tabakat-i Nasari* in *The History of India as Told by its Own Historians, The Muhammadan Period. Ghaznivide, Ghor and Slave Dynasties*, eds. H. M. Elliot and John Dowson (Calcutta: Susil Gupta, 1953), second reprint, *passim*.

own, rejecting false symbols of worship and God, "the beads of wood" and the "idols of stone," abandoning mosque and temple alike for the wider world of limitless divinity within and beyond.[5] Kabir, though born as a Muslim, was reared in the most sacred of Hindu cities, Banaras, where Ramananda's inspiring message lured him from the path of orthodox Islam. In the Punjab a historically more important religious synthesis was born with a Hindu named Nanak (1469-1538), whose early exposure to Sufism weaned him from polytheism and caste, and who subsequently became the first *guru* of the Sikh ("disciple") faith. Like Kabir, Nanak taught the unity of God and the brotherhood of man. In the final analysis he equated God with truth, and stressed the importance of a *guru*'s guidance to disciples seeking an understanding of divine reality. Within two centuries of Nanak's death, nine succeeding *gurus* had welded Sikhism into a powerful militant faith, which to this day plays a potent role in Punjabi politics as well as Indian religious life. Ironically enough, the pacifist mysticism and socioreligious toleration of Nanak's teaching was transmuted through Muslim persecution in the seventeenth century into the faith that inspired an army of the "pure" (*khalsa*) to unyielding opposition against the Mughals, contributing greatly to their eighteenth-century imperial decline. Under the leonine leadership of the tenth and last *guru*, Gobind Singh (1666-1708), moreover, the Sikhs assumed their distinctive characteristics of dress (including turbaned headgear, iron bracelet, shorts, and dagger) and ritual practice (especially the proscription against cutting their hair), which in appearance at least give them an aura of caste exclusiveness and separatism rather than universal toleration.

Islam and Hinduism borrowed from each other in many areas besides the ideological. Mass conversion of low-caste Hindus to the Muslim faith could hardly be expected to lead overnight to the total rejection of ingrained social and religious habits. Throughout Muslim India local cults, enjoining worship at the shrines of saints and resorting to superstitious rituals like those designed to exorcise demon deities, survive to this day as legacies of pre-Islamic practice. The more important ceremonies of Hinduism, such as those connected with marriage and death, were never totally abandoned, but instead became Muslim in name while remaining Hindu in form. Caste itself, with its taboos concerning food pollution and endogamy, did not

[5] See *One Hundred Poems of Kabir*, tr. Rabindranath Tagore (London: Macmillan & Co., 1954), p. 72.

disappear among Hindu converts; to the contrary, it began to infiltrate the hitherto undifferentiated Islamic society, and Muslims in India were soon divided into four groups: Turks, Pathans (or Afghans), Sayyids, and Shaikhs. Within each group sub-groups emerged, among which intermarriage and interdining became progressively more rare.

Hindus who gave up their faith continued to wear the ornate jewelry and enjoy the hotly seasoned food equally foreign to Islam. Among the Muslim aristocracy, Indo-Persian elegance in the form of embroidered silk robes, jewels, and gilded swords made the Sultan's court at Delhi no less luxurious than that of the Caliph at Baghdad; both sharply contrasted with the primitive simplicity of Arabian garb. In the Punjab, Hindus adopted the tight-fitting coats and trousers of their Muslim masters, and Rajput as well as Punjabi women still often wear slacks under their loose flowing skirts. Hindus easily weaned from their faith were less willing to give up their after-meal *pan* (areca nut chips wrapped in betel leaf), which also became a Muslim favorite. In language and art the two civilizations also merged to some extent. Urdu, now one of Pakistan's national languages, emerged around Delhi as a union of Hindi syntax and vocabulary with Persian loanwords and the *nastaliq* script of Arabia. Spoken Urdu is as closely related to Hindi as English to American, though in written form the national languages of India and Pakistan are alphabets apart and are written and read in opposite directions. Indo-Islamic architecture of the sultanate period reflects both harmony of artistic form and craftsmanship, surviving as the most tangible evidence of Hindu-Muslim cultural syncretism. The minars (towers), tombs, and mosques of this era, which decorate the Delhi plain in such profusion, were of course monuments to Muslim religious and temporal power, yet many were designed and erected by Hindu artists and craftsmen whose genius for workmanship in stone was unrivaled the world over. The remarkable Kutb Minar, completed in 1232, was constructed of the stones of some twenty-seven Hindu temples around Delhi. Erected as a symbol of Muslim conquest, it now illustrates the inextricable blending of the two great religions, with the form of one rising out of the substance of the other. Muslim mystics adopted Hindu music as stimulus to their meditations. Rajput painting was enriched with motifs drawn from Persian poetry and art. The very system of *purdah*, now thought of as epitomizing the social status of Muslim women, was unknown in Islam prior to its contact with India;

it probably resulted from Muslim emulation of Rajput seclusion of women.

Muslim Administration During the Sultanate

It was, however, in the interrelated realms of political and economic administration that the most important practical syncretisms of Islam and Hinduism occurred. According to Islamic law the faithful belong to one universal state or community (*umma*), presided over by Allah through His terrestrial representative, the leader (*imam*) chosen by the community as a whole, who is called the caliph. Theoretically, the caliph would lead the armies of Allah in holy war against all infidels. As the dimensions of Islamic conquest grew, however, one man alone could not direct all military and civil affairs, hence regional armies acquired quasi-autonomy under their own sultans. At the dawn of the Delhi Sultanate, the Turko-Afghans who ruled northern India paid their formal respects to the Abbasid Caliph, acknowledging Baghdad's theoretical suzerainty, though reigning in fact as independent monarchs. When the Mongol invasions overthrew the caliphate in 1258 and Mamluks and Ottomans began to struggle for the shattered Abbasid mantle, Delhi's autonomy was bolstered. In practice, moreover, the office of sultan became hereditary, though formal confirmation by vote of the leading nobles and the *ulama* was required. Widespread discontent with a reigning house was expressed on the field of battle or in a palace coup which, if successful, led to dynastic change. Five major Muslim dynasties ruled at Delhi during the more than three centuries of the sultanate: the Afghan ("Slave"), 1206-90; Khalji, 1290-1320; Tughluq, 1320-1414; Sayyid, 1414-50; and Lodi, 1450-1526. Not before the second reign of the Khalji dynasty was the banner of Islam carried south of the Vindhyas, and never throughout the sultanate era was all of India brought under Muslim rule. In the final years of the fourteenth century when Timur swept across the Indus plain to sack Delhi, Tughluq power shifted its center to the South. Hindu kingdoms, including empires of southern India like that of the Cholas (through the thirteenth century) and Vijayanagar (1336-1565), continued to exist on much the same pattern of polity as before the Muslim conquest.

The sultans established an administrative system for the sultanate that incorporated both Islamic experience outside of India and aspects borrowed from the traditional Hindu system. Like the Hindu *raja*, the sultan was an autocratic monarch limited by the sacred law as interpreted by leading Islamic scholars. He was assisted by a ministerial council headed by the chief minister (*wazir*), initially in charge of both civil and military affairs, though later burdened primarily with administration of the finance department. There was usually a deputy chief minister as well, and a noble with direct control over the military administration of the realm. Army recruitment and finance was controlled by a general. Other ministers of the central bureaucracy included the chief justice; head of the state secretariat; director of the secret service; and controller of religious finance and pious foundations. The imperial household and court was almost a state in itself with its army of guards, retainers, craftsmen, and slaves under the supervision of the sultan's paymaster and director of ceremonies. In size and complexity as well as general character the sultanate's bureaucracy strikingly resembled that of traditional Hindu kingdoms. By the reign of Firuz Tughluq (1351-1388), a converted Hindu Brahman, Makbul, almost ran the state as *Wazir* Khan Jahan until his death in 1372.

The Muslim army in India evolved into a true example of the synthesis of Hindu and Muslim ways. Though the cavalry, so important in the Turko-Afghan conquests, remained an elite corps and a Muslim monopoly, an elephant branch, which was massed behind the infantry composed mostly of Hindus, soon emerged as the bulwark of Islamic military supremacy. We know of cannon used in southern India before the end of the fourteenth century, and guns were widely diffused before the arrival of the Portuguese by the end of the fifteenth century; however, the sultanate was not sufficiently well equipped with an artillery corps to withstand the potent fire power of Babur's cannon train, one of the major factors in the Mughal victory of 1526.

By the time of the Tughluqs the sultanate was divided into twenty-four provinces, each of which was placed under the civil control of a governor and secured militarily by a centrally appointed general. The provinces were subdivided into rural districts, and they in turn into groups of villages. As a rule villages and sub-districts were left to govern themselves so long as they paid the land revenue upon which the state relied so heavily for its support in this as in all other epochs of Indian history. The state's share of all produce varied from between one-fifth to one-half during this era, and the special tax levied on Hindus was usually added to the regular land assessment. Other revenue was collected on such things as imports, mines, and the spoils of war, but the total of these never approached the value of taxes on agriculture. In adhering to traditional Hindu methods of revenue assessment and collection, and by relying mostly on Hindu accountants and intermediaries in the state revenue department, the sultans of Delhi simply showed themselves aware of the first axiom of successful rule in India: the interdependence of monarch and peasantry. Much of the land was "assigned" or "granted" to tax-"farmers" in remuneration for loyal allegiance to and military support of the sultanate. Many of these assignees and grantees were local Hindu chiefs, and this expedient confirmed their right to their hereditary realms. As distance from Delhi increased central authority weakened, and greater dependence was placed upon indigenous allies. Lands immediately surrounding the capital belonged to the sultan, supplying the daily needs of the palace. India's rural population in this era came to be called by the Arabic word *ra'iyat* (herd), which was converted into *ryot*, and remains our generic term for the Indian peasant.

In political, economic, social, religious, and aesthetic areas of behavior, then, highly eclectic institutions and customs emerged, revealing how flexible and in some respects compatible Hinduism and Islam could be. In other ways, however, familiarity fostered only a greater degree of mutual withdrawal, antipathy, and orthodox insularity. By the advent of Mughal rule Hindus by and large still viewed Muslims as foreign (*feringee*) rulers, and Muslims viewed Hindus as infidel second-class (*dhimmi*) subjects. History afforded the Mughals the opportunity either of binding the two civilizations more firmly into one, or driving deeper the wedge of difference dividing them.

Mughal Rule

In two respects the sixteenth century marked a crucial turning point in Indian history, bringing Mughal rule to the North and Portuguese power to the western littoral. The Portuguese were the advance guard of western Europe's more ambitious penetration; the Mughals ushered in the final and most important phase of the Muslim epoch. As had happened so often before in Indian history, Central Asia served as the rugged training ground for the Mughal invaders, who rode down from the north-west passes to plunder and remained to rule. Babur, "The Tiger" (1483-1530), descended from Timur the Turk on his father's side, and Chinggis Khan the Mongol on his mother's, founded the Mughal Empire. His *Memoirs*[6] give us a vivid account of the adventures of one of history's most intrepid and fascinating figures, who succeeded in carving an empire for his heirs out of northern India only after failing to retain the Central Asian principality left him at the age of twelve by his father. While but an émigré prince in Kabul, Babur assumed the title of emperor, then ventured forth to find a land worth ruling. The Napoleon of his age, he proved himself a master of artillery as well as men, routing the numerically far superior army of the last of the Lodi sultans on the historic plain of Panipat in 1526. Delhi and Agra became his twin capitals. The Rajput coalition failed to dislodge him a year later at Khanua, and under his grandson Akbar (1542-1605) the Hindu Rajputs became bulwarks of an empire rivaled in Indian history only by those of the Mauryas, the Guptas, and the British.

Akbar ("The Great") looms with Ashoka and Nehru as one of the greatest rulers of India, strong enough to make his personality and power felt throughout the land, wise enough to recognize that religious toleration and cooperation are surer pillars of power than military might and tyranny. His reign marks the high point of Hindu-Muslim harmony in this epoch. However, it is a source of caution as well as hope, for while demonstrating the possibility of social cooperation among two such diverse cultures, its evanescence and the bigotry and violence that followed it underscore the tenacity of darker currents of hatred, which seem only to grow stronger while awaiting their moment of reassertion. Akbar's enlightened policy of fostering communal cooperation had three aspects: political, economic, and religious. Politically he cultivated Hindu allegiance by marrying Rajput princesses (the first of these brides became mother of the next Mughal emperor, Jahangir) and appointing Hindus to the highest posts in the empire if they were qualified. By remitting the tax on Hindus in 1564, Akbar removed the major source of their economic discontent with Muslim rule. He remitted other discriminatory taxes as well, including those imposed on pilgrims, who flocked to sacred places and shrines during Hindu festivals. Such acts of grace had religious as well as economic implications; in addition, Akbar launched a frontal assault at his court against the discriminatory practices of *sunni* Islam and in 1579 stripped the *ulama* of its preponderance of religious

[6] *Memoirs of Zehir-ed-Din Muhammed Babur*, trs. J. Leyden and W. Erskine, rev. by L. King (London: Oxford University Press, 1921), 2 vols.

power. The "Infallibility Decree" of 1579 gave Akbar ultimate religious as well as temporal power, or, to put it another way, all of the prerogatives of caliph. This evoked a vitriolic attack from many of the *ulama*, who thought the emperor wanted to place himself on a pedestal of equality with The Prophet. Whether or not Akbar did in fact establish his own syncretistic divine religion is still in doubt,[7] but by making himself the final arbiter in religious controversy and stimulating doctrinal discussion among the proponents of all faiths at his court he certainly broke through the limitations of Islamic orthodoxy. As a *sufi* mystic during the latter part of his life, Akbar, evolved an eclectic personal faith based on elements drawn from Zoroastrianism and Hinduism as well as Islam.

Under Akbar's vigorous leadership the empire expanded in all directions, incorporating provinces that had broken free of the sultanate, like Gujarat (in 1573), Bengal (in 1576), Kashmir (in 1586), and the Deccani states (by 1601). Akbar reorganized the bureaucracy, establishing thirty-three salaried grades of officials (*mansabdars*), from the rank of "commander of ten horse" to that of "commander of 5,000," and carefully selected the best men he could find for the higher positions of power. Liable to assignment for service in any province of the empire, these *mansabdars* helped unify the imperial administration far more effectively than the sultanate had. The *mansabdari* system, derived from Persian practice, may be seen as the prototype for British India's civil service. Provincial administration was also improved considerably and regularized throughout the empire. The governor or *subahdar*, as he came to be called, was appointed by central authority, as were the revenue collectors, paymaster, district officers, and city magistrates. The two latter grades of officials came under the *subahdar*'s direction. Villages and *parganas* (which in British times are called *tehsils* or *talukas*) remained autonomous.

Mughal revenue collection was based on more careful land surveys and assessment than any undertaken during the sultanate. In Akbar's reign the regular imperial share was one-third of the gross produce, paid in cash value over most of northern India. Flexibility of tax remission in times of famine or other natural distress was the rule, and with Hindus like Todar Mal in charge of the imperial revenue depart-

---

[7] S. M. Ikram, *Muslim Civilization in India*, ed. A. T. Embree (New York: Columbia University Press, 1964), pp. 160-165, argues that he did not; but Vincent Smith, *Akbar the Great Mogul* (Oxford: Clarendon Press, 1919), pp. 213ff., insists he did.

ment greater understanding and sympathy was shown for the plight of the predominantly Hindu peasant population. (British rule drew heavily upon Mughal methods in this as well as other areas of administration.) Akbar's greatness, therefore, rests not only on the spirit of toleration he fostered among contending communities, but also on the extent to which he helped restore political and economic unity to a disorganized subcontinent.

The succeeding reigns of Jahangir (1605-27) and Shah Jahan (1628-58) have usually been called the "golden age" of Mughal rule because of the lavish expenditure on courtly arts and the magnificence of the architectural monuments constructed during them. The naturalistic miniature painting of Jahangir's day and the forts, mosques, and mausoleums (most famous of which was the Taj Mahal, completed at Agra in 1645) erected under the auspices of Shah Jahan are recognized as the finest masterpieces of Mughal art. However, such artistic extravagance cost more than even an imperial treasury could pay without strain. The cost of protracted warfare, especially in the later years of Shah Jahan's reign, when he vainly sought to recapture the Bactrian region of what is now Afghanistan from Persian control, was even more debilitating. Moreover, during Jahangir's reign bubonic plague was first definitely known to have spread its shadow across India (1616-24), and in the early years of Shah Jahan (1630-34) one of India's worst famines desolated the Deccan, helping deplete the state treasury. Then too the reaction of Islamic orthodoxy against Akbar's religious eclecticism, which had assumed serious proportions as early as the 1581 "Mullah revolt" in Bengal, was given fresh impetus by the Naqshbandi order and its influential leaders like Shaikh Ahmad of Sirhind (1564-1624). By Shah Jahan's reign the reaction received ample imperial patronage, and Mughal armies were sent to expel Portuguese Christians from Bengal in 1632, and to subdue *shi'a* kingdoms in the Deccan a year later, ostensibly for political, though equally for religious, reasons. The *ulama* and orthodoxy, however, had yet another reign to wait before Akbar's policy of equal toleration for all faiths was totally abandoned.

Aurangzeb (1618-1707), the fifth child of Shah Jahan and his uniquely immortalized beloved, Mumtaz-i-Mahal, cut his way to the imperial throne in 1658 over the body of his eldest brother, the enlightened Dara Shikoh. Last of the great Mughals, Aurangzeb also proved to be the most cunning and bigoted emperor of Indian history. His long reign of intolerance and terror, while superficially extending the area of Mughal power to its zenith, served in fact to exhaust the state's economic and military resources and demolish the fragile structure of social and religious harmony erected by Akbar. Coldly calculating, intellectually brilliant, a puritan by temperament, and first and foremost a zealous Muslim, who thought his primary duty the unrelenting extension of the *Dar-al-Islam,* Aurangzeb was supremely capable of inspiring the loyalty of those who agreed with and admired him and the antipathy of all others. He inaugurated a reign of unsurpassed religious austerity and doctrinaire orthodoxy by stripping his own court of song, dance, painting, poetry, and wine. Then he sought to impose Islam's pristine morality upon the realm by appointing censors of public morals in every major city to punish Muslims who fell below his own rigid puritanical standards. Next, he launched a relentless attack upon Hinduism, outlawing Hindu fairs and festivals in 1668, and using imperial troops to demolish Hindu temples and schools of learning. Not since the raids of Mahmud of Ghazni had so many of northern India's great temples been razed and replaced by mosques. The jeweled icons of India's holiest places of worship were laid before the mosques of Agra to be stepped upon by Muslims going to their prayers. In 1671 Aurangzeb tried to administer India without Hindu help in his imperial services, but he found this totally impractical and was forced to rehire many of the clerks thrown out of office. Determined, however, to abide by the letter of *sunni* law, he revoked all taxes (other than the traditional alms) imposed upon Muslims, and then reinstituted the hated tax on Hindus in order to balance his budget.

The last of the great Mughals did not have to wait long before reaping the harvest of his policy. Disaffection fanned rebellions throughout the empire. Peasants of the Mathura District rose in defiance of Mughal desecration of their temples in 1669; although they were crushed within a year they rebelled again. The *Satnamis* (True Names) of the Punjab, peasants influenced by the Sikh faith, revolted in 1672. The Sikhs themselves soon joined the revolt, especially after Aurangzeb sought in vain to convert the ninth *guru,* Tegh Bahadur (1621-1675), who was finally beheaded after prolonged torture at Delhi. Thereafter, Gobind Singh devoted himself to avenging his father and his faith, and transformed the Sikhs into an army of the pure, a caste of "lions" (*Singhs,* henceforth the surname of all Sikhs) dedicated to destroying Mughal power. By the end of Aurangzeb's reign, *Guru* Gobind had enlisted more than 100,000 sturdy soldiers from the Punjab and Kashmir in his holy war against Mughal tyranny. He had, moreover, the supreme satisfaction of outliving his mortal enemy by one year. The martial tradition he instilled among the Sikhs has never died. The Rajputs, whose loyalty Akbar labored so diplomatically to assure, rose in revolt after 1679, and with the aid of Aurangzeb's own son (also named Akbar) almost deposed the despotic monarch in 1681.

The strongest and most debilitating threat to Mughal dominance, however, emerged in this era from the Deccan region of what is now Maharashtra. Shivaji Maharaj (1627-80) had founded the Maratha "nation" by carving a Hindu kingdom out of the rugged "badlands" of southern India's plateau. This kingdom posed the greatest single challenge, not only to Aurangzeb's rule, but to that of his many successors throughout the first half of the eighteenth century. Few monarchs of Indian history were as daring, shrewd, and successful as Shivaji, who was contemned by his enemies as little more than a "mountain rat," worshipped by his followers as divinity incarnate, and hailed after his coronation in 1674 as *Shiva Chhatrapati* (Lord of the Universe). Until 1665 Shivaji was deemed unworthy of direct Mughal attention, but in that year Aurangzeb sent a formidable army against him under the command of the Rajput general, Jai Singh, temporarily quelling the Maratha rebellion. Shivaji was lured, in fact, to Agra as a Mughal *mansabdar* of 5,000 the following year. Proximity to the emperor only increased his alienation, however, and after a harrowing escape from Mughal imprisonment, he returned to his homeland to incite a "national" revolt among Hindus of the Deccan. Shivaji was imbued with the fervent conviction that his destiny was to restore *svarajya* ("self-rule") to a Hindu land enslaved by Mughal tyranny. The flame he ignited was passed on to his son, Sambhaji, and burned indeed with so fierce a light throughout Maharashtra that it continued into the epoch of British rule, blazing forth again during the Nationalist movement under leaders like Bal Gangadhar Tilak.

For the last quarter century of his life, Aurangzeb moved his court and capital to the Deccan, dedicating himself and all the military and financial resources of his empire to crushing the Marathas and the last of the Shiite kingdoms of the South, Bijapur and Golconda. His shifting capital traveled like a "plague of locusts" across the impoverished land, winning every battle, until by 1690 the Mughal caliph could claim all the territory from Cape Comorin to Kabul for Islam. Yet the victory proved as shortlived as it was costly. Maratha armies dissolved into the very hills and mud-walled villages, which nurtured Maratha horsemen and their attendants till the Mughal power had moved on. Then they reappeared, ever stronger, always more confident of their skill in the guerrilla tactics they had so naturally evolved. By 1705 Aurangzeb, at eighty-eight, was too tired and ill to do more than retreat to Ahmadnagar, where he waited quietly for death to deliver him from his burdens early in 1707. The Marathas were now poised on the threshhold of imperial expansion. After 1714, dawn of the *peshwai* era of Maratha history (when the *peshwas*, Brahman hereditary prime ministers at Poona, became the actual leaders of the Confederacy), Hindu power spread in the wake of the bankrupt Mughal Empire's collapse.

The disintegration of the Mughal Empire in the first half of the eighteenth century was the fruit of Aurangzeb's fanatical ambition. No fewer than five Mughal "emperors" shared the precarious throne at Delhi-Agra between 1707 and the battle of Plassey in 1757 (which may be considered the start of the British epoch). By 1712 the emperor had become a puppet of his leading courtiers. In 1724, the imperial *wazir*, Nizam-ul-Mulk (1669-1748), left the capital in disgust at its degradation, to carve his own kingdom out of the Deccan at Hyderabad, which survived till 1947 as the greatest Muslim principality of India. The Marathas, however, were the major legatees of Mughal decline. By 1729 they had pushed their borders north into Malwa, Bundelkhand, and Gujarat, riding forth unopposed to levy their "taxes" over peasants no longer "protected" by imperial troops. In these new domains Maratha generals created their own kingdoms. At Bundelkhand the *peshwa* was within easy striking distance of the Ganga-Yamuna heartland of northern India, and by 1738 his armies had ranged to the suburbs of Agra and the mighty gates of Delhi. A year later, Perso-Afghan invaders led by Nadir Shah swept across the Indus plain to conquer and plunder Delhi in the grim heat of April, returning beyond the Hindu Khush with the peacock throne of the emperor's Red Fort. Robbed of his regal chair as well as his provinces, the Mughal emperor had little more than his hollow titles left. The next twenty years witnessed the devastating power struggle between Marathas and Afghans for the mantle of the northern Indian empire. Lesser kingdoms watched apprehensively from the South and East (Oudh, Bihar, Bengal, and Orissa had become almost independent states under their Mughal governors), while the Hindu and Muslim giants moved into position for their final confrontation at Panipat in

1761. Indian history's third fateful battle on that blood-drenched plain north of Delhi robbed Maratha power of its finest fighters, some 200,-000 in all, cut down in a matter of hours by Ahmad Shah Durrani's Afghan force, which itself sustained irreparable loss. The only true victors of Panipat indeed, were the British, for by exhausing one another in battle Marathas and Afghans left a void, of which Europe's foremost power in India was by then ready and able to take advantage.

Muslim emperors continued a pretense of power for fully a century after the epoch of Muslim rule in India actually ended. Persian remained the official language of administrative and legal affairs until 1834. The visage of the "Grand" Mughal continued to appear on British-made coins in India until then as well. Robes of investiture continued to be granted regally from Delhi to "vassals" whose real power far exceeded that of the shadow monarch who still lingered in the palace until 1857. Noble Muslim families staunchly dreamed of the resurrection of empire. Scholars of Islam issued learned *fatwas* (opinions or "briefs") on all aspects of public life. The roughly one-quarter of India's population descended from invaders and converts to Islam remained faithful to the laws of Allah, and waited no doubt for the ultimate vindication and total victory of the *Dar-al-Islam*.

But a new epoch had dawned. New rulers, a new faith, and new ideas had entered India, temporarily ousting the old and adding vital ingredients to the compound Hindu-Muslim civilization of eighteenth-century India. In the nineteenth and early twentieth centuries these new influences were destined to transform India radically.

FOUR

British Conquest and Rule

Though the British were not the first Europeans to win a foothold in India, they succeeded where their Western rivals all failed. Their victory was due to slow and patient penetration, which bore fruit only after more than a century and a half of continuous contact with India. Moreover, they learned from the errors of earlier Western arrivals, benefiting from techniques evolved after long experience by the Portuguese, Dutch, and French. The British epoch of Indian history may be seen as the final fruition of some two and a half centuries of European experimentation and penetration in South Asia. Its roots go back to late-fifteenth-century Lisbon.

Portuguese Power in Asia

The scent of spice lured Western Europeans to Asian waters. Pepper, cloves, and nutmeg, needed to make palatable the decaying meats of Europe's markets, were incentives to Henry the Navigator and his school of sturdy seamen. Religion was also a spur, for Portuguese Catholics resented giving "infidel" Muslims, the middlemen who brought Asian spices to Western Europe, exorbitant profits. Vasco de Gama's successful trip around the tip of Africa and across the Indian ocean to Calicut in 1498 climaxed some eighty years of Portugal's "national" effort to gain direct access to Asian spices, and the start of an era of Western intrusion in India.

For most of the sixteenth century Portugal reigned supreme over the Indian ocean. Portugal's empire in Asia was based on command of the sea routes between the sources of spice production and Lisbon; her interest in India was commercial, not territorial. The territory she grabbed on India's west coast provided harbors for loading vessels with spice accumulated the year round in both India and the "Spice Islands" (Maluccas and Bandas), and strategic bases from which Portuguese naval units could patrol the major routes. Cochin and Calicut were the most important *entrepôts* on the Malabar coast, while Goa became the Indian captial of Portuguese power under Alfonso d'Albuquerque's viceroyalty (1509-1515). Driven by a fanatical ambition to destroy Islam, Albuquerque dreamed of diverting the headwaters of the Nile to dry up Egypt and of invading Mecca itself. He settled, however, for driving Muslim carriers from Indian waters, establishing naval bases at Ormuz on the Persian Gulf and Socotra near the Red Sea, besieging Aden, capturing Malacca, Diu, and Colombo, and turning South Asian waters into Portuguese private property. The geo-political scheme Albuquerque devised gave his nation, whose total population was barely one million, a monopoly over the world's most lucrative international trade during the first eight decades of the sixteenth century. After Portuguese power in Asia waned, moreover, Albuquerque's strategy was emulated almost in its entirety, first by the Dutch, then by the British. Singapore, Colombo, Bombay (rather than Goa), and Aden became the key points in Britain's blueprint of Asian naval dominance. Goa, Diu, and Daman long survived the collapse of Portuguese influence in India only because of British protection. Ironically enough, the first European power to rise and fall in India was also last to leave, finally driven from Goa by force in 1961.

The Portuguese also bequeathed two other important techniques to their Western European successors. They hired Indian soldiers who were trained and led by Portuguese officers. The French and British modeled their military establishments along precisely the same lines. (*Sipahi*, the Indian term for "police," was converted by the British into *sepoy*.) Also, Albuquerque negotiated the first European "subsidiary alliance" treaty with the king of Ormuz in 1507. As an expedient designed to give the European "ally" the reality of power but none of its more onerous burdens, this Portuguese prototype of later British treaties with Indian princely states contained three major clauses. First, the local "king" acknowledged himself a "vassal" of the Portuguese sovereign; second, he granted territory within his domain on which the Portuguese could erect a fortress and commercial warehouse for storing produce; finally, he agreed to pay an annual sum sufficient for maintaining a Portuguese armed force in his kingdom, which ensured that the "subsidiary ally" remained loyal to his European overlord. The system proved singularly effective: it required the minimum number of scarce European personnel; it involved no expense; and it aroused the least possible amount of popular animosity, since to all outward appearances the local ruler and his courtiers remained in power.

For all their political and military astuteness, however, the Portuguese failed in India. Their failure was in part attributable to their small home population and the growing interest in Asian trade of mightier nations. Equally detrimental to Portuguese success in India, however, was the fanatical religious zeal motivating so many of her *conquistadores*. Jesuits, arriving at Goa in 1542, labored relentlessly at trying to "save" Indian "heathen" from perdition. Their mission proved as fruitless as it was frustrating. Those who converted, obviously did so more for reasons of material benefit than spiritual salvation. Portuguese techniques of proselytizing, which included piratical attacks against Mughal ships filled with pilgrims destined for Mecca, only backfired. The British cleverly offered to escort these vessels instead, thus ingratiating themselves with Muslim administrators at the expense of the Portuguese.

When Portugal came under Spanish domination through the "personal union" of Philip II in 1580 the Catholic empire in Asia seemed about to begin a new era of dynamic growth. Spain was more interested, however, in New World gold than Old World spices, and Goa received less attention from Lisbon after 1580 than it had before. More important, Spain closed Lisbon to Dutch merchants after 1594, and this stimulated the Dutch to engage in the spice trade. The British also intensified their efforts at breaking the Iberian monopoly on the high seas at this time. In 1587 Sir Francis Drake's capture of the *San Filippe*, from which he plundered some £100,000 worth of Indian cargo, helped launch the fateful attack by Spain's Armada in 1588. In the wake of the Armada's defeat, Dutch and British seamen began their intrepid invasion of Asian seas in earnest.

Dutch and British Power in the Indies

On December 31, 1600 the "Governor and Company of Merchants of London Trading into the East Indies" was chartered by Queen Elizabeth. Over 200 Englishmen had contributed close to £70,000 as the initial capital behind this venture. The royal charter granted Governor Thomas Smythe and his twenty-four "committees" of London merchants a monopoly on all trade between the Cape of Good Hope and the Straits of Magellan for fifteen years. Four ships were outfitted the following year, a humble beginning for what was to become the administrative as well as mercantile agency of Britain's empire in

India. Ironically enough, the Company's early voyages were aimed not at India, but at the far wealthier sources of spice beyond: Bantam and Batavia in Java, Amboina in the Bandas, and the Molucca (Spice) Islands. By the time British vessels reached these ports, however, they found their Dutch friends already busily trading there.

Several factors help account for the initial lead of the Dutch over the British. In the late sixteenth century Antwerp had emerged as the home of Europe's most advanced school of cartography as well as a world leader in the adoption of modern business and, especially, banking techniques. The Dutch, moreover, were somewhat more generally experienced in sailing than the English. Most important of all, however, was the sense of rivalry and animosity motivating the recently independent Dutch states to struggle wherever possible against Spanish tyranny. In 1595 the Dutch sent their first expedition east. Goa reacted to this daring invasion by deploying Portuguese men-of-war to the Indian Ocean, and in 1598 the Dutch launched twenty-two mighty galleons in five separate fleets to run the Portuguese blockade. Once they reached Southeast Asia, the Dutch were most warmly received; the people there had grown sick of Portuguese and Spanish intolerance. Lucrative profits from these initial voyages stimulated greater investment at home. In 1602 merchants of Amsterdam, Rotterdam, Delft, and other major ports of the Netherlands, organized the *Vereenigde Oostindische Compagnie* (United East India Company) with ten times the capital raised in London and some seventy-six directors. This truly national enterprise was granted the monopoly of all trade between Good Hope and Magellan for twenty-one years by the States General of Holland. By 1605 some forty Dutch ships of the V.O.C. were plying the spice routes of Asia. Larger and better armed as well as more ably manned than their Portuguese rivals, these Dutch vessels swiftly took command of the high seas. Allied at first to the British by antipathy to Iberian Catholicism, the Dutch freely opened their Southeast Asian ports to British vessels. By 1610, however, Anglo-Dutch cooperation had become bitter competition in the Spice Islands.

Jan Pieterszoon Coen (*b.* 1587), the Albuquerque of Holland, was determined to convert Java and the adjacent islands into spice plantations run purely for Dutch exploitation. As governor-general of the Netherlands Indies in 1618-23 (he held the position again in 1627-29), Coen set himself the task of driving his English competitors from Spice Island ports. By 1619 the Dutch, centered at Batavia (now

Djakarta), were engaged in open war with the British based at Bantam. Mutual Anglo-Dutch interests in Europe dictated a truce under which the two nations were to share the wealth of Southeast Asia. But Coen was far too ambitious to accept any such diminution of his power for very long. In February 1623 he had ten Englishmen stationed at Amboina beheaded after a star chamber trial for "conspiracy"; this intimidated the British into withdrawing from the Spice Islands once and for all. The incident proved a blessing in disguise for Britain, since by discouraging further concentration on Southeast Asia it stimulated the development of British enterprise in what at the time seemed a poor second choice for commercial purposes, India. The Dutch, on the other hand, found their Spice Island monopoly so lucrative that they paid less attention to India, except for efforts at weakening Portugal's position there, especially by blockading Goa in 1639 and ousting the Portuguese from Colombo (Ceylon) in 1658. By the mid-seventeenth century Holland had become the world's foremost power, controlling the key points on the major sea route between Western Europe and Asia: at the Cape of Good Hope, Ceylon, Malacca, and Batavia.

Like the Portuguese, the Dutch, with a total population of under two million, were at first content to be a great commercial rather than territorial power in Asia. Experience, however, soon taught them that continued commercial expansion required stable sources of supply, which could only be assured by territorial control. Restive Spice Islanders began revolting against Dutch rapacity for profits after 1650, and before the end of the seventeenth century the Dutch proconsuls in the Indies had begun to develop their notorious "plantation system" based on slave labor and rigid administrative domination over the territory involved. It was from the Dutch that British imperialists learned the importance of territorial acquisition and its natural gifts of revenue as well as internal stability, essential to maintaining a properly balanced trade.

British Merchants in India

The first half-century of British contact with India was an era of meager mercantile expansion, in which British expectations of grandiose profits were frustrated by Dutch and Portuguese competition as well as Mughal indifference. This early period began in 1608, when London's first ship to India arrived at Surat (north of Bombay at the mouth of the Tapti), and lasted until 1658, when a revitalized East

India Company embarked on its "golden age" of profit. London merchants had hoped that the Grand Mughal would welcome an opportunity to trade with Englishmen, but found him as indifferent to such a proposal as their counterparts of the nineteenth century were to find the emperor of China. India in the seventeenth century was quite self-sufficient economically, an exporter of manufactured as well as raw materials, whose only really elastic demand was for specie. As Sir Thomas Roe, Britain's first official ambassador to India, complained, "Europe bleedeth to enrich Asia." In an era of prevailing mercantilist philosophy, of course, the export of specie was viewed as little less than a national crime, and Roe's mission was to negotiate a treaty of trade more favorable to British commercial interests. His failure was a reflection of the economic imbalance differentiating India from England in the seventeenth century. Indian spices, indigo, cotton cloth, silk, and saltpetre were in demand throughout Europe and Asia, while English woolens were hardly of use in semitropical climates.

Denied equality of trade, British merchants were content to linger in India by the grace of Mughal *firmans* (edicts of permission to trade within strictly prescribed limits), eagerly taking advantage of whatever opportunity presented itself to serve the Mughals in other ways. Surat became the first center of British interest in India, remaining the west coast headquarters of British power on the subcontinent until 1687, after which it was superseded by Bombay. Surat allowed British merchants easy access to Agra indigo and Gujarat cotton cloth, but not to the spices of Malabar. The latter remained under Portuguese control, and the British soon concentrated their fire power on Portuguese rivals in the Indian ocean, taking Ormuz in 1622, and escorting Mughal pilgrim ships from Surat after 1629. By the 1630 Treaty of Madrid, Portugal agreed to allow British merchants free access to pepper ports in the South, and after 1635 British ships were given direct entrée to Goa for the purchase and loading of spices. Soon after that Portuguese pirates started harrassing Mughal ships in the Bay of Bengal off India's east coast, and in 1639 the Surat Council of English merchants was called upon by the Mughal court to negotiate a truce, thereby serving the emperor in a diplomatic as well as military capacity. Thus, the initial phase of British penetration in India was characterized by willing subordination to Mughal needs rather than bellicose arrogance.

In the early part of the seventeenth century, however, Mughal power did not extend to the southeast coast of India (the Coromandel coast), and after 1611 British ships began probing this region in search of produce and markets for trade. Here they were eagerly welcomed by local chieftains, but found themselves faced with powerful Dutch opposition. The Dutch had established their headquarters at Pulicat (some thirty miles north of what was later Madras) in 1609. Initially they refused to cooperate with the English, but by treaty arrangement after 1619 gave British merchants permission to trade at Pulicat in return for support of half the armed garrison there. The Coromandel coast produced no spices, but was a flourishing center of cotton weaving. To reduce their specie drain, British merchants invested in cloth production, carried the cloth to Bantam, where it was much in demand, and sold it at considerable profit for spices there, so developing a specie-saving triangular trade. They had learned this technique from the Dutch, but the latter were also busy buying slaves along the Coromandel coast for their Spice Island plantations. After the Amboina incident the English left Pulicat to search for an independent center of power in the immediate vicinity. After more than fifteen years of wandering they settled at Madras in 1639. A fort was erected at once and christened St. George, and by 1658 all British settlements in Coromandel and Bengal came under the direction of the governor at Madras and his council.

Bengal, which from 1757 until 1911 was the center of British India, was not opened to British traders until 1651. Situated at the outlet of the Ganga, draining the wealthiest and most populous region of India, Bengal was a coveted viceroyalty of the Mughal administration, a formidable center of Mughal power. In 1632 the Portuguese had been driven from this region by Shah Jahan's army. Less than two decades later the British were permitted to trade in it only by special dispensation from the Mughal viceroy, thanks to the personal supplication of an English doctor, Gabriel Boughton, in attendance at the viceregal court. Establishing themselves at Hughli, slightly north of the Dutch center of Chinsura (also along the Hughli River, one of the Ganga's tributary outlets), the British developed a brisk trade in silk and saltpetre, shipped downriver from the interior of Bengal and Bihar. The English could purchase silk so much cheaper in Bengal than from their earlier Persian source of supply that by 1655 Bengali silk had preempted the market, while the saltpetre of Patna had long been in great demand throughout Europe for gunpowder. By 1658, then, British merchants had attained three toeholds on the coasts of western, southern, and eastern India. They had proved themselves adroit at negotiating with local as well as central Indian authorities, had initiated a triangular trading pattern with India and Southeast Asia, and were busy extracting several commodities other than spices for which an ever-growing demand had developed in Europe. Surprisingly enough, during this early era of trial and keen competition in India, the British Company was faced with its greatest difficulties at home.

Englishmen unconnected with the Company viewed its monopoly and the specie drain attending its continued pursuit of Asian trade as something of a national calamity. They thought a small group of London merchants greedily pursuing their own profit were undermining the security of the state. To maintain its monopoly privileges the Company was obliged to remit periodic "gifts" to the Crown. Here too were competitors. From 1635-49, for example, a rival company, Courten's Association, bought the patronage of Charles I and sent its own ships to India in direct defiance of the older Company's charter. Resorting to indiscriminate piratical tactics in Indian waters, this Association's ships plundered Mughal as well as Portuguese vessels, exposing the Surat Council of Englishmen to harsh Mughal reprisals. By 1640 the East India Company's stock had fallen to almost half its face value. In desperation, London merchants appealed to Parliament, but initially the latter felt little sympathy for the plight of any product of royal prerogative. Under Cromwell's Commonwealth, however, the situation changed radically, and in 1657 a national charter restored the Company's solvency, and marked its transition to a permanent joint stock basis of incorporation. The assets of both British competitors for the Indian trade were merged, and direction of the United Company's affairs was placed in the hands of a governor and committee of twenty-four. Revitalized by Commons, its stock bolstered by eager new subscribers in the City, the Company embarked on a new phase of vigorous and profitable expansion in 1658, the very year in which Aurangzeb came to power in Delhi.

For the British, the first half of Aurangzeb's reign was a golden age of rising dividends. Charles II turned Bombay, part of Catherine of Braganza's dowry, over to the Company in 1661, and after 1687 this excellent insular port replaced Surat as the Company's west coast capital. As an island, Bombay (unlike Surat) was impervious to Maratha raids, and it proved the one natural port of British India capable of sheltering modern ocean-going vessels without costly dredging.

Fortified and defended by cannon, Bombay managed to withstand all seaward assault as well, and it quickly became India's first commercial city, a position it still holds.

Expanding trade encouraged the British to build new factories in Bengal, and Mughal repressive measures against English merchants in this region led to the first clash of arms in 1686. The British were as yet no match for Mughal might, and Job Charnock, governor of Bengal's council, was obliged to retreat from Hughli with his men, falling back down-river some twenty-seven miles to a spot later known as Calcutta. A few years later the puny British garrison was forced out of Bengal entirely, sailing for Madras, while the Bombay-based fleet harassed Mughal shipping until Aurangzeb agreed to a truce whereby the British were permitted to return to Calcutta in 1690. The strategic utility of Britain's three-pronged base on Indian soil was thus early demonstrated, and British power in one garrison was often to be used later in bolstering the waning fortunes of another. Within a decade of Charnock's return to Calcutta in 1690, Fort William had been erected there and more than a thousand British inhabitants were settled in what soon became British India's bustling capital.

Few Englishmen of the seventeenth century could have foreseen the singular good fortune of their countrymen on Indian soil during the next century. Yet to write of the growth of British imperial power in India as nothing more than expansion in a fit of absentmindedness would be inaccurate. By the latter decades of the seventeenth century several Englishmen at home and abroad had the vision to anticipate a future for British interests in India far grander than the present appeared to warrant.

Anglo-French Rivalry

Two major themes dominated the history of India in the first half of the eighteenth century: Mughal disintegration, and Anglo-French rivalry along the fringes of a collapsing empire. To Indian aspirants for the Mughal dominions the former seemed by far the more important. The outcome of the Anglo-French conflict, however, was destined to decide who the true successors to Mughal imperial might would be. While Marathas, Afghans, Rajputs, Mughals, and Sikhs wore each other out in indecisive warfare, the European rivals were left relatively free to determine between themselves whether Britain or France would inherit an Indian empire.

Colbert's ambition had stimulated the founding of a French East

India Company in 1664, and ten years later François Martin chose Pondicherry (some eighty-five miles south of Madras) as the capital of French power in India. While the English were busy erecting Fort William at Calcutta, moreover, the French settled at Chandarnagar, some twenty miles north on the Hughli. They had already constructed a warehouse at Surat, thus duplicating the British tripod pattern. Franco-Dutch conflict in Europe, however, almost completely eliminated French outposts in India at the turn of the century. Then after 1720 a nationally supported French "Perpetual Company of the Indies" was born, and in the 1730's the French enjoyed their most prosperous decade of Indian trade. Till 1744 the French and English in India were leading commercial competitors, but after news of the official outbreak of the War of the Austrian Succession reached India they became military combatants.

The Anglo-French struggle for power was focused initially on the Coromandel coast where it raged, with brief intervals of truce, from 1744-61. The war's first round went to the French, whose daring admiral, Mahé de la Bourdonnais, sailed through an English blockade to capture Madras in 1746. Fortunately for the English, Admiral de la Bourdonnais would not allow the brilliant French governor of Pondicherry, Joseph François Dupleix (1697-1764), to command his fleet, and instead of remaining at Madras withdrew to Mauritus Island. The personal antipathy dividing de la Bourdonnais and Dupleix mortally undermined the French position. Yet Dupleix was an empire-builder of such stature that he almost managed to realize his ambitions in southeast India without the royal fleet. Promising Anwar-ud-din, then *nawab* of the Carnatic, to capture Madras for him in return for his neutrality, Dupleix drove the British from their Coromandel capital a second time in October 1746. He then balked at turning over Fort St. George to the *nawab*, and proved himself in fact master of the former rather than his servant. An army of over 10,000 poorly disciplined Indians sent to seize Madras was routed by a compact, well-trained force of some seven hundred sepoys, led by about two hundred Europeans. Few people in India or Europe took note of this battle of St. Thomé, but it was a portent of the swiftly changing balance of power between armies commanded by Europeans and those led by Indians.

Dupleix understood the implications of his early victories, and saw that an empire was within reach if he could but eliminate his English rivals and use the might at his disposal to support otherwise impotent claimants to viceregal thrones. By 1747 the English had been reduced to one small outpost south of Pondicherry, Fort St. David, and but for the treaty of Aix-la-Chapelle (1748) which restored Madras to them, they might have left India altogether. To the diplomats in France, however, Madras seemed small enough a concession for the return of so much of their captured terrain in North America. Dupleix was defeated more by his own countrymen at home than his enemies on Indian soil. Nonetheless, he continued to play a brilliant game on the chaotic chessboard of southern Indian politics, and by mid-century the French were masters of both major capitals of southern India. However, the British quickly learned to play their rival's own game. Still and all, in 1751 an astute observer of the relative positions and strengths of French and British forces in southern India would have seemed correct in predicting total French victory. Fort St. David and Madras, Trichinopoli and Tanjore, were more nearly islands of British resistance to the fast-running French tide than the keystones of an empire-to-come. Yet this prognosis would have reckoned without the unpredictable individual factor which, in the person of Robert Clive (1725-74), did so much to turn the tide.

Clive was the prototype of those rambunctious and untutored young Englishmen whose tempestuous temperaments would most likely have led them to some lock-up in London, but who were instead shipped off to the colonies to win fame and fortune. He was a malcontent, an outsider, a brooding bully, who tried to blow out his own brains in a Madras counting house before deciding that he preferred blowing out the brains of others. Viewed in another light, he was a born soldier, a natural military genius, irrepressible, inexhaustible. He loved nothing better than a good fight. No one had to order him to lead a charge. No one could hold him back. Indeed, when all his battles were won and his fortune secure, when at last, on the eve of his fiftieth year, he faced the prospect of a long and leisurely retirement at home, he found the future so grimly dull that he attempted suicide again, and succeeded.

Just when the French position was strongest, when a ring of steel blockaded most of the British Indian troops at Trichinopoli, when Madras and St. David were at their lowest point of morale, Clive, intuiting that the best defense is an offense, convinced his governor to let him launch an attack upon Arcot. It worked perfectly; Arcot was taken by surprise. Clive and some 500 troops held the capital of a region, controlling almost two million people for fifty days in the fall of 1751. The daring escapade electrified southern India, demoralizing the French, bolstering flagging British spirits, starting legends about England's "heaven-sent general" throughout the subcontinent. In June 1752 Clive and his men marched south to relieve Trichinopoli. The superior French force surrendered, and the British puppet was proclaimed *nawab*.

Dupleix was hardly beaten as yet, but each report of even a minor French defeat was magnified by the directors back home, who had waited in vain for profits ever since their independent-minded proconsul had embarked on his expensive empire-building enterprise, and in 1754 he was ordered home. A treaty of Indian truce was drawn up by the French in 1755, and a year later, with the start of Europe's Seven Years War, the balance shifted heavily in Britain's favor. By 1761, with the British conquest of Pondicherry and its destruction as a military stronghold, French power along the Coromandel coast was shattered. Two years later Dupleix died in poverty and disgrace, his foresight and vision unappreciated. The British were wiser; they recognized the ingenuity of their greatest rival. Clive paid his enemy the sincerest of compliments by building the foundation of British India according to the blueprint of power drafted by Dupleix.

The British in Bengal

After 1704 Bengal, while remaining nominally a province of the Mughal Empire, became in fact an independent kingdom. Under Aliverdi Khan (1740-56) the British were left unmolested in their trade throughout this most wealthy domain, but Siraj-ud-daula, the old *nawab*'s grand nephew, who succeeded to the throne in 1756, had other ideas. He considered the British merchants bothersome leeches on his land's riches, and decided to remove them directly. First he drove the Company's factors from Kasimbazar, then marched south to Calcutta in the torrid month of June, 1756, capturing Fort William with remarkable ease. The aftermath of the British garrison's ignominious retreat was the celebrated "Black Hole" incarceration of somewhere between sixty and one hundred and fifty British prisoners from dusk till dawn in a room fourteen by eighteen feet with only two barred air holes. Hardly more than twenty of the prisoners emerged alive. The martyrdom of the others helped kindle flames of self-righteous retaliation and determination in the minds of many generations of British youth sent out to "civilize" India. More immediately, a retaliatory expedition set sail from Madras with Clive and some 2,000 soldiers in October. By year's end Calcutta was back in British hands, but the Company was no longer to rest content with trade alone. Clive soon learned that the impetuous young *nawab*'s rash manners had provoked Hindu bankers as well as Muslim nobles, and he perceived that Bengal was as ripe for revolution as the Deccan had been a few years before. Mir Jafar, the former *nawab*'s brother-in-law, was particularly disaffected, and Clive used the Mir's ambition to his own advantage, turning him into a puppet of British power. In June 1757 Clive led hardly more than 3,000 soldiers (most of them Indian) north toward Murshidabad, stopping in a mango-grove at Plassey to engage Siraj-ud-daula's treason-infested army the next day. Mir Jafar kept his bargain by withholding the most potent cavalry force from the field, thereby permitting the British to win the day and to become masters of the most coveted region of the collapsing empire. The political change inaugurated by Plassey marks the dawn of the British epoch in India.

At first the Company was satisfied with the substance of power, leaving its formal shadow in the hands of Muslim *nawabs* at Murshidabad, whose tenure lasted only as long as they obeyed British orders and abstained from interfering with trade. Clive himself was appointed a Mughal *mansabdar*, extorted some £250,000 from Mir Jafar, and was granted a substantial private estate, whose revenues he reaped annually for life. An era of legalized plunder by British factors in Bengal unmatched in the recent history of India for its rapacity and greed, had begun. The French were disarmed at Chandarnagar, the Dutch isolated at their Chinsura fort, the Mughal helpless on his precarious throne at Delhi. As governor of Fort William from 1758-60, Clive was virtual king of Bengal, and when he returned to England in 1760 he was hailed and reviled, his fortune more fabulous than any ever amassed by a single subject of the king in so brief an interlude. He purchased a controlling share of the Company's stock, as well as a seat in Commons, becoming the envy and idol of every young Englishman of negligible means, all of whom now dreamed of marching the high-road to glory in London via the battlefields and bazaars of India.

Clive set the tone for his subordinates, giving them a target at which to aim. The young apprentice or writer who joined the Company for the passage east received a salary so small it would hardly pay for the clothes he wore, yet each man knew that if he played the game wisely once in Bengal, using his influence and opportunities for the purpose of private trade rather than Company service, he could earn a fortune. Indian moneylenders were always eager to become the creditors of the white Sahibs, who held the keys to power. Indian peasants and weavers, merchants and laborers, were always ready to serve the vigorous young men whose fearless and godlike manner had marked them out as a caste apart from and higher than all others. For the young men of England after 1760 the universal cry of ambition was "Go East." India's bountiful tree of golden pagodas (the standard coinage of Madras, later displaced by the silver rupee) stood waiting to be shaken. One needed but a stout heart and a purse large enough to hold the spoils.

Even Mir Jafar could not accept such rapacity for more than a few years. He had to be pensioned off in 1760, replaced by his son-in-law, Mir Kasim, whom the British hoped would be more docile. He proved himself quite the contrary, however, conspiring with Shuja-ud-daula, *nawab-wazir* of Oudh, and his hostage-master Shah Alam, the Grand Mughal, to drive the British plunderers from North India. The confrontation came at Baksar, on the south bank of the Ganga between Patna and Banaras, in October 1764. It was the Mughal army's last great stand against British fire power, and the victory of the latter more than confirmed the ascendancy won at Plassey. After Baksar the Company was formally granted control over all revenue collection in Bengal by the emperor himself. The *nawab* remained in charge of civil administration, but without revenue to run it now found himself totally dependent upon Fort William, which in turn had all the funds but none of the responsibility for maintaining law and order. This "dual government," as it came to be called, was probably the worst system of rule ever foisted upon an Indian region. Power was irresponsible, and those with responsibility were bankrupt. The population at large suffered from unsurpassed extortion without receiving any vestige of official protection. Only individual Englishmen, who amassed personal fortunes, benefited from the system. The Company itself was now so ill-served that instead of reaping profits from its new kingdom it was faced with a growing deficit, and in 1767 could not remit £400,000 called for by the British Treasury. The glaring inconsistency of individual wealth and corporate insolvency raised a hew and cry in London for parliamentary inquiry into East India affairs. This investigation was still in progress when a devastating famine scourged Bengal from 1770 to 1772, obliging the Company's directors to approach Parliament for an urgently required loan of one million pounds. Commons finally recognized that something was very rotten in Bengal, and decided it was high time to intervene.

Lord North's Regulating Act of 1773 was the first major intrusion by the home government of Britain into the administration of British India. It marks the beginning of a gradual transfer of real power over India from Company to Crown, which was to be officially consummated in 1858. Parliament was in no rush in 1773 to assume more immediate responsibility in India than was considered absolutely necessary; Britain's colonies in North America provided more than enough troubles for most members to worry about. Yet something had to be done with Bengal, and especially its financial plight. The Regulating Act limited the Company's dividend rate to 6 per cent; provided for the appointment of three new councillors to the governor of Fort William by Parliament to act as "honest brokers" for the sizable loan granted; established a Supreme Court of British judicature at Calcutta; and, implicitly most important of all, empowered His Majesty's high treasurer with the right to review all records of the Company's revenue and copies of all letters and dispatches passing between its directors and its servants in Fort William on matters of general administration. It also imposed certain restrictions on election to and qualification for the Company's court of directors, and gave Bengal the leading administrative position among the three British presidencies in India by promoting the governor of Fort William to the rank of governor-general and giving him certain powers over Madras and Bombay. The dual system had thus become triplex, and in some measure confusion and misrule were compounded; yet order and a clearer definition of responsibility gradually emerged in Bengal. Those who came to plunder remained to rule. This new approach largely resulted from the labors of Fort William's first governor-general, Warren Hastings (1732-1814).

Hastings had been partly reared in the Company's service, having come to Calcutta as a "writer" (of Company letters and ledgers) at the age of seventeen. Orphaned as a child, precociously bright, and armed with a classical education before he shipped east, Hastings found his true home in India and quickly immersed himself in the study and mastery of its complex culture and diverse languages. He was by temperament more a scholar and mystic than a soldier-diplomat, yet above all he was a loyal Company servant, qualified by long and intimate knowledge of India to direct the Company's establishment in Bengal after 1772. His primary concern throughout the twelve years during which he guided the government of British India was to strengthen the Company's position, financial and political. He did not fear responsibility, and strove to check the selfish grasping of merchants who never looked beyond their own immediate profit. A famine-stricken, rack-rented Bengal could hardly provide lucrative trade, and Hastings understood that in the long run what was good for Bengal would be good for the Company. The administrative reforms he introduced were all designed to give Indians a better opportunity to live according to their time-honored traditions, customs, and legal systems. He knew enough about India to appreciate how different its heritage was from that of England, and he was practical enough to know that differences like these could not be abolished by fiat or force. Although Hastings was accused of so many sins and crimes by Edmund Burke and others in the course of his impeachment trial before the Lords, which dragged on for almost a decade (1786-95) until his ultimate acquittal, his standards of public morality were surely not abnormal for his age. He was a realistic administrator, not a reformer nor an idealist. He was interested in achieving results, and used whatever means were available. He could be ruthless, vindictive, dishonest, aggressive—but always in order to serve his Company and strengthen its growing empire. More than Clive, he deserves to be remembered as the father of British India, having raised, as he himself put it, "a great and weighty fabric, of which (when he first took command) all the parts were yet loose and destitute of the superior weight which was to give them their mutual support." [1]

By renting Company troops to the *nawab-wazir* of Oudh to use in suppressing the Rohilla Afghans in 1774, Hastings bolstered Oudh as a buffer protecting Bengal from northwestern invasion, while winning the alliance of the great "country" power neighboring his own. By dispatching an army from Bengal on an unprecedented march across central India to relieve the Bombay presidency in 1778, when it was most humiliatingly defeated by the Marathas, he restored British prestige and power in western India and proved himself a governor-general in more than title only. But for this timely action, the Marathas, then recovering from their defeat at Panipat twenty years earlier, might in another decade have proved too powerful for the

[1] Hastings' "Review of his Administration," 1765, quoted in Ramsay Muir, *The Making of British India* (Manchester: University of Manchester Press, 1923), p. 157.

British to overcome. In southern India as well, Hastings saw to it that British possessions and influence suffered no diminution, but rather grew. The triple alliance of the Maratha confederacy, Hyderabad, and Mysore, instigated by the French and concluded in 1778, was designed to oust the British first from Madras, ultimately from all of India. Hastings did not underestimate the danger of such unified Indian opposition, and he first used diplomatic means to divide or neutralize it.

Opposition to Hastings, both within his own council and in Commons, was bitter and strident throughout his era of rule. Britain was at this time sustaining her worst military defeat in modern times at the hands of American "rebels," and the Whig opposition to Lord North and George III feared that much the same sort of thing was about to happen in India. The hew and cry in Parliament for tighter controls over East India Company affairs became irresistible by 1784, when the younger Pitt's India Bill was enacted, leading Hastings to resign and return home to face his decade of trial.

The India Act of 1784 gave Parliament, through a newly established board of control, supervisory power over "all the British territorial possessions in the East Indies, and over the affairs of the Company.[2] In effect it did to the Company what the Company's subsidiary alliances had earlier done to indigenous princes. The Crown—i.e., Parliament—hereafter retained ultimate power to control Indian affairs, while leaving the immediate administration of such matters in the hands of Company servants, still appointed by and nominally responsible to the court of directors. His Majesty's privy councillors on the board of control were granted full access to all East India papers, and final control over all civil and military operations in British India. This board thus functioned as the constitutional precursor of Whitehall's India Office (established after 1858), and its president was in fact, though not in name, the Cabinet forebear of the secretary of state for India. Henry Dundas (1742-1811), whose ideas inspired Pitt's Act, led the new board with Scottish ingenuity and vigor for the first eighteen years of its existence, and by his astute management guided British India through its arduous transition from one among several competing powers in India to almost complete paramountcy over the subcontinent. First of all it was necessary to restore British and general European financial confidence in the government of In-

[2] Pitt's India Act (24 George III, c. xxv) of 1784, quoted in *ibid.*, p. 171.

dia.[3] The Marquess Cornwallis (1738-1805) was sent out as governor-general in 1786 to fulfill this vital function.

Cornwallis was an English country gentleman, with all of the strengths and shortcomings associated with that singular breed in its finest form. His probity and integrity were beyond reproach. He was brave, self-confident, naïvely simple in outlook, mediocre in intellect. He sincerely believed that his mode of life, his ideas, and his criteria of judgment for all things were the final products of human evolution, invariably admirable, universally applicable. Unlike Hastings, he was the king's man rather than the Company's, and instead of seeking to rule Indians with the aid of as many Indians as possible, he introduced British officials everywhere in the higher ranks of the bureaucracy, and sought to apply British law, British standards, and British customs to every realm of Indian life. He Anglicized the Indian army as well, and for almost a century after his administration no Indian was permitted to serve as a commissioned officer in the British military establishment. The Regulations of 1793, which came to be called "the Cornwallis system," set high moral standards for the Indian civil service, prohibiting British covenanted servants from engaging in private trade, and raising salaries high enough to induce them to work for the government instead of themselves. The more flagrantly corrupt officials were fired, and European confidence in the Company's solvency was restored. Cornwallis' land revenue policy, the first of his forty-eight Regulations, fixed a permanent annual assessment of some three and three-quarter million pounds on all lands within the Company's Bengal presidency. The Mughal tax-collectors (*zamindars*) were given title deeds to property in the hope, as far as Cornwallis at least was concerned, of inspiring them with all the virtues of British country squires. Actually, most of the original *zamindars* were soon displaced by moneylenders for failure to repay loans secured with the collateral of property deeds. Instead of living on their estates, moreover, many of these new landowners remained as absentee holders in Calcutta, reaping windfall profits as the yields of their huge holdings doubled and quadrupled over the next several decades while the "permanent settlement" demand by government stayed the same. One valuable political by-product of Cornwallis'

[3] Holden Furber, *John Company at Work. A Study of European Expansion in India in the Late XVIII Century* (Cambridge: Harvard University Press, 1951).

policy, at any rate, was the emergence of a powerful and prestigious group of Indians in Bengal, wholly loyal to the British *raj* for the best of financial reasons. Thanks in good measure to the *zamindars'* loyalty, Bengal remained mostly quiescent during the War of 1857-58, thus helping British India to survive its severest ordeal.

By the end of the eighteenth century the British government of India was thus well established along the lines on which it continued to develop for the next fifty years. The pattern formulated in Bengal was to be duplicated elsewhere as new provinces were incorporated into the empire. The governor-general at Calcutta, responsible both to the court and board in London, was assisted by councillors, civil and military, in the central administration of daily affairs. British district officers, originally (1786-93) charged with the combined duties of police magistrate, revenue collector, and judge, were sent into the hinterland to keep order and transmit revenue. After 1793 at least two British civil servants were assigned to each district; one as magistrate-judge, the other as collector (from 1817 on the functions of magistrate-collector were united, while justice remained in independent hands). The young Englishmen who ruled districts often containing as many as a million people, all relied heavily on Indian interpreters, assistants, clerks, and personal servants. At the district and subdistrict levels administration continued on much the same lines as those established by Mughal rule, and within villages ancient autonomy prevailed. The British in India, by virtue of color, language, religion, and custom, easily fit into the traditional pattern of Indian society as a "caste" of foreign rulers. In the Company era, however, most Englishmen consorted with their Indian "housekeepers" and thereby gained a more intimate knowledge of Indian habits and attitudes than their successors of the post-1858 Crown era of strict racial segregation. Nonofficial British merchants, of course, penetrated the interior in pursuit of trade, and as Britain began to lead the world in industrialization, British machine-made fabrics outsold Indian handspun cloth, setting in motion a silent but pervasive revolution within India's economic structure, which was to have as far-reaching implications as those of the political upheaval so dramatically under way.

Though the Act of 1784 declared all "schemes of conquest and extension of dominion in India" to be "repugnant to the wish, the honour and policy of this nation," such pious pronouncements did not stop the process of empire-building initiated by Clive. Richard Colley Wellesley (1760-1842), who arrived at Calcutta in 1798 to govern British India on the eve of Napoleon's invasion of Egypt (the first stop on his intended march to India), more than doubled the territory under British control within the seven years of his reign. Motivated by the francophobia guiding British diplomacy of his day, Wellesley wasted no time in striking to stamp out French influence among rival Indian powers. By 1801 the only remaining power capable of challenging total British hegemony over India was that of the Maratha pentarchy. By then, however, the Maratha's greatest general, Mahadji Sindhia (1727-94), and their shrewdest diplomat of the century, Nana Phadnis (1742-1800), were both dead, leaving Wellesley at a considerable advantage in contending with their less vigorous and talented successors.

The Maratha leaders, like all of their Indian contemporaries of the eighteenth century, had never learned the importance of sustained cooperation in their struggle against Western powers. The British conquest of India was, indeed, as much the product of Indian lack of unity or any true spirit of Nationalism at this time, as it was a result of British policy, power, or gifted leadership. Had Maratha rivals joined forces rather than fighting each other for dominance of the pentarchy, British power might well have been contained, and possibly even rolled back in the first decades of the nineteenth century. Instead, the leading Maratha generals sponsored rival claimants to the *peshwa's* office, and Wellesley resorted to the well-tested technique of using the claimant temporarily out of power as the puppet behind which a British army was to advance into Poona. Baji Rao II, ousted from his throne in 1802, served the British cause from his exile on Bassein, signing a subsidiary alliance with the British there in December. This treaty marks the *de jure* fall of Maratha power, though it was not until 1818 that the final Maratha defeat was in fact sustained on the field of battle. Wellesley himself had long since been driven to resign and return home after losing the confidence of the Company's directors by his costly conquests and haughty indifference to Leadenhall Street. But the trail he had blazed was completed in 1818, when the fourth Anglo-Maratha War ended and the era of British paramountcy over India was begun.

The four remaining decades (1818-58) of the first century of the British epoch were marked by the consolidation of British power, and the inauguration of socio-religious and material reforms, which in turn stimulated multi-faceted intellectual and violent political responses throughout the newly conquered subcontinent.

Consolidation of the British Raj

After 1818 no single Indian power was capable of challenging British paramountcy. The Sikhs under Ranjit Singh (1780-1839), the one-eyed Lion of the Punjab, had consolidated their grip over the region west and north of the Sutlej, which they retained (together with Kashmir) till the late 1840s. The Amirs of Sind were independent until 1843. On the frontiers to the west, north, and east, moreover, hostile Afghan tribes, Nepali Gurkhas, and Tibeto-Burmans posed irritating and often dangerous local threats to neighboring British settlements, just as the tribal peoples and recalcitrant princes of central India did. But a new *raj* had succeeded the *mughal's*, and the wars it fought after 1818, with the exception of the one in 1857-58, were battles of expansion and consolidation rather than struggles for survival.

Burma was absorbed into British India's empire after wars concluded in 1826, 1852, and 1885. Britain's imperialist motivation in this direction was earlier commercial penetration and its subsequent protection. Private British merchants had established commercial outposts along the Arakan and Tenasserim coasts in pursuit of their triangular "country" trade in the eighteenth century, and by 1795 Calcutta sent an envoy to the Court of Ava seeking permission to post a British resident at Rangoon to supervise Anglo-Burmese trade. The "Hermit Kingdom" of Burma, however, refused to acknowledge British traders as equals, thereby bringing itself to the brink of war with the East India Company in 1798. In 1802 Wellesley offered the Burmese a subsidiary alliance treaty, and a resident was again sent to Rangoon, but relations deteriorated after 1811 when British troops were engaged in fighting over a border dispute around Chittagong. The "turbulent frontier" [4] remained a source of continuing irritation till Lord Amherst (governor-general from 1823-28) sent his gunboats up the Irrawaddy to seize Rangoon. The original British plan was to advance as far north as the capital at Ava, but stiff Burmese opposition, deleterious climate, disease, and widespread sepoy unrest convinced the British to content themselves in 1826 with the acquisition of Burma's coastal provinces, the promise of Burmese withdrawal from Assam and Manipur State, and a substantial indemnity. Burma balked at fulfilling its treaty obligations, however, and after 1840 the

[4] John Galbraith, "The 'Turbulent Frontier' as a Factor in British Expansion," *Comparative Studies in Society and History* (January 1960), II, 2, pp. 150-168.

British severed diplomatic relations. At this time British troops were too busy in the west to bother with Burma, but in 1851 gunboat diplomacy was reintroduced by "combustible Commodore" Lambert, and Rangoon was occupied by British Indian troops in April of 1852. The wealthy southern half of Burma was annexed, and in 1862 the three commissionerships of Pegu, Arakan, and Tenasserim were incorporated into British India as a new province. Southern Burma under British rule became the world's foremost exporter of rice. Isolated and impoverished, Ava to the north was left to enjoy its precarious independence till 1885. Thereafter, all of Burma remained part of the British Indian Empire until 1935.

British expansion to the west was undertaken primarily for strategic rather than commercial reasons. Francophobia had declined with Waterloo, but its place was soon taken in British diplomatic minds by an equally virulent strain of russophobia. In the 1830s Russia expanded under Tsar Nicholas I into Central Asia, and Whig statesmen like Lord Palmerston saw the specter of Russian influence stretching into Persia and across Afghanistan itself to the very highroad into India. George Eden, the Earl of Auckland (governor-general from 1835-42), was the unfortunate and inept director of the first British attempt to "defend" India against Russia by taking control of Afghanistan. Shah Shuja, the deposed Durrani Amir of Afghanistan, expelled from his Kabul throne in 1809, and since then living on a British stipend in Ludhiana, was the straw man Auckland chose to support against Dost Muhammad, the popular Barakzai monarch of Kabul. The pretense was Russian intrigue at the Afghan court. An unholy triple alliance was formed between the Company, the Sikhs, and the powerless Shah in 1838, and plans were laid for a two-pronged assault against Afghanistan. Ranjit Singh's Sikhs were to march from Peshawar over the Khyber to Kabul, while Auckland's doomed Army of the Indus was to traverse Sind and invade Afghanistan across the Bolan to Kandahar, then North to Kabul. Ignoring the advice of all who knew better, Auckland went ahead with his megalomaniacal scheme early in 1839. The Company's splendid army advanced irresistibly. Dost Muhammad fled from Kabul and his hated cousin was restored to the throne. Then the troubles began, for no Afghans came to Shah Shuja's support. He ruled by British bayonets alone. The army of escort became, perforce, a permanent army of occupation immersed in a seething sea of Afghan hatred. The conquered capital became a prison for its martial masters. Throughout

Afghanistan rebellion spread, and the garrison isolated at Kabul was finally forced to flee a hostile country in utter desperation in January of 1842. Snow covered the high passes and Afghan tribesmen who waited with cold fury, holding their fire till the straggling lines of that once glorious British army appeared. Of 16,000 who started the long retreat, one man, half dead, completed the journey to Jalalabad, while somewhat more than 100 prisoners were returned to Kabul to be liberated later. The attempt was a total failure; never before nor since did British arms in India sustain so unmitigated a defeat. Auckland was replaced as governor-general by the president of the board of control himself, the Earl of Ellenborough (1700-1871).

Psychological desperation dictated the next aggressive show of British force. In a vain effort to recover prestige lost in Kabul, British troops overwhelmed the Amirs of Sind in 1843. Two years later they marched north against the Punjab, wresting Kashmir from Sikh control in 1846. Gulab Singh (1792-1858), a Dogra Hindu Rajput general of Jammu, shifted his allegiance from the Sikhs to the British during this first Anglo-Sikh war, and was rewarded for his treachery by the latter with nominal control over the state of Jammu and Kashmir. It was this same unpopular dynasty that reigned in Kashmir in 1947 at the outbreak of the violent struggle for that state between India and Pakistan. The Punjab was not totally incorporated within British India until after the second Sikh war, ending in 1849.

By the early 1850s, then, British India had attained its frontier dimensions, and though wild dreams of Afghan conquest continued to infatuate later diplomats and generals alike (two subsequent wars were fought with Afghanistan, in 1878-80, and 1919), the *raj* never expanded beyond the Hindu Khush. Internal political consolidation, however, was pursued with a vengeance during the energetic governor-generalship (1848-56) of the Marquess of Dalhousie (1812-60). Invoking a British legal "doctrine of lapse," by which the domain of an Indian prince was brought under the direct administrative control of the British Government of India whenever no natural heirs survived a reigning monarch, Dalhousie incorporated some 150,000 square miles of quasi-autonomous princely territory into the *raj*. Great Maratha principalities like Satara (in 1848), Jhansi (in 1853), and Nagpur (in 1854), and Rajput kingdoms like Udaipur (in 1852), were thus brought to sudden, unexpected, and to Indian minds, unjustifiable ends. Hindu law had always equated an adopted heir with natural issue for purposes of inheritance. Indian princes and their newly unemployed courtiers viewed Dalhousie's action as nothing more than official plunder sugarcoated with jargon from codes of law they neither accepted nor understood. Indeed, several millions in sterling were annually added to the Government of India's revenue as a result of "lapse." Some 20,000 hitherto tax-free estates were also confiscated by the British from aristocratic Indian families, whose title deeds to their property were either lost or found faulty. Ancient noble titles and their pensions were, moreover, left to "lapse" with the death of each incumbent. The *mughal* emperor himself was almost stripped of this final remnant of his sovereignty by the mighty leveling and unifying bulldozer of British power, driven by the same tough-minded young governor-general who introduced the railroad and telegraph to India. Then, in the last year (1856) of his reign, Dalhousie discarded the Company's subsidiary alliance treaty with the *nawab-wazir* of Oudh, and ordered direct annexation of that kingdom. Thus, British power ruled some 700,000 square miles of the subcontinent. Indians were no longer deceived by pageantry and outward display into believing themselves still under the rule of their indigenous monarchs. Nor were the British content with mere absorption of land, for behind the military and political bulldozers marched an army of teachers and missionaries, indeed, reformers of every variety.

Reform and Renaissance

British power in India early revealed a fundamental ambivalence in attitudes toward the purpose of Indian empire. Most Company merchants had come East solely for profits and trade, and the rule they sought to establish in India was one designed best to further their own aspirations. With notable exceptions like Charles Grant, 1746-1823,[5] they did not wish to transform India into a mirror-image of England, but rather to learn the intricacies of Indian cultures and habits so as to be able to manipulate them for selfish advantage. Clive was a crude example of this mercantile mentality, Warren Hastings a more sophisticated one. Hastings had encouraged men like Sir William Jones (1746-94), the Supreme Court Justice of Bengal (whose genius for language led to his monumental discovery of the Indo-European linguistic family, which unites Sanskrit with Greek, Latin, German, and English) to start the Asiatic Society of Bengal in 1784

[5] See Ainslie Embree, *Charles Grant and British Rule in India* (London: George Allen & Unwin, 1962).

for very practical reasons. English translations of Hindu law codes were required before Englishmen could enforce them. Englishmen not connected with the Company directly, on the other hand, were made aware of Indian problems, of famine and plunder, superstitious ignorance and barbaric behavior, through parliamentary oratory, which stirred profound feelings of sorrow and anger, stimulating passions for reform. Others, like Cornwallis, simply wanted to see India raised up to the British standard of administrative excellence. As the Crown took more and more interest in controlling the Company's India, the reformist current in British thinking became increasingly vocal and powerful. By the first decade of the nineteenth century a substantial segment of influential British opinion insisted that Great Britain's primary business in India was fostering education rather than trade, and saving souls more than making profit.

This reformist current was stimulated by contemporary intellectual, religious, and economic reform movements within England herself. Utilitarianism and its French-inspired adjunct, positivism, provided theoretical support for the administrative reformers of British India in the early part of the nineteenth century. Evangelicalism inspired social and religious reform movements of a fundamental nature. Laissez-faire economic theory bolstered the British lobby for free trade in its vociferous struggle against monopolistic Company privilege. By 1813, when the Company's charter came before Parliament for renewal, all three of these swelling currents of opposition to the old, narrow view of British India's destiny were articulated during heated debate. The result was abolition of the Company's trade monopoly with India (though not as yet with China); the opening of British India to missionary activity (though missionaries as well as private merchants still had to obtain licenses from the directors or the board of control); the allocation of a modest sum (£10,000 annually) for education and the encouragement of learning among Indians; and the appointment of a bishop of Calcutta and three archdeacons. The Company retained its patronage privileges and rule of the territories it had conquered, but the sovereignty of the Crown over British India was for the first time explicitly asserted. A wave of new British migration followed, opening floodgates of change within India.

Reform, however, could not be expected overnight. For one thing, intimate contact with daily life in India engendered caution among foreign rulers, especially in such sensitive realms as social and religious reform. Then too, it took the new arrivals from England time to become accustomed to the Indian scene, to learn some of the languages, and appreciate better the precise nature of the ills they were to assail. British missionaries, of course, had come to India before the founding of the Calcutta diocese in 1814. The Baptist Missionary Society, started in 1792, had sent William Carey and others to Calcutta a year later, but the Company refused to permit them to work on British terrain, and they were thus obliged to set up headquarters and their press at the Danish enclave of Serampore in Bengal. The London Missionary Society, founded in 1795, also attempted to proselytize in Calcutta, but was obliged to focus its early efforts in southern India instead. In 1799 the Church Missionary Society, overseas arm of the Established Church of England, was founded, and in 1813 the American Baptist Mission sent its representatives to Bombay. Nonetheless, early missionary efforts in India were confined mostly to study, translation, and social service activities. Agitation for specific reforms in Hindu customs started only in the 1820s, by which time Indians themselves had been enlisted in the cause.

Ram Mohun Roy (1772-1833), a Brahman employee of the East India Company, justifiably revered as the father of the Hindu Renaissance, was the founder of the *Brahmo Samaj* (Brahma Society), a reformed offshoot of Hinduism. The Samaj owed much of its inspiration to ideals of Christian brotherhood as well as to the monistic philosophy of the Upanishads. It became a highly influential lobby for social as well as religious reform, sponsoring Western education, publicizing the demands of Indian intellectuals, and supporting British Liberal legislation. Roy himself visited England in the last years of his life as the personal deputy of the Mughal Emperor to the Crown, and testified on his countrymen's economic grievances and social aspirations before a committee of Parliament. After Roy's death, his friend and disciple Debendranath Tagore (1817-1905), the poet Rabindranath's father, led and expanded the Samaj. Similar Hindu reformist sects subsequently emerged in other parts of India.

Secular reformers imbued with Utilitarianism were even more successful than the evangelicals in stimulating change within India. Though taking self-interest and individual pleasure as his motivation, Bentham inspired his disciples with zealous concern for the enactment of "scientific legislation" designed to make as many people throughout society as happy as possible. James Mill (1773-1836) transmitted Bentham's ideas to several generations of Indian civil servants who were reared at the Company's college at Haileybury on his *History of British India* (published in 1817). As examiner of India correspondence for the Company (between 1819-36) Mill, moreover, was in a key position to implement directly many of the reforms he believed essential to Indian progress. Considering Indian civilization retrograde and barbaric, Mill favored paternalistic legislation formulated by enlightened, though autocratic, English rulers to any form of popular sovereignty. The codification of law, impartially applied throughout India, was an essential platform in the Liberal approach to India's plight, and after passage of the Charter Act of 1833, Thomas Babington Macaulay (1800-59) was sent to Calcutta as the first legal member of the expanded council of the governor-general.

The "Liberal Charter," as the Act of 1833 came to be called, was drafted in the heyday of Whig and Liberal ascendancy in London, and stands as a milestone of radical change in the history of British India. Since it was passed in the very year in which slavery was abolished throughout the British Empire and the first Factory Act drafted, the generous spirit of humanitarianism that suffuses it is hardly surprising. The victory of free trade was now complete, the Company's monopoly totally abolished. India was opened without restriction to British settlement. The governor-general in council was for the first time officially recognized as governor-general of India, rather than Bengal. Hereafter, a unified British Indian government was to pay increasing attention to the needs, if not as yet the aspirations and desires, of its vast populace. The ground was thus laid for an ever-expanding legislative arm within India itself. Perhaps most significant of all, at least in terms of the inspiration it provided for later Indian Nationalists, was the Act's articulation of an overall British policy toward India of equality of opportunity.

Had this policy been implemented with the same spirit in which it was drawn up much of the bitter subsequent national struggle might well have been avoided. Between the letter of the law and its application fell the shadow of individual British disagreement, ignorance, and, too often, arrogance. Perhaps it was simply too much to expect any despotic government, howsoever benevolent, to subordinate its own interests and privileges to those of its subjects. Certainly, many British Liberals tried their best to act with total impartiality.

Macaulay, who was first assigned the job of augmenting the Liberal Charter, personally believed in representative government, yet agreed with Mill that for India as yet it was totally out of the question. Much of the problem was that Indians themselves neither understood nor desired such a system. They had never been educated to appreciate its merits. A tutelage era of paternal despotism was first required, yet during that interim period government would have to sponsor an educational program designed to create, as Macaulay argued, "a class of persons, Indian in blood and colour, but English in taste, in opinion, in morals and intellect."[6] The controversy, which raged between those who favored "Oriental" education in government-supported institutions of learning, and the "Anglicists" advocating Western education, was resolved partly by Macaulay's weighty Minute in favor of the latter in 1835. Thereafter a new breed of Indian intellectuals began to emerge from lecture halls and classrooms in which they imbibed the language of Milton, Burke, Bentham, and Mill, and protein ideas of freedom, liberty, legal rights, and happiness. In seeking to equate what they learned with the society in which they lived many were frustrated and profoundly bewildered, others inspired to advocate sweeping reforms, still others infuriated and impelled toward rebellion. The seed thus planted bore a strange and wonderful variety of intellectual fruit. One important effect was to cut off the rising generation of Indian leadership from its rich and inspiring cultural heritage, severing ties that had permitted India to endure the worst shocks of invasion and foreign conquest. Yet those roots would be searched for again, somewhat later, to be used in revitalized form to nourish a national political awakening. Macaulay's policy was by no means purely altruistic; the government of India needed servants in great numbers, who could act as translators and mediators between its alien officials and the population at large. Yet Macaulay himself was Liberal enough, idealistic enough, to recognize the full implications of what he proposed. By codifying, liberalizing, and unifying India's Penal Code in 1835, Macaulay sought to translate Benthamite theory into social practice. Bentinck's administration sponsored further reforms. English displaced Persian as the legal language of the land in 1835, and the visage of the British monarch displaced that of the Mughal Emperor on Company coins. The *raj* had come of age, venturing boldly into every sphere of Indian life, private as well as public. The 1840s, as noted, were years of further military expansion,

[6] Quoted in de Bary et al, *op. cit.*, p. 601.

culminating with Dalhousie's administration and the forward march
of internal consolidation, coupled with technological and scientific
innovation.

Before coming to India, Dalhousie had served as president of Britain's Board of Trade, where he became vitally concerned with the
development of railroad transport. Determined to carry on this work
in India, he strongly advocated the construction of a massive rail net
across British India, and India's first railroad track was laid under his
auspices in 1853. The East India Railway, at first designed to link
Raniganj coal mines with Calcutta, was introduced to facilitate economic expansion rather than transportation. Dalhousie also pressed
for the development of an Indian telegraph system, inaugurating the
first line between Calcutta and Agra in 1853, and transmitting the
first telegraph message some 800 miles along it less than five months
later. By the time he left India more than 4,000 miles of telegraph
line were in working order; thanks to this fact Calcutta was promptly
alerted at the outbreak of hostilities in 1857. A Public Works Department was initiated to stimulate major irrigation projects, the greatest
of which, the Ganges Canal, was opened in 1854. The Indian Postal
Service was expanded and the cost of mailing greatly reduced.

All of these projects invigorated India's economy and gave fresh
impetus to private business investment. The industrial evolution of
modern India dates from this era of dynamic growth and vigorous
change under government leadership. India's first modern cotton-
cloth mill, the Bombay Spinning and Weaving Company, started
production in 1854. Mining, especially of coal, was stimulated by
government-subsidized rail transport to ready markets. Free government land grants of up to 3,000 acres in Assam started India's
plantation tea industry, and by the century's end Indian tea had displaced China's almost entirely on the British market. Tanning and
coffee industries blossomed in the South. Steam transport was beginning to displace sail, thereby rapidly expanding the volume of India's
overseas trade. Thanks to the Crimean War, which cut off the supply of Russian hemp to Dundee, the demand for Bengal's jute bur-
geoned, and the first Indian jute mill was opened at Calcutta in
1854. Business had never been better, Indian revenues never so high
as they were on the eve of Dalhousie's departure.

The mechanism of government had also been improved by the
Charter Act of 1853, thanks to which some six additional members
were added to the governor-general's council when it met for purely

legislative purposes. This was the first major step in the long transition from legal member to Legislative Assembly and Parliament in India's constitutional history. This Act also replaced the old Company system of patronage with regular civil service examinations open to all "natural-born subjects of the Queen." Theoretically any qualified Indian or young Englishman without "connections" could now set his foot on the ladder leading to the top of the bureaucratic pyramid.

Dalhousie's policy on social and religious reform was as progressive and vigorously paternalistic as his program of economic development. His government passed a Caste Disabilities Act in 1850 making it illegal to deprive any convert to a faith other than his ancestral one of his paternal inheritance. This was, of course, designed to protect Hindu converts to Christianity from the hitherto effective threat of economic sanction wielded by Hindu caste *panchayats*. Orthodox opposition was strenuously outspoken, but incapable of deterring the "Christian" British Government. To foster Western education a Presidency College was established at Calcutta in 1854, and again with disregard for traditional custom, female as well as male students were encouraged to apply. Finally, in 1856 the Hindu Widows' Remarriage Act was passed, granting official permission to Hindu widows wishing and able to remarry. Not since the abolition of *sati* had any single legislative measure aroused so strident a cry of popular reprobation; it was generally felt that government was intruding in an area of sacrosanct private religious belief, attacking the very citadel of Hinduism by undermining its control over the most momentous of life's sacred rituals. Yet fearless Hindu reformers like Pandit Ishwara Chandra Vidyasagar (1820-91) were brave enough to advocate the measure, and Dalhousie supported it strongly, leaving its final passage to his successor, Lord Canning.

Despite the protest raised by such reforms, Dalhousie felt at the end of his eight years in office that there was good reason to anticipate a bright future for British India, which would present "in each successive year, a happy record of peace, prosperity and progress." [7] History proved him overly optimistic.

The War of 1857-1858

Many were warning that the pace of change was too swift. Important groups within Indian society were being too brashly ignored, too

[7] Minute by Lord Dalhousie, February 28, 1856, from *Parliamentary Papers*, 1856, No. 245, quoted in Muir, *op. cit.*, p. 378.

completely alienated. The deposed princes poisoned all ears around them with talk of "faithless" British promises and treaties torn to bits by men without honor. The landed aristocrats, whose estates had always been freeholds, were now assailed by low-born tax collectors and bullied by beardless young men in a foreign tongue. Brahmans and Muslim Maulvis spoke of Christian rulers desirous only of converting all Indians to their English religion. Merchants and craftsmen saw their livelihood undermined by British competition and foreign manufactured goods. Teachers and scholars found the labors of a lifetime no longer valued in a society run in a language they could not understand, according to principles and ideas they feared and hated. Most dangerous of all the sepoy soldiers had grown restive. By 1856 their morale was at an all-time low, just when their number proportionate to British troops in India was at its all-time high.

Ultimately, everyone knew that the British had conquered India by the sword, and held India by the sword. Yet it was not entirely their own sword, for by 1857 less than one of every six soldiers in British India's army was European, while in the largest of the three presidency armies, that of Bengal, the ratio was nearer to one in seven. The sword had become blunted with grievances, rusted by disaffection. Some of the many reasons were low pay and no promotion beyond the ranks of petty officer, inferior British commanders, and excessive engagements in hostile and distant lands like Afghanistan and Burma. Indeed, some regiments of the Bengal army had mutinied four times in little more than a decade preceding 1857. As early as 1806 the Madras army had mutinied at Vellore for religious and political reasons. Yet in 1856-57 three separate and extremely volatile causes of sepoy discontent had been introduced for the first time, precisely when the Crimean and Persian wars had siphoned an inordinate number of British regulars out of India.

First, and in some respects foremost, of the reasons inciting Bengal sepoys to revolt was the annexation of Oudh. Approximately one third of the Bengal sepoys were high caste Hindus (Brahmans and Kshatriyas) of Oudh, who considered the annexation a treacherous and hostile act of British rapacity. To call what occurred in northern India in 1857 simply a "mutiny" is to ignore entirely the widespread, almost national character of the rebellion against British rule which occurred in Oudh. The aristocracy of that once great kingdom had the support (active or passive) of practically all the large landowners, soldiers, and peasants of their usurped domain. Had the British indeed taken control of the region to abolish the inequities of the past, perhaps traditional ties of loyalty would have been less sturdy. But British rulers proved themselves even more greedy and shameless in the early months of their power than the former ruler and his cohorts had been. A second cause of sepoy disaffection was passage of the General Service Enlistment Act in mid-1856, which made it mandatory for any soldier in the Company's service to fight overseas if necessary without special compensation. High caste Hindus of the Bengal army were particularly offended by this Act, since Hindus had always considered travel across the "dark waters" tantamount to the loss of caste through pollution. With growing British involvement in Burma, Persia, and China, moreover, it seemed probable that more fighting would in the future take place beyond India's frontiers.

The final straw came with the greased cartridges issued for use with the new and more efficient breach-loading Enfield rifles. Sepoys were instructed by their drill masters in the time-serving technique of biting off the greased tip of the cartridge in order to pour in the powder with one swift operation, while holding the rifle nestled under their other arm, then snapping the barrel shut. The ordnance experts who devised this method failed to reckon with Hindu and Muslim religious sensitivity. Rumors swiftly spread throughout the ranks that the grease was a compound product of pig and cow fat. Christian officers had invented the technique, devout Hindus and Muslims were told, for the sole purpose of tricking sepoys into tasting forbidden fat, which would in effect pollute them irrevocably, robbing them of their own religious status and leaving them all vulnerable to conversion by eager missionaries. In January of 1857 sepoys refused to accept the new cartridges at Dumdum. Two months later a regiment was disbanded at Barrackpur when it mutinied against direct orders to load its new arms. British officers, who at first refused to believe that their troops were superstitious enough to accept such rumors seriously, now made strenuous efforts to prove that all cartridges issued with the Enfields were greased only with the purest vegetable fats. Such professions of innocence served merely to bolster earlier suspicions. Irrational fears could hardly be eliminated by rational arguments, tours of fat-producing factories, or scientific tests. The anxiety of the sepoys was symptomatic of deep-rooted distrust. Wilder rumors began to spread with equal success—the Christians were pouring cow and pig fat into sepoy wells; officers wanted all soldiers to eat at a common "mess" in order to defile the Brahmans among them; generals were in the employ of the Church. Nothing could restore tranquility and trust once such gnawing doubts and fears were planted in the minds of superstitious men. Disaffected Hindu and Muslim preachers did their best to fan the flames, hovering on the outskirts of army cantonments, introducing mysterious symbols among the troops, a lotus passed silently from hand to hand till it had been held by each man in the regiment, or *chapatis* (unleavened wheatcakes) passed along without being eaten, like sacred amulets, whose touch alone imparted strange power. Some petty officers watched these rituals and shuddered, reporting to their British commanders that it seemed a terrible conspiracy was underway. But most of the British colonels and generals were unruffled, supremely confident that their men would prove "true to their salt." All that was needed perhaps was a bit more stringent discipline. Sepoys who refused orders were publicly stripped of their martial insignia and sent home in disgrace to wait like dry tinder in their villages for the spark of ignition.

The explosion came at Meerut, the great military cantonment north of Delhi, on the tenth of May, 1857. Thousands of sepoys had stood at attention for hours on the ninth under a blistering sun while more than sixty of their comrades were manacled with irons for having refused to taste grease, and led off at bayonet point to the guardhouse. The last sepoy bonds of loyalty and discipline were smashed. Outraged troops of three regiments rose as one man that fateful Sunday to massacre every officer in sight, liberate their imprisoned peers, and race South with the cry, which in World War II was echoed as the battle shout of Subhas Bose's Indian National Army, "*Chalo* Delhi! (Let's go to Delhi)." The Mutiny had begun. It soon became a full-scale war, raging for more than a year across the great heartland of northern India's Ganga-Yamuna plain and the central provinces, engaging Britain's largest overseas expeditionary force of the century, and costing India close to one hundred million pounds in material loss alone.

Three great cities became the major focal points of battle: Delhi, Kanpur, and Lucknow. The sepoys, who arrived at Delhi, easily took control of the city, which was almost devoid of British troops, and convinced the octogenarian Mughal, Bahadur Shah II, that they had come to restore him to his rightful position. Younger and more ambitious courtiers, who had long waited for just such a moment, eagerly proclaimed the Mughal restoration, issuing edicts in the emperor's name, exhorting the populace at large to rise in "holy War" against

British tyranny. The lead thus taken by Delhi Muslims convinced the British that the revolt was primarily a Muslim plot. The deposed king of Oudh, after all, was Muslim too, and by May thirtieth rebellion had spread to Lucknow, capital of Oudh. Henry Lawrence (1806-57), chief commissioner at the time and one of the shrewdest Britishers of his day, stocked the residency building with supplies and retreated behind its walls with his entire Christian community. Lawrence himself was soon killed, but the residency fortress held out until it was finally relieved in November, 1857. Delhi was retaken by a mighty Anglo-Sikh army, sent from the Punjab by Henry's brother John Lawrence (1811-79), under the dauntless command of John Nicholson, who was mortally wounded leading the charge through a breach blasted in the Kashmir gate. Old Bahadur Shah was captured and shipped off to Burma, his sons shot to death without provocation or trial by a British captain, who thus took it upon himself summarily to end the longest and most powerful dynasty of Indian history.

At Kanpur, it was Maratha rather than Mughal leadership that rallied popular support. The sepoys of Kanpur revolted in June and besieged General Wheeler and his force of some 400 behind the entrenchment of a poorly selected compound. After more than a fortnight of siege, Wheeler surrendered on the promise of safe conduct down river for himself and his garrison, but after entering their small boats they were mercilessly cut down in a treacherous cross-fire. Only four escaped to tell the tale, which provoked equally barbaric reprisals by the British forces that reached Kanpur in mid-July. The city was recaptured by the Gwalior sepoys in November, however, and only permanently restored to British control a month later.

Less concentrated battles were fought at Banaras and Allahabad, indeed throughout Oudh and the northwest provinces. In central India the war continued under Maratha leaders well into 1858. Sporadic outbursts in Maharashtra never resulted in any mass uprising or major battle. Madras remained passive. The Punjab stayed loyal, as did most of Bengal. Lord Canning (1812-62), governor-general and first viceroy (1856-62), officially proclaimed the peace on July 8, 1858, but though the war itself was relatively brief, its legacy was long and pervaded every aspect of British Indian life.

Later Nationalists and many Indian historians to this day speak of what the British call "the mutiny" as their "first war of Indian independence." Actually, it was more than the one and less than the

other. Nehru came closest to the truth in writing of this "great revolt" as essentially "a feudal outburst," the *ancien régime*'s "last
despairing effort to drive out foreign rule." [8] Had the spirit of Indian
Nationalism inspired the struggle all of those revolting would have
joined forces. But Marathas and Mughals, Hindus and Muslims were
still jealous and suspicious of one another, despite many examples of
Hindu-Muslim unity in this year of travail. Then too, the nobility
and aristocracy, who had attracted dissident soldiers and civilians to
their banners like human magnets, hardly stood ready to lead their
followers toward the promise of a new India. They looked backward
rather than ahead. Their every impulse was to restore the old, not
to build from the ashes of conflict a new nation. From the pages of
histories written on this era no one figure emerges with the vision or
stature of a modern national hero. There were as yet no Gandhis or
Nehrus to offer India a true alternative to the British *raj*, nor were
the people at large prepared to follow such a clarion call had it in
fact been sounded. The war was instead an inchoate protest of frustration, fear, anxiety, and hatred, a blind lashing out against forces
and policies half understood, passionately rejected, violently resented.
It failed, moreover, for positive as well as negative reasons, for unlike
their enemies the British were united, self-righteous, confident of
their "civilizing" mission in a backward society, bolstered by the
sinews of science and such technological military superiority as the
very Enfield rifle that both started the war and helped finish it.

But though British rule survived its most serious challenge, the
Company could not. Parliament lost confidence entirely in the "old
men" of Leadenhall Street. India had become too great and vital an
imperial enterprise to be left in the hands of merchant princes. And
so on November 1, 1858, the governor-general, who thereafter became
the Crown's viceroy as well, read Victoria's Proclamation at Allahabad, announcing the formal and complete transfer of power over
British India from Company to Crown "for divers weighty reasons."

[8] Jawaharlal Nehru, *The Discovery of India* (New York: John Day, 1946),
p. 324.

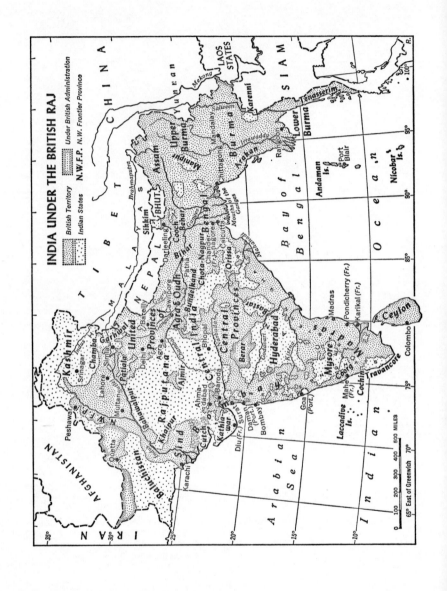

INDIA UNDER THE BRITISH RAJ

British Territory
Indian States
N.W.F.P. N.W. Frontier Province
Under British Administration

FIVE

CROWN RAJ, NATIONALISM,

AND PARTITION

The ninety years (1858-1947) during which India was ruled directly by the British Crown, that is, Parliament, may most conveniently be studied in three major chronological periods divided at 1885 and 1920. The first of these eras was dominated by the legacy of 1857 and the fundamental changes in governmental policy, mental attitudes, and economy coming as the "aftermath of revolt."[1] In 1885, with the founding of the Indian National Congress, the growing political consciousness of India's New Men acquired an integrated institutional form, which until 1920 remained primarily "loyalist" or cooperative in its approach to British rule. After 1920 Congress adopted a nonviolent, "noncooperation" platform, to which it adhered by and large until the attainment of independence in 1947. During this latter era, moreover, in good measure as a result of the new Congress approach, Muslim nationalism in India, which had been slowly gaining popularity, developed in rapid strides, leading to partition of the subcontinent and the birth of Pakistan.

Crown Raj and the Legacy of 1857

The cataclysmic upheaval of 1857 resulted in many fundamental changes in the administration, policy, and society of British India. Perhaps least dramatic was the formal transfer of power from Company to Crown, for by and large the same personnel remained at administrative posts, carrying on the everyday business of government in much the same manner as before. The most important immediate change made by the Government of India Act of August 1858 was that "all . . . powers and duties in anywise relating to the government or

[1] See Thomas R. Metcalf, *The Aftermath of Revolt. India, 1857-1858* (Princeton: Princeton University Press, 1964).

revenues of India" [2] were hereafter vested in "one of Her Majesty's Principal Secretaries of State," and through him, of course, in the British cabinet responsible to Parliament. The court of directors was abolished, though seven of its members were elected to serve on a Council of India (totaling up to fifteen members in all, eight of whom could be appointed by the Crown), created to assist and advise the new secretary of state at Whitehall. The dethroned Company thus retained influence of an advisory nature, which during the tenure of a weak or disinterested secretary of state could become quite powerful. The secretary of state was obliged to lay before both houses of Parliament an annual account of the financial conditions of India, and during the "East India budget debate" which ensued in the chambers of Westminster as a result, Indian affairs were brought to the regular, though brief and often bored or uninformed, attention of the British public. Legally and by implication these changes in the home government's machinery were momentous, potentially radical. In practice, however, the ship of so massive a state could only be swung around slowly, if indeed the man at the helm desired to change its course in the first place. Most early secretaries of state were content merely to reiterate in periodic despatches the "great principle" that constitutionally "the final control and direction of the affairs of India rest with the Home Government." [3] The full and effective implementation of this sweeping power invested in the parliamentary government of Great Britain would have to await the significant half decade of change introduced by Whitehall's most brilliant secretary of state for India, John Morley, whose "Era of Indian History" [4] lasted from 1906-10.

The legacy of 1857 was most clearly apparent in the total reversal of British policy toward princely Indian states. Dalhousie's policy of annexation was abandoned; Victoria's Proclamation specifically assured "the native princes of India that all treaties and engagements made with them by or under the authority of the Honourable East India Company are by us accepted, and will be scrupulously main-

[2] Government of India Act, August 2, 1858, clause III, quoted in *The Evolution of India and Pakistan, 1858-1947. Select Documents*, ed. C. H. Philips (London: Oxford University Press, 1962), p. 5. Hereinafter cited as *EI & P*.

[3] As the Duke of Argyll (Secretary of State from 1868-1874) did on November 24, 1870, quoted in *EI & P*, p. 13; and Lord Salisbury (secretary of state from 1866-1867 and 1874-1878) did on May 31, 1876, *ibid.*, p. 15.

[4] My forthcoming monograph on "The Morley Era of Indian History, 1906-1910," deals with this period and Morley's policy in detail.

tained." [5] The doctrine of lapse was repudiated, and special documents were drawn up by the British government for each of the Indian princes confirming the legality of succession by an heir adopted according to Hindu (or Muslim) law. While the paramountcy of the British Crown was asserted and given titular implementation after 1877, when Victoria was proclaimed Empress of India at Delhi, Indian princes were hereafter handled with kid gloves by viceroys, who were eager to stay on the best of terms with "the natural leaders" of Indian society. The political unification of India so boldly pursued in the 1850s thus came to a grinding halt, and was in fact reversed with the reinvestment of states like Mysore to heirs of the deposed Hindu dynasty in 1881. Because of this cautious reaction to Dalhousie's progressive policy, some 562 princely states survived as a political patchquilt of semifeudal enclaves until 1947.

The same timidity prompting this policy put an end to all bold official innovation in areas of social and religious reform. More than three decades were to pass before government ventured again, and even then most cautiously, to outlaw religious practices known to be detrimental to the health and well-being of certain segments of Hindu society. As a result Indian reformers were stimulated to take the initiative in working to cure the ills of their own society. The great strides made during the past century, especially among Hindus, toward female emancipation and equality, the elevation of depressed castes and tribes, and the establishment of a broader based educational system, were by and large the product of individual, and public nonofficial, efforts of a heroic nature. Individual Britishers often helped with private encouragement and support, but the government's attitude was predominantly one of aloof indifference.

Military reform was a different matter entirely. The Company armies were abolished, and all forces came directly under Crown control. The entire policy of recruitment and the apportionment of military personnel was revamped. After 1858 practically no Brahmans nor indeed Indians of any caste or religion residing in Bengal and the united provinces (Oudh and the region west) were considered suitable for military service. Recruitment concentrated on the so-called "martial races" of the Punjab, Rajputana, and Nepal, who had served loyally under British command in helping to win the war. Sikhs, Gurkhas, Jats, Rajputs, and Pathans became the back-

[5] "Proclamation by the Queen in Council to the Princes, Chiefs, and People of India," November 1, 1858, quoted in Muir, *op. cit.*, p. 382.

bone of the "native army," and were as a matter of policy to be mixed promiscuously through each regiment. Never again would entire regiments of Brahmans or Kshatriyas of one region be left to blister as one man against particular grievances to their caste or region of birth. All "scientific branches of the service" were to be kept strictly in British hands, especially the artillery regiments. The ratio of British to Indian soldiers was not to be permitted to fall below one to three, and was usually maintained at one to one. John Lawrence, whose heroic efforts in 1857 were rewarded by his appointment as viceroy from 1863-69, warned the secretary of state as late as 1867 that "the events of the Mutiny have excited a distrust, indeed I may say a hatred, between the two races which perhaps may never subside, and which has certainly not of late years decreased." [6] He estimated that India could "never" be held securely with under 40,000 British troops. At the time more than 60,000 were in fact garrisoned there to some 120,000 Indians. The cost of this enormous machine by which India was retained within the Empire was more than seventeen million pounds annually by 1878, approximately one third of the total revenue of British India.

This military legacy of distrust shackled India with an economic burden more crushing than any ever sustained even at the peak of Mughal tyranny. The entire cost of Britain's war effort in 1857-58 was charged to India's budget as well, and for four years after the debacle annual deficits of over thirty-five million pounds (roughly equivalent to the total revenue) piled up. To meet these expenses new and heavier taxation was introduced, and a population already ground low by poverty found itself pressed still more severely by foreign rulers who proved themselves as greedy in peace as they had been rapacious in war. By this era, moreover, India's hitherto self-sufficient subsistence agricultural economy began to feel the effects of a commercial agricultural revolution[7] which tied it to the vagaries of the world market. The Crimean War, as already noted, had stimulated jute production in Bengal. The American Civil War performed the same function in developing western India's cotton production, since British mill-owners turned to India for their raw

---

[6] Lord Lawrence to Lord Cranborne, January 4, 1867, quoted in *EI & P*, p. 509.

[7] See D. R. Gadgil, *The Industrial Evolution of India in Recent Times* (London: Oxford University Press, 1944), rev. ed.; and Daniel H. Buchanan, *The Development of Capitalistic Enterprise in India* (London: Macmillan, 1934).

material supply after the American South ceased to export its key commodity. Between 1861-65 the price of raw cotton trebled in India, and the acreage devoted to its growth more than doubled, displacing food grains. When the market collapsed after the war peasants found themselves overstocked with cotton, undersupplied with food. Indian speculators in Bombay were equally ruined, and depression of a previously undreamed of magnitude gripped that great city. Tied now to Britain's industrial revolution, India rode the economic tiger of boom and bust. Peasants borrowing heavily during years of prosperity were displaced en masse from their hereditary holdings when they suddenly found themselves unable to meet the demands of moneylenders, who used British law courts to support their claims for money or land. A new class of landless laborers thus emerged, growing to alarming proportions in the latter part of the nineteenth century. Armies of these laborers were impressed into service on the swiftly expanding tea and coffee plantations run by private British enterprise. Others were shipped as indentured servants to East Africa, establishing Indian colonies in Natal, the Transvaal, and the Cape, and providing a source of growing racial irritation within the British Empire and, incidentally, the initial testing grounds for Gandhi's techniques of nonviolent resistance.

Though modern Indian industrial development had initially been sponsored by British official and private efforts, the industrial lead early taken by England coupled with India's colonial status and the victory of the Manchester School's free trade policy combined to thwart rapid expansion of Indian industrial capacity. Ironically enough, by the late nineteenth century India's economy was more predominantly agricultural and village-based than it had been at the start of the century. In 1800 an estimated 10 per cent of India's population was urban, while by 1870 that figure had fallen to below 9, primarily because so many indigenous craftsmen were forced to fall back on the land for support when they could no longer compete with the pressure of foreign manufactured imports. Entire industries, devoted to producing fine textiles, metalwork, and shipbuilding, were rendered obsolete and uneconomical by cheap British imports. No guardian national state raised protective tariff barriers in their defense. Indian noble patronage declined precipitously. Few British industries emerged on Indian soil to hire the displaced craftsmen, for most of the great industrial products, including all railroad equipment and tracks, telegraph wires, and even coal, were shipped half-way around the world to Indian ports in British-made and manned bottoms. With the rapid advance in steam transport that followed the opening of the Suez Canal in 1869, the passage to Bombay from London was reduced from about three months to less than one. Foreign trade expanded greatly, and with more than 5,000 miles of rail linking India's interior to major ports by 1869, the process of distributing imported manufactured goods throughout the countryside and extracting raw materials for export overseas accelerated phenomenally. Peasants, who had never used cash before, were now being paid in silver for grain and sugar cane as well as cotton and jute, transported rapidly out of their regions by smoke-bellowing monsters, which brought them cloth and utensils, trinkets and ploughs to be purchased for cash. Villagers, who had always relied on traditional barter agreements with their neighbors for all the things they needed, suddenly found themselves dependent on producers and distributors they had never seen and with whom they had no direct way of communicating. Every failure or temporary dislocation in the new, impersonal system brought tragedy in its wake.

For India's peasant population 1868-78 was a decade of unprecedented famine and epidemic disaster. The over-all population of the subcontinent actually decreased by several millions between 1870 and 1880. The Deccan and southern India were worst hit between 1876-78, but hardship of almost equal dimensions devastated Rajputana in 1868-69, and Bengal in 1873-74. The initial cause of famine was of course natural failure of the rains, but late nineteenth-century famines assumed such staggering proportions (those of 1895-1900 were to prove even more calamitous) because of the commercial revolution. Peasants became more vulnerable as mutual bonds of intervillage dependence eroded and local storage of grain was reduced owing to the inroads made by a cash economy and world market. The scourges that visited India's countryside in these years of suffering can hardly be imagined, even by those of us reared on Dante's descriptions of *Inferno*. Little wonder that the Deccan was racked in those years by violent peasant uprisings.

The least tangible legacy of 1857 was more significant than any of the others. It was a basic change of heart and mind, racial in essence, that divided Britishers from Indians. The atrocities committed by both sides during the conflagration were never forgotten. Fortunately, individual Englishmen in positions of power, both in Calcutta and London, were magnanimous enough in mind and character to rise above the meanest of avenging temptations. Lord Canning, then viceroy, was the finest example of such true nobility, and for his insistence that civilization was after all preferable to savagery he won what was meant to be the invidious sobriquet of "Clemency" Canning from his countrymen in Calcutta, which has endured as his most honored title. Victoria's Proclamation, moreover, reiterated the promise of equality of opportunity articulated in 1833, and expressed "our earnest desire to stimulate the peaceful industry of India, to promote works of public utility and improvement, and to administer its government for the benefit of all our subjects resident therein. In their prosperity will be our strength, in their contentment our security, and in their gratitude our best reward." Yet these were rare exceptions to what became the rule of vengeance, growing racial antipathy, and the "white man's burden" mentality of most Englishmen on the spot. White enclaves appeared outside all of India's major cities in the era of Crown *raj* and the "camp" (as the cantonment area came to be called) with its British club was designed to remain as remote from "native India" as possible. Tight little islands of England in miniature emerged above the dark ocean of a despised and "depraved" India, and English women accompanied their men bravely to what everyone hoped would be as brief a tenure of colonial exile as possible. More rapid transport and the cable linking Britain to India after 1870 brought home much closer to the civil servant than it had ever been in the previous century, and leave time was now usually spent for the most part on a steamer rather than on a trip "up-country." Natives were kept at a safe and cool distance, for which of them, after all, could truly be trusted? Officers never forgot the sublimely stupid faith their predecessors had placed in troops who murdered them in their sleep. Women never lost the vision of violated English ladies hacked up and stuffed with their children into a Kanpur well. Mass phobia, a compound product of fear and hatred, infected generations of Anglo-Indians, just as it poisoned the hearts of many Indians as well. Army-of-occupation and occupied-nation mentalities grew side by side, breeding despotic repression among insecure rulers, and fanatical terrorism among their embittered subjects.

The psychological legacy was slow to subside. Sensitive and intelligent British minds could not, of course, long harbor feelings of blatant intolerance. The separation of "races" predicated on specific violent action acquired the theoretical trappings of spurious scientific justification. Natives *were* different, and fundamentally *inferior* to Europeans, especially Englishmen. The exalted phrases about equality of opportunity in the Liberal Charter and the Queen's Proclamation became embarrassing promises, which had somehow to be explained away, or better still ignored by more sensible practice and application. The competitive examination path to the I.C.S. posed a potentially large problem, yet administering the examinations only in London and making the maximum age of applying candidates twenty-two made it possible to keep all but one Indian candidate from passing during the first fourteen years of selection. After 1869, however, several more Indians managed to reach London at a tender enough age to learn English well enough to overcome the great obstacles, and so in 1876 the age limit was reduced to nineteen (the minimum age was set at seventeen), thereby effectively excluding all "natives." A year later the viceroy, Lord Lytton, a cultivated and creative gentleman-poet and diplomat, challenged the very theory of racial equality of opportunity. He suggested as an alternative the creation of a subordinate "native service," as distinct from the British "covenanted service" as the native city was distinct from the camp. Though rejected by Whitehall, the idea alone reflected how pervasive and potent British racial arrogance remained two decades after the war.

On the other hand, the Liberal viceroy of the half-decade 1880-84, George Fredrick Robinson, the Marquess of Ripon (1827-1909), and his legal member, Sir Courtney Ilbert, earned the unrelenting contempt of their fellow-Englishmen and the unabated affection and admiration of the Indians for their sponsorship and support of the famous Ilbert Bill of 1883. The bill was designed simply to remove from the legal code of British India "every judicial disqualification which is based merely on race distinctions," [8] by empowering Indian judges to try cases involving Englishmen as well as Indians in the countryside. The British enclave opposed this bill with such vitriolic, united, and publicly vocal fervor that, when finally enacted in 1884, it ensured "European British" subjects trial before a jury at least half European in complexion. The racists had won their batle, but forced as they were by this "treasonous" threat to their dominance to fully expose their basest motives and fears in press and from public plat-

---

[8] C. P. Ilbert on "The Principles and Purposes of the Ilbert Bill," 1883, from "Abstracts of Proceedings of the Legislative Council, 1883," pp. 92-95, quoted in *EI & P*, p. 122.

form, they inadvertently trained a generation of English-educated Indians in the tactics of political agitation. The power of unified public pressure had been clearly demonstrated on Indian soil for the first time. The potency of press and platform were bitterly, but usefully, revealed. Government, for all its martial and despotic power, had been forced by civil agitation to retract its own legislation. Surely if a handful of British planters, publicists, and lawyers could accomplish that, India's millions could achieve much more. Ripon was sent off in 1884 with tumultuous cheers and the spontaneous, heartwarming gratitude of millions of humble men who knew and cared little more about him than that for some strangely obscure reason called "principle" he had championed their cause, the still-undefined struggle against the inflexible bigotry of his own master race. A year after he had gone, the Indian National Congress was born.

Indian Nationalism—the First Phase

Though Indian Nationalism first achieved unified institutional form in 1885, its roots may be traced provincially back to the early part of the nineteenth century. The impetus to pervasive reform imparted by the introduction of Western learning has already been noted. Men like Ram Mohun Roy hardly dreamed of displacing the *raj* they served with a nation state of their own, yet by asserting their critical talents in appealing for economic and administrative as well as social reforms, they proved that Indians had ample capacity to help manage themselves along the very lines of government laid down by British initiative. An emulative mainstream of new Indian leadership thus emerged in Bengal, and shortly thereafter in Bombay as well, inspired by English thought and institutions to press for reforms not only in Hindu religion and social customs, but also in the British management of Indian affairs. These Indians thought of themselves as British subjects; while accepting British rule as "providentially ordained," they insisted upon their right to help make and keep it proudly British. Initially at least they were willing to accept British promises in good faith, loyally trusting that when their apprenticeship in Western ways was duly completed, they would be given equal opportunity to join their tutors in the great partnership of promoting better government for backward Indians. Only gradually did they learn, by bitter disappointments over decades of struggle, that British officialdom more readily helped those who helped themselves, and that holders of despotic power were reluctant to turn over its reins to anyone else. Thus, what started as faithful and patient supplication moved through a phase of more urgent petition-ing and polite public pleas, to demands for political rights and partner-ship, leading ultimately to independent Indian rule.

This pre-Nationalist period, however, also gave birth to a reaction-ary response against British rule and the Western learning it had foisted upon Indian intellectuals. The most extreme exponents of that response led or joined, as earlier noted, the violent upheaval of 1857-58. To their way of thinking, British rule at its best was a foreign tyranny which had to be ousted by force, fraud, or guile. There was no well-planned conspiracy, however, nor unity of purpose as to pre-cisely how the political surgery would be performed, or what would replace it. The result was chaotic, mostly ineffective, violence fol-lowed by worse despotism than before. While 1857-58 put an end to mass military assault against British rule, it did not deter the leaders of Indian opinion hostile to Crown *raj* from political activity of a basically revolutionary character. Though it may sound contradictory to call the same movement both reactionary and revolutionary, the twin impulses were reconciled by predominantly Hindu revivalist motivation, which fired some political leaders among the new middle class to raise the revolutionary cry of "India for the Indians" (first sounded in Bombay as early as 1879), attributing all of India's ills to British rule. Concentrating as it did on an anti-British, anti-white line, this revivalist mainstream became militantly nationalistic. Yet because of its inherently communal religious orientation, equally divisive, it alienated large segments of Muslim opinion. Liberal re-formers, moreover, of the emulative frame of mind were reviled as lackeys of British imperialism and "traitors" to their own heritage by these generally orthodox Hindu extremists.

The first provincial organization resembling a public political lobby on British-inspired lines, the British India Association of Ben-gal, was founded in 1851. Shortly after that, the Bombay Association appeared, as did the British Indian Association of Oudh. Limited in membership to wealthy landholding and business interests, these small but influential bodies of nonofficial opinion strove to influence legislation most directly affecting their own property rights. In the 1870s somewhat broader based provincial bodies like the Poona Public Society and the Madras Native Association enlisted the public efforts of Western-trained lawyers, teachers, and government workers as well in pressing for reforms ranging from diminution of taxes to the employment of more Indians in the various services. Thanks to the labors of Mahadev Govind Ranade (1842-1901), the Poona Public Society had become the premier public organization of India by the eve of the founding of Congress, whose initial meeting it hosted and helped sponsor. A profound student of economics and history, Ranade wrote many essays and books on both subjects, striving to enlighten his countrymen as to their own weaknesses so that they might devote their energies to labors of constructive reform rather than wasting themselves on negative rhetoric. He guided the Society along practical lines of action directed at the sources of British power, not merely its servants in India, memorializing Commons to repeal the repressive Vernacular Press Act, passed by Lytton's administration in 1878, and entering the British political arena for the first time by openly supporting the Liberal Party during its 1880 campaign. His prestige and influence in Western India, both with officialdom and the enlightened Indian community at large, was unique for his time. Not least important of his contributions was the inspiration and political training he imparted to Gopal Krishna Gokhale (1866-1915), his foremost disciple.

Gokhale, who was dubbed *Mahatma* (Great-souled One) by his greatest political disciple, Gandhi, was, like Ranade, a Chitpavin Brahman. He revered Ranade as his *guru* throughout life, emulating what he accepted as his teacher's primary message: "work and sacrifice for the motherland." As a young man he was inspired by the self-sacrificing zeal of another youthful Chitpavin as well, Bal Gangadhar Tilak (1856-1920). But the paths of political action blazed by Tilak and Gokhale in this first phase of Indian nationalism quickly parted over fundamental differences about the character of the new nation.

Attracted more by the lore of Hinduism than Western education, Tilak, who received his B.A. from Elphinstone College in 1876, had focused his study on Sanskrit and mathematics (in high school he became specially interested in astrology). Returning to Poona at a time of famine and depression, Tilak was unable to find suitable employment, and his personal disaffection toward British rule heard an eloquent echo in the passionate Marathi prose of the young essayist Vishnu Krishna Chiplunkar (1850-82), a Poona high school teacher, whose journal *Nibandhamala* ("Garland of Essays") was the most popular literary organ of the day. Chiplunkar "threw off the chains" of his government job in 1880, and protested in print that "Our Country's Condition" had degenerated because of British rule to "that of a prostitute," while "our grand and minor kings are almost like pawns in a game of chess." Joining forces in 1880, Chiplunkar and Tilak started a "New English School" in Poona, a pioneering Indian venture in education, to which Gokhale allied himself in 1884. The "Indian Jesuits," as these ardent young men called themselves, extended their educational efforts throughout the Deccan by establishing the Deccan Education Society in 1884, and the still-flourishing Fergusson College at Poona a year later.

By 1885, then, many "New Indians" were busily engaged in numerous provincial endeavors of public protest, publicity, and educational self-strengthening. The Parsi community of Bombay and the Brahmans of Bengal were as precocious as Poona's Chitpavins in providing able new leadership capable of articulating Indian aspirations. The Bombay Parsi Dadabhai Naoroji (1825-1917), "Grand Old Man" of Indian politics, opened the first Indian business enterprise in England in 1855. Dadabhai's interest in economics stimulated the development of his famous "drain theory" of British economic exploitation of India, which became one of the battle-cries of Indian nationalism and found passionate advocates among Nationalist leaders, including Nehru, to the very eve of independence. A Parsi barrister, Pherozeshah Mehta (1845-1915), helped direct Congress in its early phase of growth. The Bengali Brahman Surendranath Banerjea (1848-1926), who early won admission into the *sanctum sanctorum* of the I.C.S. only to be summarily dismissed for "improper conduct," turned his talents to political agitation, founding the Indian Association in Calcutta in 1876. Banerjea, whose lead in the post-1905 partition protest earned him the popular name of "surrender-not," convened an Indian National Conference at Calcutta in 1883 to counteract anti-Ilbert Bill agitation. His Conference met again in 1885 at the same time that Congress was begun in Bombay, but thereafter the forces of India's political awakening were united.

Individual Englishmen played as important a role as enlightened Indians in the founding of India's National Congress. Allan Octavian Hume (1829-1912), who joined the I.C.S. in 1849 and served India officially until his retirement in 1882, thereafter embarked upon his career of more important unofficial service to the Nationalist movement. Early in 1883, Hume circulated a letter to the graduates of Calcutta University reminding them that "Whether in the individual or the nation, all vital progress must spring from within, and it is to you, her most cultured and enlightened minds, her most favoured sons, that your country must look for the initiative." [9]

The first Congress met in Bombay in December, 1885, attended by seventy-three representatives and about ten unofficial participants, from every province of British India. Nearly all the delegates were Hindus, only two being Muslims, and most were lawyers or journalists. Professions of loyalty to the *raj* rang from the rostrum, but all who attended the Congress and those outside aware of its inauguration realized that a new era of national self-consciousness had dawned in India. Only two years later, at the third Congress in Madras, more than 600 elected delegates, eighty-three of them Muslims, flocked to the *pandal* (festive tent) at which the annual sessions were held. In addition to giving Indian leaders from distant regions an invaluable opportunity to exchange ideas and discuss their grievances, the annual Congress meetings served as a unified lobby for the presentation of Indian demands to government through a series of resolutions passed on the final day of each session. These Congress resolutions, even though often totally ignored by officialdom, form a skeleton history of early Indian political aspirations and grievances. Between 1885 and 1905 the most important and recurring themes stressed in Congress resolutions included the call for more strenuous government action in abolishing poverty; the introduction of more Indians in all branches of official service; greater representation of Indian opinion on all legislative bodies, central as well as provincial and local; reduction of military expenditure and taxation; expansion of educational facilities, including those required for technical training; abolition of the Council of India at Whitehall; extension of the Permanent Revenue Settlement beyond Bengal; and the removal of onerous disabilities from Indians residing in Africa. Though mocked by Lord Dufferin (viceroy from 1884-88) in 1888 as a "microscopic minority" [10] drawn from the "very few thousands" of English-edu-

[9] William Wedderburn, *Allan Octavian Hume. Father of the Indian National Congress, 1829-1912* (London: T. Fisher Unwin, 1913), p. 50.
[10] Briton Martin, Jr., *New India, 1885. A Study of British Official Policy and the Emergence of the Indian National Congress.* Ph.D. thesis, University of Pennsylvania, 1964.

cated Indians in a land of some 200 million voiceless peasants, and wishfully believed by Lord Curzon (viceroy from 1899-1905) to be "tottering to its fall" [11] in 1900, Congress survived and indeed flourished.

This institution, which became the major vehicle leading India to independence, was by no means devoid of factional internal stresses, in addition to grave strains from external official pressure. The reformist and revolutionary (or moderate and extremist) groups already described continued to struggle within Congress for their respective platforms. Anxious to avert any open split over questions of religious reform, the leadership early agreed to limit Congress debate and resolutions to political and economic problems, specifically excluding all socioreligious issues. This decision led Ranade and his followers to organize the National Social Conference in 1887, a group designed to press for change in those very areas placed beyond the purview of Congress. Naturally many members of Congress joined the Conference as well, and indeed until 1895 the annual sessions of both groups were held in the same *pandal*, the Conference convening after Congress adjourned. In 1895, when Poona was venue of the meetings, Tilak and his orthodox Hindu supporters stirred so incendiary an opposition to this use of Congress quarters by the Conference that Ranade, always ready to "bear and forebear" in the hope of preserving peace, agreed to convene his Conference elsewhere.

The reactionary-revolutionaries had won a major victory, reflecting the growth of their power. Actually, a new political party of extreme Hindu Nationalism was forming within the ranks of Congress. Tilak himself had parted company from Gokhale and his reformist colleagues in the Deccan Education Society in 1890, turning from education to journalism as his medium of nationalist agitation. In 1891 he led the reactionary Hindu opposition to Sir Andrew Scoble's bill to amend the penal code by raising the age of females (married or unmarried) with whom intercourse would be defined as rape from ten to twelve years. The "age of consent" controversy, which blazed in the wake of this timid official attempt to defend the health of child brides, rekindled all of the passions and fears stirred by the abolition of *sati* and legalization of widow remarriage. Tilak used his vernacular press, oratorical talents, and ingenious knowledge of Hindu legal texts to remarkably effective advantage in mounting

[11] Lord Curzon to Lord Hamilton, November 18, 1900, quoted in *EI & P*, p. 151.

mass protest meetings and stimulating a flood of petitions to government opposing this official invasion against the "ancient and powerful fortress of Hindu society." When his agitation had proved ineffective, Tilak labored to organize the substantial support he had rallied to mount continued attacks against the white Christian *raj*. In 1893 he helped to revive annual public festivals commemorating the birth of the popular Hindu diety Ganesh, which drew crowds of peasants to large Deccan cities like Poona for some ten days of celebration, entertainment, and historically disguised political speeches. Groups of martially trained young Hindus marched behind bands through the crowded old towns during these festivals, often provoking violent Muslim reactions when they passed near a mosque. The ensuing communal rioting only stiffened orthodox adherents of both major religions in their long-standing mutual antipathy.

In 1897, on the night of the diamond jubilee celebration of Victoria's coronation, political assassination was added to the arsenal of Hindu extremism with the murder of two British officials in Poona. Several of Tilak's speeches and editorials had helped inspire the young Brahman assassins, but no direct complicity could be proved; however, Tilak was subsequently jailed for sedition, which confirmed his implacable hatred for the *raj*. Anarchist groups emerged at various centers in the Deccan, and after 1905 in Bengal and Punjab as well. Despite Gandhi's protracted preaching of nonviolence, violence remained a factor in the Nationalist struggle, winning its champion spokesman in Subhas Bose during World War II, and leading to the murder of Mahatma Gandhi following India's attainment of freedom.

The first partition of Bengal in 1905, carried out with indecent haste and without due consultation of respected Indian opinion, added a new dimension and several new tactics to the Nationalist movement. Though the British protested that the scheme was purely administrative in inspiration, Hindus of Calcutta generally interpreted it as an insidious attempt to weaken their power and undermine Congress influence by dividing the Bengali "nation" along communal lines. The new province of Eastern Bengal and Assam, born on October 16, 1905, contained a Muslim majority. Hindus everywhere considered it the result of an official policy of divide and rule. George Nathaniel Curzon (1859-1925), one of the most brilliant and energetic viceroys of British India, had a special talent for sponsoring the least popular measures for the best of administrative reasons—greater efficiency. With some eighty-five millions Bengal was indeed an unwieldy provincial unit, and even anti-partition leaders readily agreed that some form of division was desirable. The division made, however, not only separated Hindus from Muslims, but cut through the heart of the Bengali-speaking region of this multilingual province. A few more months of consultation and reappraisal might have made all the difference, but by 1905 Curzon was far too embittered to consult anyone, least of all Indians.

The partition immediately resulted in intensified anti-British agitation throughout India. Leaders of the anti-partition movement in Bengal called for a boycott of all British imports, introducing a new plank of enonomic pressure into the Congress platform. Public bonfires fed by British cloth, symbolic revivals of ancient Vedic sacrifices for the goal of political salvation, lit the sky over India for decades after. To replace the burned foreign produce, a *svadeshi* ("of our own nation") movement was launched, vigorously stimulating indigenous industry. Wealthy Indian merchants, who until this time had stayed aloof from Congress agitation, now added substantial support to the Nationalist movement. Parsi industrialists like Jamsetji N. Tata, father of India's steel industry, became leading financial backers of Congress. The boycott of goods was soon extended to English education as well. Curzon's policy of paternalism and strong central intervention in every sphere of Indian life had brought the universities of Calcutta, Bombay, and Madras more tightly under the control and direction of British officialdom after 1903. With characteristic indifference to Indian sensibilities, Curzon had castigated the senate of Calcutta University in a bluntly worded convocation address which alienated most leading Indian intellectuals from government policy. Indian political leaders now proposed "national" education to replace the "denationalizing" Western learning that had so long served to exalt British traditions while ignoring the roots and achievements of Indian culture.

The last quarter of the nineteenth century had witnessed growing interest in ancient India and Hindu religion and philosophy. Stimulated in good measure by Western Sanskritists and amateur archaeologists, this renaissance attracted brilliant indigenous exponents. The *Arya Samaj* (Aryan Society), founded in Bombay in 1875, called for a return to the purity and unsurpassed greatness of the Aryan epoch, by asserting Aryan primacy in every field of human endeavor.

By the end of the nineteenth century Hindu preachers were eager to "conquer the world" with the spirituality of Hinduism, founding missions in Europe and America to spread the gospel of Vedanta and turn the tide of Western materialism. Instead of feeling ashamed of their heritage, Hindus were told to take pride in the genius and beauty of Upanishadic idealism and the teachings of Vedantists. It was the West, suffering traumas of material despair and industrial dehumanization, that needed to learn from India, not the reverse. India's spiritual ethic of tranquility and psychic calm would one day save mankind from the monstrous society it had manufactured. Many Westerners agreed; foremost among them were Madame Helena Blavatsky and an American colonel, Henry Steel Olcott, co-founders of the Theosophical Society, originated in New York City in 1875. They were soon joined by the singularly dynamic Englishwoman, Annie Besant (1847-1933), who directed the Society's Indian headquarters at Adyar, outside Madras, after 1886. Viewing religion as the highest expression of intellectual endeavor, and Hinduism as the highest form of religion, Theosophy helped inflate the self-image of Hindus, who had long felt ashamed of their own heritage. The political implications of this restoration of ego were quite important, since if Indians had indeed been capable of attaining the pinnacle of human enlightenment several thousand years before, why then should they have to endure any period of British tutelage before being ready for self-government? Mrs. Besant did in fact become a leading figure in the early Nationalist movement, founding her own Home Rule League in 1915, and presiding over Congress in 1917. In 1910 she helped Pandit Madan Mohan Malaviya start the Hindu University at Banaras, where instruction at the highest level in all subjects was offered in Indian languages alone. The program of National Education included the creation of numerous technical schools, thus linking it directly to the Svadeshi movement.

Finally, in the wake of partition, Congress adopted a new ultimate goal, *svaraj* (self-government) patterned after the model of "the United Kingdom or the Colonies." This bold demand rang from the Congress rostrum for the first time in 1906. A major split between reformist and revolutionary parties within Congress hereafter developed over the time schedule and tactics to be employed in attaining this generally accepted goal of colonial self-government or dominion status. Gokhale and his followers favored a policy of loyal cooperation with the British home government and its dominant (after 1906) Liberal Party, leading to gradual reforms in the "constitution" of British India, which together with expanded education and public responsibility would help prepare India to receive total power to govern herself. Tilak and other extremists wanted their "birthright" of *svaraj* immediately, and advocated the use of any tactics, legal or illegal, to hasten British departure.

The Liberal Party's victory in 1906 ushered in an era of reforms for India. John Morley (1838-1923), Gladstone's biographer and leading lieutenant in the long struggle for Irish home rule, took command of the India Office at Whitehall, and soon initiated a program of comprehensive reform in Indian government. Reversing the policy of Curzon, whose strong will had guided Indian affairs from Calcutta for the preceding half-decade, Morley introduced a Liberal program of "peace, retrenchment, and reform," the bywords of his political mentor. He sought out and welcomed Indian advice, and valued most highly his protracted discussions with Gokhale, his leading unofficial adviser on India. Though thwarted at every stage by a stiff-backed bureaucracy, which confused responsible rule with surrender of rightful power and progress with weakness, and hampered by a mediocre viceroy (Lord Minto, the fourth Earl, 1905-10), Morley managed to introduce several very significant reforms. First, he struck a blow for racial equality by appointing two Indian members to his own council in 1907-8, and an Indian member to the viceroy's Executive "holy of holies" in 1909. Thereafter, at least one Indian would be present at all meetings of the most exalted and powerful councils of government, and British racial arrogance would be tempered while Indian pride was bolstered. Coming after half a century of racial conflict and policies based on belief in white supremacy, the importance of placing "a Native in the seats of the Mighty," Morley knew, could hardly be exaggerated. He suspected, in fact, that at root Indian unrest and disaffection with British rule were racial far more than political, and as such more difficult to reconcile. Nonetheless, he sponsored pervasive political reforms as well, which were introduced after passage of the Indian Councils Act of 1909.

By an Act of 1861 the maximum number of additional members appointed to the viceroy's Executive for the purpose of making laws and regulations had been raised to twelve, with at least half of these to be nonofficials. Several members of the Indian aristocracy were at this time appointed by the viceroy to serve in this legislative capacity.

Legislative councils were, moreover, created for both Bombay and Madras, each of which could contain up to eight additional members appointed by the governor. Nothing further was done for more than three decades by way of expanding the councils and their power, though at the first Congress session a resolution was passed calling "admission of a considerable proportion of elected members" to expanded councils "essential." Three years later Lord Dufferin's committee on provincial council reform recommended expansion of provincial councils to include some thirteen members selected from among Indian chiefs, princes, and the wealthiest landholders, as well as some twenty-three members of a proposed "second division" to be elected by municipal committees and local boards and appointed in part so as to provide adequate representation for "minority interests" (especially Muslims). These proposals of 1888 also included the review of India's annual budget by legislative councillors, and "consultation" on matters of provincial interest. The Indian Councils Act of 1892 incorporated some of these recommendations as well as others, increasing the Central Council's additional membership to a maximum of sixteen, and those of Bombay, Madras, and Bengal to twenty. The budget was thrown open to annual discussion and questioning, though no amendments could be proposed, nor supplementary questions asked. In implementing this Act, Lord Landsdowne (viceroy 1888-94) suggested the introduction of indirect "election" to councils of several of the new additional members, whose names could be submitted to the viceroy for official nomination, after they had been elected by certain representative bodies (corporations, boards, university senates, and chambers of commerce). As a result of this formula, which satisfied both the Liberal and Conservative parties in Parliament, some thirty-nine Indians were "elected" to central and provincial councils for the first time. Men like Gokhale were thus brought within earshot of the viceroy and his governors. Gokhale's annual critiques of the budget, though they could not immediately affect fiscal allocations, did influence the finance member's calculations for the following year, and served as precise statements of responsible Congress demands and models of excellence for the instruction of future generations of Indian officials and political leaders.

The Act of 1909 initiated a new kind of association of Indians with Britishers in the fashioning of legislation for British India. It was indeed the first tentative step on the path toward responsible parliamentary government for India. The principle of election of members to councils was now directly introduced, and though the initial electorate was miniscule (based on property or educational qualifications), anyone familiar with the constitutional history of England realized that once a principle wedged open a parliamentary door, public pressure would soon complete the task of swinging it fully ajar. In 1910 some 135 newly elected members took their council seats throughout India as the first self-chosen representatives of their own people. Maximum additional membership on the Central Legislative Council was escalated to sixty; while in Bombay, Madras, Bengal, East Bengal and Assam, and the United Provinces the total was raised to fifty; in all other provinces of British India to thirty. At the provincial level, moreover, the official majority was abolished, establishing another vital new precedent opposed to the bitter end by bureaucrats, who rightly sensed that their days of despotic rule were now numbered, but carried over most strenuous objections by the Liberal secretary of state. The executive councils of Bombay and Madras were also expanded to include Indian members. Powers of the legislative councils were enhanced along lines of British parliamentary practice with the introduction of supplementary questions, permission granted to members to propose resolutions, and extended opportunity provided for debate and amendment of the annual budget. The viceroy and governors retained ultimate veto power over all legislation yet, as Gokhale put it to the Madras Congress in welcoming the 1909 reforms, "hitherto, we have been engaged in agitation from outside: from now we shall be engaged in what might be called responsible association with the administration . . . as practical men we should be satisfied with the scheme."

Congress itself had split openly at Surat in 1907. With their new "Nationalist" party, Tilak and Pal abandoned the moderate leadership of Gokhale, Mehta, and the "Conventionists" to wander their own way for nine years. Most of those years Tilak spent in prison exile in Burma; he was found guilty of sedition a second time in 1908, and sentenced to six years at Mandalay prison. The cult of the bomb had been added to that of the pistol in 1908, and terrorist activity continued sporadically around Bengal, the Punjab, and the Deccan. Minto's inept government resorted to increasingly harsh repression, which from the distance of Whitehall Morley could only challenge, question, and eventually overrule, but hardly stop. Unrest fed on the poison of mistrust; disaffection grew and racial tension continued, despite symbolic measures of good faith like those already noted. The new reforms, while allowing men on both sides of India's armed camp to build a bridge of cooperation and mutual confidence, could not in themselves transform an atmosphere charged with hatred into a garden of love.

At this very time, moreover, Muslims began to acquire independent political consciousness, adding further conflict and stress to what was already a movement sorely divided against itself. Though the Muslim quarter of India's population was slower than the Hindu majority to generate leadership capable of articulating Muslim "national" demands of a modern sort, Islam had always provided sufficient doctrinal mortar to bind its Indian faithful into a separate brotherhood. While that sense of Islamic community was more accurately supranationalist than nationalistic in aspiration, it was nonetheless strong enough to make the Muslims of India feel distinctly different from the Hindus, Sikhs, and Christians around them. Because it was Muslim rule the Company had displaced, the Muslim aristocracy and intellectual elite hardly rushed to support the new *raj*, or take advantage of its exotic educational opportunities, with anything like the alacrity early shown by Hindu subjects, particularly in Calcutta. Instead, Muslims sulked in their tents or actively labored to revive Islam in India, restore Mughal rule, and oust the Christian usurpers of Muslim power. Throughout the second quarter of the nineteenth century local outbreaks of holy war against the foreign rulers raged under Muslim revivalist banners from the Punjab to Bengal. Peasant uprisings among the faithful were particularly severe in the 1840s in northeast India, and in some measure the war of 1857-58 may be seen as the culmination of this movement. Indeed, the Muslim Wahhabis remained active through the 1870s, and it was an Afghan convict of this sect who assassinated Lord Mayo (viceroy from 1869-72) during his visit to the Andaman Islands, the sole successful attempt on the life of a British governor-general.

After 1858, however, most Muslim revivalists were content to abandon violence and bide their time, concentrating on study and the propagation of their ideas. The *Dar-al-Ulum* (Abode of the Ulama), founded at Deoband (about one hundred miles north of Delhi) in 1867, served as the intellectual breeding ground for Muslim scholars dedicated to the restoration of Islamic polity in India. Among those trained there were some of the later "Nationalist" Muslim leaders of Congress, most notable of whom was Maulana Abul Kalam Azad

(1887-1958), who presided over Congress during World War II and was minister of education, natural resources, and scientific research in the Nehru cabinet.

The emulative movement of Muslim reformers began with the "Urdu-revival" [12] around Delhi during the second quarter of the nineteenth century, and attained institutional form in 1863 with the founding of a Muhammadan Literary Society. The foremost Muslim champion of British rule in the nineteenth century was Sir Sayyid Ahmad Khan (1817-98), who had entered the Company's service in 1838, remained staunchly loyal during the war of 1857-8, and published a famous pamphlet (*Causes of the Indian Revolt*) in 1873, which attributed the great upheaval to Hindu rather than Muslim inspiration. Intellectually eclectic and modernist in outlook, Sir Sayyid did much the same for Islam, stressing its similarities to Christianity and laboring to reform its social customs, as Ram Mohan Roy had earlier done for Hinduism. Inspired during a visit to England in 1870 by what he saw of Oxford, and encouraged by leading Conservatives, among them young Theodore Beck, Sir Sayyid started the Muhammadan Anglo-Oriental College at Aligarh in 1875. Beck became the first principal, Sir Sayyid the secretary, of this pioneering center of higher education in English and Islamic learning, which trained leaders of a modern political party of Indian Muslims started in 1906.

The Muslim League, like Congress, was a product of joint Anglo-Indian inspiration. Sayyid Mahdi Ali, known as Mohsin-al Mulk (1837-1907), who succeeded Sir Sayyid as secretary of Aligarh, convened a deputation of thirty-five influential Muslims, led by the Aga Khan, to explain to Lord Minto the "special . . . national interests" of the some sixty-two million Indian Muslims, in October 1906. The deputation, whose warm reception had been assured by the labors of interested Englishmen, insisted that "we Mohammedans are a distinct community with additional interests of our own which are not shared by other communities." [13] Minto's reply was more than cordial; after stating "I am entirely in accord with you," he declared

[12] Wilfred C. Smith, *Modern Islam in India. A Social Analysis* (Lahore: Minerva Book Shop, 1943).

[13] Address presented to Lord Minto, October 1, 1906, at Simla, reproduced as Appendix B in Ram Gopal, *Indian Muslims. A Political History (1858-1947)* (Bombay: Asia Publishing House, 1959), pp. 331-332. For an account of the genesis of the Muslin League see Syed Razi Wasti, *Lord Minto and the Indian National Movement, 1905 to 1910* (Oxford: Clarendon Press, 1964).

as viceroy that "any electoral representation in India would be doomed to mischievous failure which aimed at granting a personal enfranchisement regardless of the beliefs and traditions of the communities composing the population of this continent," [14] thereby committing the government of India to the system of separate electorates as part of the proposed reform scheme. He further promised "the Mahommedan community" that they could "rest assured that their political rights and interests as a community will be safeguarded in any administrative reorganization with which I am concerned." The die was thus cast for an officially sponsored pattern of political communalism, which served to bolster the sense of religious difference between Hindus and Muslims in British India that terminated in the partition of an entire subcontinent. The Act of 1909 introduced this "separate electorate" formula by setting aside a specific number of seats on all legislative councils for "Muslim" members, who were to be elected by qualified Muslims voting as a separately enfranchised block. The Acts of 1919 and 1935 expanded the system to include other minority religious groups as well. Shortly after leaving Lord Minto, the Aga Khan's Muslim deputation organized itself into the Muslim League, the Party, which in 1947 assumed control over the government of Pakistan.

By 1910, therefore, the historic ground was prepared, which led to the dual terminal points of the British epoch, independence and partition. Before World War I, however, both goals appeared quite remote, and few in India or England fully grasped the implications of the constitutional changes initiated at the close of Morley's era. Congress and the League labored to reach a rapprochement on the question of representative apportionment, evolving a scheme approved by both at Lucknow in 1916, the year in which Congress itself was reunited. The First World War, moreover, evoked a remarkably unified response of loyal support for the *raj* from almost every segment of Indian society. Men and money poured forth to defend Britain when she most needed help. Almost one million Indian troops were sent to the western front. A princely loan of £100 million was swiftly subscribed. Thousands of British civilian and military officers were drained from India to serve in Europe and Africa, yet the populace remained staunchly calm. Even Tilak sent a message of personal loyalty to the viceroy and the Crown. Gandhi subordinated his principles of nonviolence to the urgent need of the hour, and toured north-

[14] Appendix C, *ibid.*, p. 338.

ern India recruiting troops to defend the *raj*. Indian industry enjoyed a period of rapid development. Coal output jumped to over fifteen million tons in 1914. The Tata Iron and Steel Company, whose plant at Jamshedpur in southern Bihar was started in 1908, received vigorous official stimulus once the war began, and by 1916 India produced 100,000 tons of steel. (By World War II Jamshedpur was the largest single center of steel production in the British Empire.) Cotton cloth production in the Bombay-Ahmadabad region boomed as well, as Indian mills were called upon to help dress Allied armies. During the half decade of war the number of registered business enterprises in India more than trebled, and their capital value quadrupled. Wheat was exported in unprecedented quantities from the Punjab breadbasin. Inflation followed the process of sudden economic growth. The government appointed a commission in 1916 to consider the over-all problems of stimulating India's economy so that the subcontinent could more rapidly produce urgently needed sinews of war. A munitions board was created in 1917, and ordnance plants syphoned landless laborers to urban centers in such large numbers that the earlier trend toward deurbanization was finally reversed.

The war brought in its wake many new ideas and aspirations as well. For India and the world 1917 was a year of ideological excitement and the greatest of idealistic expectations. Wilson's fourteenth point, with its promise of self-determination for peoples everywhere, seemed a message of hope to India's political elite. More exciting still was the solemn declaration voiced by Sir Edwin Montagu (1879-1924), Morley's India Office protégé, who as secretary of state for India (1917-22) told Commons on August 20, 1917, that the policy of His Majesty's government was now one of "increasing association of Indians in every branch of the administration, and the gradual development of self-governing institutions, with a view to the progressive realization of responsible government in India as an integral part of the Empire." Here at last was the promise of dominion status, the very goal toward which Congress had been agitating for more than a decade. Before the year ended, however, the Bolshevik Revolution seemed to prove that Europe's era of despotism and colonial tyranny had finally reached its end.

Small wonder, then, in the light of India's response to the war effort and the hopes generated by 1917, that the Great War's aftermath brought disillusion and despair to the Indian scene. The influenza epidemic of 1918, which cost India an estimated five million lives, seemed a portent of the bleak political prospects ahead. Instead of freedom, the armistice brought only an extension of martial law throughout India with passage of the "Rowlatt Acts" of 1919. Congress leaders denounced these "black Acts" as proof of British ingratitude and duplicity, for now that Indian aid was no longer urgently required to save the Empire, officialdom reverted to its prewar despotic mentality. Indians could continue to be deported or imprisoned for any length of time by "preventive detention" powers first taken by the government of India in 1818. The Peace Conference at Paris stirred further resentment, for India was not directly represented there despite her massive battlefield losses. After demobilization Britishers who had served abroad returned to their I.C.S. posts, displacing Indians who had acted effectively in their absence. Indian peasants returned to their villages in the Punjab to face the same sort of harsh treatment that had always been their lot in life, only now they remembered that for years they had been granted equal opportunity to die beside similar men in distant trenches. For most new industries, the immediate aftermath of the war was depression, yet prices remained inflated, especially as a result of food scarcity. But the tragedy that sent a shudder of rage through the subcontinent and caused Congress to abandon its basic policy of cooperation and loyalty to the *raj*, occurred at Amritsar on April 13, 1919.

The Punjab, major recruiting ground for the Indian Army since 1858, had provided some 400,000 soldiers during World War I, and because of its proximity to Afghanistan, as much as the martial nature of its people, was considered by British strategists as potentially the most volatile province in India. Ever since 1907, moreover, vigorous political agitation had developed in this third major center of Congress influence. Curzon's paternalistic land policy was pursued with a vengeance by his disciple, Sir Denzil Ibbetson, whom Minto appointed lieutenant-governor of the Punjab. Lala Lajpat Rai (1865-1928), a member of Congress since 1888, became head of the Arya Samaj, which grew into a militant political as well as reformist religious force in the Punjab early in the twentieth century. He launched so effective a campaign of mass opposition against Ibbetson's unpopular Punjab Colonization Act of 1907 (subsequently vetoed by the viceroy) that he was summarily arrested and deported to Burma that very year. This deportation roused a flood of protests from Commons as well as from moderate leaders of Congress like Gokhale. Morley himself was scandalized by Ibbetson's autocratic arrogance, and finally secured freedom for the man who had overnight become a national hero, backed by Tilak for the presidency of Surat's abortive Congress. Thereafter, the Punjab remained a center of political ferment, including Pan-Islamic agitation, as well as revolutionary terrorist activities like the attempted assassination of Lord Hardinge of Penshurst (viceroy from 1910 to 1916), during his state entry into Delhi in 1912. Sikh revolutionaries like Har Dayal, founder of the *Ghadr* ("Mutiny") Party, which raised funds in the United States for weapons shipped to the Punjab, sought German support during World War I for an Indian "uprising." Canada's refusal to allow the Japanese *Komagata Maru*, a vessel packed with more than 350 Sikh peasants, to land with its unwelcome émigrés added fuel to the Punjab scene in 1914. (As subjects of the British Empire, Indians naturally expected privileged opportunities of residence within British Dominions. Instead they were made acutely conscious of the "second class" subjectship to which they had been relegated by their skin color. Canadian, South African, and Australian laws against Indian immigration became increasingly sensitive sources of Nationalist discontent. Anti-Indian legislation in white Dominions was to emerge as the major argument later used by Indians opposed to the idea of independent India's joining the Commonwealth.) Afghan ambitions and open encouragement to Muslim revolutionaries of the Punjab, just following the war, gave the British real cause for anxiety in this province by 1919. Yet what happened at Amritsar, sacred capital of the Sikhs, in April of that year can hardly be explained as anything but the terrorized behavior of a madman, who happened unfortunately to be the general in command of the Punjab military establishment.

After several riots, which came in the wake of the "preventive arrest and deportation" of two Arya Samaj leaders a few days earlier, General Reginald E. H. Dyer posted an order prohibiting all public meetings in Amritsar on April 12. On the thirteenth, learning of a mass meeting being held in a garden, the General drove with some fifty trusted soldiers to the one narrow entrance of the garden, deployed his troops across the width of the twenty-foot opening, and without so much as a word of prior warning, ordered them to open fire. He made them continue firing until their ammunition, some 1,650 rounds in all, had been used up about ten minutes later. Within the walled garden, which was under five square acres in area, were approximately 10,000 unarmed men, women, and children with no place to hide, no exit, no defense. When the human target practice had finished, some 400 lay dead, and another 1,200 were wounded. Few of the bullets had gone astray.

Testifying later before an official commission set up to review this massacre, General Dyer explained that he had given the crowd no warning or order to disband since he considered it essential to produce "a sufficient moral effect, from a military point of view, not merely on those who were present, but more especially throughout the Punjab." He did in fact produce a moral effect of a different kind throughout India. No leader of Congress or the Muslim League had ever succeeded as well as General Dyer in weaning millions overnight from their loyal allegiance to the British *raj*, and their ultimate faith that the spirit of "fair play" lay at the root of British behavior, however arbitrary or despotic such behavior may have seemed in the past. Men like Motilal Nehru (1861-1931), father of India's first prime minister, the wealthiest barrister of northern India, more English in dress, manner, and mental habit than most officials of the Crown, could no longer stand silent on the sidelines of India's struggle. The impact of Dyer's bullets, his inflexible defense of what he had done, and the reward he received upon returning to England of a jewelled sword inscribed with the words "Saviour of the Punjab" were more than the most patient and passive of Indian minds could abide.

Ironically enough, the same year brought to fruition Montagu's long labors at hammering out new reform legislation built on the base established by Morley, but far more ambitious and liberal: the Government of India Act of 1919. Had it come a year earlier most Indians would have welcomed the Act's substantial concessions of power as a long stride toward the promise of dominion status. The Central Legislative Council was now to be transformed into a bicameral legislature: a Council of State with a maximum of sixty members, no more than one-third official; and a Legislative Assembly with a total of 140 members, 100 elected, and no more than twenty-three, of the remaining forty, official appointees. At the provincial level, the principle of dyarchy was to be introduced, converting legislative councils (again all greatly expanded in size) into partially responsible miniature parliaments with several ministers of each governor's executive council representing the elected majority in the legislature, each given full control over a "transferred" department of state. The most critical subjects, like law and order, revenue, and finance, were to remain "reserved" for official administration. Here at least, however, was "half the loaf" of the parliamentary responsibility for which Congress had been clamoring, and the explicit promise that if the system worked effectively, the remaining half would be given within a decade. At least 70 per cent of all provincial legislatures were to be comprised of elected members. Franchise requirements were liberalized to qualify several million Indian electors instead of the few thousands hitherto permitted to vote. Local boards and municipalities were "as far as possible" to be placed under "complete popular control." Recruitment for the I.C.S. was hereafter to be simultaneously carried out in India and England. The salary of the secretary of state for India and all operating expenses of the India Office were to be transferred from the Indian to the Imperial Treasury budget. An Indian high commissioner, responsible to Delhi rather than Whitehall, was to be sent to London to direct the purchase of all stores for India. An advisory chamber of princes was to be established for regular consultation by the viceroy on all matters affecting princely interests. Fnally, after ten years of testing the new system of government, a parliamentary commission was to be created to consider the next stage in this progressive devolution of power from British to Indian agency.

Coming in the wake of Amritsar and the Rowlatt Acts, all of these generous concessions and grand promises sounded hollow to Indian ears. The disenchantment and disgust that preceded the reforms served to negate their impact and subvert their value. National loss of faith could not be restored by mere act of Parliament. Congress turned from the path of continuing cooperation with the *raj*, which had been an axiom of its program and annual professions over the past thirty-odd years, to follow the lure of a different cry on a path as yet untrod. A remarkable new leader emerged on the Indian scene to issue his call for mass nonviolent noncooperation starting from August 1, 1920.

Noncooperation, Independence, and Partition

The new leader of Congress was Mohandas Karamchand Gandhi (1869-1948), a Hindu Vaishya of Gujarat, who went to London at the age of nineteen to study law. He returned as a barrister after three years, but was so shy and morally scrupulous that he could not succeed at the legal practice he started, and soon left India again, this time for Natal in South Africa, hired by some Indian merchants in

Durban to represent their firm. For the next twenty years South Africa was Gandhi's home, and while there he developed the technique by which he later led Congress and India to independence.

The reasons for Gandhi's impact on recent Indian history may never be accurately defined. Though few historical figures were so frank or prolific in writing about their own experiences, aspirations, and foibles, and no other individual in all of Indian history has evoked nearly so much scholarly attention, the secret of Gandhi's charismatic power over his countrymen remains enigmatic. We can at best allude to certain characteristics of his life and thought that helped stimulate mass responses, and generate selfless loyalty, devotion, indeed adulation, among hundreds of millions of followers. The man himself, however, was far greater than the sum of these effects. Most obvious of the attributes which come to mind in trying to probe the secret of Gandhi's leadership are truth, compassion, courage, and simplicity. Others have possessed most, if not all, of these qualities, some men more. Few, however, succeeded in developing each as intensively as did Gandhi. He made them all part of his religious credo. Truth in fact was the essence of his faith, its realization the ultimate goal of his life, as the title of his autobiography, *The Story of My Experiments with Truth*, indicates. The Sanskrit word for truth, *satya*, originally meant "the existent" or "real," and those who lived entirely by the laws of *satya* were supposed to attain supernatural powers. Gandhi named his technique of struggle *satyagraha*, literally "hold fast to truth." Perhaps he was inspired in part by John Stuart Mill's dictum that one man and the truth comprised "a majority," though he need only have relied upon the ancient Sanskrit phrase which has subsequently become the national motto of India, *satyameva jayate* (truth alone conquers). Gandhi equated truth with God. But he did more than pay lip service to an abstract concept of Platonic ideal. He worked to live by his beliefs, to close the normally wide gap between theory and practice, to do what he professed, calling upon others only to do what he himself did. He refused to accept any facile arguments of expediency for differentiating the means employed in a political struggle from the end desired. Freedom did not justify murder, nor deception of any sort. Untruth in the supposed service of independence was no less sinful, Gandhi insisted, than in the employ of individual greed. Seasoned politicians considered him a dreamer, a naïve idealist, unfit for the rough and tumble of political bargaining and the machinations of civilized society. Tilak, the supreme "realist" of Indian nationalism, once rebuked Gandhi for arguing that politics must be based on truth, chiding, "My friend! Truth has no place in politics." Gandhi begged to differ, insisting that "it betrays mental laziness to think that the world is not for *sadhus* [*saints*]." To the contrary, until all mankind exerted "a desperate attempt" to follow the path of sainthood, striving to conquer "hate by love, untruth by truth," the world was destined to suffer untold hardship and meaningless strife. "Even toward a villain, truth," Gandhi insisted in 1920, and he never changed his mind.

Compassion, or love, was another of the qualities he treasured highly, and it too was part of the secret of his genius and phenomenal magnetism. Once when asked to define his ambition in life, he replied that it was "to wipe every tear from every eye." The only title he ever received was *Mahatma*, "Great-Souled One," a spontaneous gift of love from those who knew the man, and understood what he wanted to achieve. He was more than a political leader. The world he worked to create, in fact, would have no need of politicians. He was a social reformer in the broadest sense, or as skeptics would put it, a Utopian. His aspiration was for "the uplift of all," the liberation not only of India from colonial subordination to Britain, but of all mankind from bondage to violence and mechanized, impersonalized society. He dreamed of a universal brotherhood in which peace and plenty would abound. It was, he confessed on the eve of his assassination, the dream of "my early youth," [15] a "paradise" in which "there will be neither paupers nor beggars, nor high nor low, . . . Where there will be no untouchability and where there will be equal respect for all faiths." This magic transformation of society was to be achieved through the agency of love, by the conscious extension among all human beings of the same instinct which impelled a mother to nourish her child. Gandhi himself was uniquely endowed with this elastic capacity of loving compassion. Nonviolence became the ethical keystone of his religion. "Truth implies love," he insisted, but a conscious merging of these two great forces of the soul would "move the world." For this reason his "method" of *satyagraha* has often been freely translated as "soul-force" in contrast to "physical" or "brute force." Compassion helps to explain the remarkable impact Gandhi made upon his "enemies" as well as the attraction of his

[15] From the transcript of his prayer meeting at Birla House, January 14, 1948, M. K. Gandhi, *Delhi Diary* (Ahmedabad: Navajivan Publishing House, 1948), pp. 341ff.

teaching to an unarmed nation of vegetarians, whose majority had so long adhered to nonviolence "as the highest religion." Before embarking upon his second great *satyagraha* campaign in 1930, Gandhi wrote Lord Irwin (viceroy 1926-31), "My ambition is no less than to convert the British people through nonviolence and thus make them see the wrong they have done to India. I do not seek to harm your people. I want to serve them even as I want to serve my own."

Courage was perhaps the least obvious of Gandhi's personal qualities, for he rarely alluded to it, and as the leader of a nonviolent army he was often accused of passivity, and by some even of cowardice. The effectiveness of his method, however, depended as much upon fearlessness as it did upon self-purification and dedication to spiritual values. Nehru once defined his message for India in two words: "Forget fear!" Those most intimately associated with him knew how courageous, how singularly tenacious, a man he was. His was the calm, quiet strength of a purified spirit, the rocklike courage of one who had no selfish motive, no mean aspiration, no crude or cunning desire. He faced death as he had so often faced assault, arrest, and long periods of prison incarceration—intrepid, confident of the ultimate vindication of his actions and aspirations. His unflinching courage inspired millions of humble and timid people to march bare-chested, without weapons of any sort, toward mounted police with steel-shod sticks, singing softly as they were dragged off to jail, until there was no more room behind bars in which to keep them all. Gandhi's life might almost be read as a conscious, arduous courtship of suffering, a heroic personal attempt to take upon himself the travail of his nation. Perhaps in that sense alone he succeeded.

Simplicity was the essence of his nature. Yet, like the simplicity of any great work of art, its achievement was the product of ingenious insight and patient labor. As a young man in London, as a lawyer newly arrived in Natal, Gandhi dressed in the fashion of high society. Pictures of him dating from this time reveal little more than an awkward, uncomfortable, young dandy, singularly unimpressive and unattractive in the most stylish garb of Bond Street. Yet for all his elegance of attire and Western erudition, Gandhi learned in South Africa that what counted most in determining his treatment by whites was the shade of his skin. The racial discrimination he personally suffered in Natal marked a fundamental turning point in his life. He became intensely aware of the plight of the more than 60,000 Indians settled in Natal, the Transvaal, and the Cape Colony at the turn of the century, who, though nominally subjects of the same British Crown as their white neighbors, were reduced to inferior legal status by a series of restrictive "Black Acts." Acutely sensitive, not only to prejudice, but to any departure from the high ideals of British equality before the law for all subjects, Gandhi decided to devote his life to resisting the anti-Indian legislation he found in South Africa, and thus labored to fashion a truly multiracial "commonwealth" of equal opportunity within the fortuitous framework of the British Empire. After 1917, when India enjoyed official representation at Imperial conferences, she regularly championed the cause of racial equality within the Empire, and after independence she became a leading critic of discrimination throughout the world from the forum of the United Nations. In 1901, Gandhi took the vows of poverty and celibacy, making the ancient Hindu ascetic concept of "nonpossession" part of his personal religion, and his entire appearance underwent as significant a transformation as had his mode of thought. He became the visual symbol of India's half-naked peasantry to a wide-eyed world at large. Much of the secret of Gandhi's hold over India's masses lay in the immediacy of their identification with him. Other leaders they admired, even adored, but always from a distance. Gandhi instead was one of them. He dressed, ate, looked precisely the way they all did. The lowliest, the poorest, the vast majority of village India, could turn to him as a brother, confident that he would empathize with their plight. Nor did power, prestige, adulation or age ever change him. Gandhi could forget self, or at least relegate it to so minor a role that nothing of the ego obtruded to weaken the impact of his message. When he visited Buckingham Palace in 1931 and was chidingly asked by reporters if he actually planned to wear his *dhoti* during an audience with the king, Gandhi said, "Some go in plus-fours, I will go in minus-fours." There were times, of course, when his penchant for the simple life evoked critical comments from weary followers among Congress' high command who had to travel hundreds of miles to out-of-the-way village retreats in order to consult their leader on matters of urgent business. As Sarojini Naidu, the poetess who became India's first female governor, once quipped: "It costs India *lakhs* [hundreds of thousands] of rupees to keep Gandhiji in poverty." Yet the value of personal precept can never be overestimated, and it was in good measure by keeping his simple image that Gandhi kept his mass following. Desiring nothing for himself, he was given everything he asked for by millions, who never once doubted the sincerity of the man, or the integrity of his motives.

What he asked for in 1920, upon launching the first nationwide *satyagraha* campaign, was the boycott of all things British throughout India. He called upon Indian lawyers to boycott the law courts; upon students and scholars to boycott British-sponsored schools; upon politicians and public leaders of every sort to boycott the legislative councils; upon voters to boycott the polls to which they would soon be invited under the new Government of India Act; upon dignitaries honored by the *raj* to boycott their titles and awards, pensions and medals; and finally, should that last extreme prove necessary, he explained that he would be prepared to call upon India's peasant population to boycott the revenue collectors by refusing to pay taxes. The response among all segments of India's population indicated Gandhi's popular support. Many of the old leaders of Congress withheld their backing from what seemed a precariously uncharted course, but the younger generation joined the movement enthusiastically. "We were full of excitement and optimism," Nehru reminisced, writing of 1921 as a year of political "intoxication." [16] By year's end some 20,000 *satyagrahis* had been imprisoned. Less than one third of the enfranchised electorate had gone to the polls. Many schools were obliged to shut down. Bonfires of foreign cloth fanned the flames of *svaraj*, and brilliant young men like Subhas Chandra Bose (1897-1945) gave up the chance to join the I.C.S., after passing the examinations, to return to India and fight for freedom. Rabindranath Tagore (1861-1941), India's Nobel laureate, "The Poet," whom Gandhi honored with the title *Gurudev* (Godly Teacher) as well, renounced his knighthood, though he could not wholeheartedly accept a campaign of chauvinistic nationalism. The most sensitive and ingenious artistic spirit of recent Indian history, Tagore was more nearly a citizen of the world than of any nation, yet he recognized Gandhi's "great-souled" character, and composed the words and music of India's anthem, *Jana Gana Mana* ("The Mind of the Multitude of the People").

Gandhi promised his followers *svaraj* in one year (by December 31, 1921). Muslims joined the Congress campaign in unexpected numbers, thanks to the impetus given Pan-Islam by the 1920 Treaty of Sèvres, which dismembered the Ottoman Empire. Muhammad Ali (1879-1930), elected president of Congress in 1923, roused the Mus-

[16] Jawaharlal Nehru, *Toward Freedom* (New York: John Day, 1941), p. 69.

lim masses of India to a fever pitch of indignation at British treachery in truncating the Caliphate, despite solemn wartime pledges to
the contrary. Together with the launching of Gandhi's first *satyagraha* campaign, therefore, the *Khilafat* movement was begun in India, and Gandhi welcomed its advent as the dawn of a new era of
Hindu-Muslim brotherhood. Indeed, many orthodox Hindus believed
that The Mahatma had been "captured" by the lure of Pan-Islam
because of the time and attention he lavished upon an issue that they
considered extraneous to India's struggle for *svaraj*. Gandhi, however,
recognized from the start that without communal unity, independence would at best bring fratricidal strife to his suffering subcontinent.
He warned his countrymen time and again that "divided we must
fall," but by 1947 he stood almost alone in resisting partition. Ironically enough, the *Khilafat* issue, which briefly generated a true spirit
of unity between Hindus and Muslims of India, served after its collapse in 1924 only to intensify earlier communal bitterness. One
cause of this bitterness was the tragic flight, which Congress helped
sponsor, of some 18,000 Indian Muslims to Afghanistan in August
1920. The Afghan government refused to admit their devout Islamic
brothers, obliging the émigrés to return over frozen passes where
many of the ill-clad and aged died, most of the rest coming home to
find themselves without property or land in their native villages.
Then in 1924, Mustafa Kamal Ataturk himself dealt the deathblow
to the entire movement by abolishing the Caliphate, leaving much
of the pent-up emotionalism and frustration of India's Muslims to be
unleashed against their Hindu neighbors. The Moplah uprisings in
Malabar were but the beginning of a long series of terrible communal
riots which shook India during the 1920s and '30s.

By 1922, when Gandhi's "year to freedom" had passed without the
promised fulfillment so eagerly awaited, The Mahatma decided to
unleash his ultimate weapon of mass peasant boycott. He warned
the Liberal Viceroy (from 1921-26) Rufus Isaacs, the Marquess of
Reading, that he would launch the boycott on taxes in the Bardoli
district of Gujarat on February 1, 1922. Sardar Vallabhbhai Patel
(1875-1950), subsequently India's first deputy prime minister, had
organized the peasants of his home region and convinced Gandhi of
the wisdom of starting his last stage of *satyagraha* with these well-
disciplined villagers. No sooner was the movement launched, however, than news reached The Mahatma of the tragic immolation of
some twenty-two Indian policemen in their headquarters at Chauri

Chaura about 800 miles to the northeast in the united provinces. An enraged mob had surrounded the building, setting it to the torch and butchering the police who desperately tried to escape. A different sort of political leader might have shrugged off the report with some words about not being able to make omelets without breaking eggs, but Mahatma Gandhi was so profoundly shocked by this violent display that he immediately called off his entire campaign, explaining that he now realized he had committed a "Himalayan blunder." India was not sufficiently prepared for nonviolent action on a nationwide scale. The spiritual ground had not been properly cleared. Younger men like Bose and Nehru received word of their leader's retreat in crowded jail cells with incredulity and despair. Others implored Gandhi to change his mind and sound the charge once more, while the nation was poised at the brink of its liberation from tyranny. But Gandhi listened instead to his "inner voice," which warned him that should British troops and officialdom withdraw tomorrow, India might suddenly be plunged into a chaos of barbarism, in which the incident at Chauri Chaura would be magnified ten thousand times. He decided instead to withdraw from political action entirely, and concentrate on what he called his "constructive program" of cotton-spinning, home-spun weaving, and social reform, especially the fostering of Hindu-Muslim unity and the uplift of *harijans* (children of God), who still lingered in the dark corridors of Hindu society as untouchables. The movement for freedom, Gandhi insisted, must first of all be "a movement of self-purification."

Determined to make the most of this cessation of militant national struggle, Britain's Liberal government at this time introduced numerous reforms along lines of greater autonomy for India. In 1923 India received full fiscal autonomy with the creation of a tariff board in Delhi, and was finally released from the leading strings of Manchester. Simultaneous examinations for the I.C.S. were held the same year in Delhi and London, and Indians were admitted to the officer cadre of the army. The new legislatures were anxious to prove themselves more than mere rubber stamps of British-sponsored policy. Many members of Congress began now to regret their boycott of these expanded representative bodies, and a group of "realists" led by Motilal Nehru (1861-1931), Chitta Ranjan Das (1870-1925), and Subhas Bose organized the Swarajist Party within Congress in order to contest the forthcoming elections. Gandhi's followers then came to be known as the "no-changers" within Congress, adherents of the noncooperation policy of boycott. The Swarajists won over forty seats in the Central Legislative Assembly in 1924, but, anxious to convince the *raj* that British rule had in fact become untenable, they used their positions primarily for obstructionist purposes.

New forces of unrest emerged after 1924 throughout British India, forces arising primarily from socioeconomic rather than political causes. The alarming increase in number and intensity of communal riots stimulated both Hindu and Muslim extremists to better organized attacks against one another. The Muslim League revived as the major party of Islam in India. The Hindu *Mahasabha* (founded in 1906) emerged in 1924 as the political arm of Hindu communalism, which at this time also acquired a militant militia with the founding of the *Rashtriya Svayamsevak Sangh* (National Self-service Society) at Nagpur. The Mahasabha and R.S.S. were in great measure heirs to the Tilak tradition of extremist and violent revolutionary tactics in the service of Hindu orthodoxy. They led campaigns of forcible "re-conversion" of Muslims, especially in southern and central India, to Hinduism. "The history of 1926," as Subhas Bose reported, "is largely a history of Hindu-Moslem strife." [17] This was also a time of growing industrial unrest and labor strikes led by newly organized unions, the first of which, the All-India Trade Union Congress, founded in 1920, was to come under Communist domination. Manabendra Nath Roy (1886-1954), a former Bengali terrorist, who helped organize the Communist Party of Mexico and met Lenin in Moscow in 1919, was the Comintern member in charge of developing the Communist movement in India, which he launched in 1922. By 1927 the Communist Party of India (CPI) was well established and embarked upon an energetic program of organizing workers' and peasants' parties. Thanks to such stimulus at a time of world economic depression, peasant societies blossomed throughout India in the early 1930s, just when Gandhi reentered the political arena at the head of his second great *satyagraha* movement.

In October 1929, Britain announced that "dominion status" was its goal for India, and government proposed the convening of a round table conference in London to decide upon the precise steps to be taken next toward its realization. Congress, however, had at this time come under the vigorous direction of a new young president, Jawaharlal Nehru (1889-1964), and at its December meeting passed

[17] S. C. Bose, *The Indian Struggle, 1920-1934* (London: Wishart & Company Ltd., 1935), p. 141.

a resolution rejecting the British piecemeal offer and calling instead for complete independence as soon as possible. The Central Committee was authorized "whenever it deems fit" to "launch upon a programme of Civil Disobedience including non-payment of taxes." January 26, 1930, was declared to be "Independence Day" (and is still celebrated annually in India as such), and throughout the nation pledges were taken to the effect that, "it is the inalienable right of the Indian people, as of any other people, to have freedom and to enjoy the fruits of their toil and have the necessities of life." [18] The Mahatma agreed to lead the campaign in March of 1930, starting on the twelfth to walk some 200 miles to Dandi by the sea in order to defy the law against making salt from sea water. The salt tax and government monopoly on salt production were among the most widespread of India's grievances, since their burden fell upon everyone. By choosing this particular form of protest, Gandhi again displayed his ingenious ability to arouse a mass following. His twenty-four day march had a compelling and cumulative effect upon public opinion throughout the land. Originally accompanied by hardly more than seventy followers, the tide swelled to thousands by the time he approached his destination. Millions more followed The Mahatma's progress in daily newspaper reports of the political foot pilgrimage. When he stepped into the sea, dipping his salt pan into the surf in symbolic defiance of the law, he was hailed by a chorus of admirers, and then followed by countless thousands all over India, who took courage from their venerable leader's example. Within months over 60,000 *satyagrahis* were jailed. Gandhi himself was arrested on May 5, 1930, and kept in prison for eight months, his second lengthy sentence.

On November 16, 1930, the first round table conference opened in London, but with no representative of Congress attending it was like a production of *Hamlet* without the Prince of Denmark. The air of unreality hovering over the conference soon became too much for the British to endure, and in January 1931 Lord Irwin (viceroy from 1926-31) ordered Gandhi released, in the hope that personal negotiation could succeed where repression had so obviously failed. By March 5, after a series of private talks, Gandhi and Irwin reached an "agreement" calling for the cessation of civil disobedience and Gandhi's participation in the London negotiations to hammer out a future constitution for India. Gandhi then attended the second round

[18] "Pledge taken by the Indian National Congress on Independence Day," January 26, 1930, Nehru, *Toward Freedom*, Appendix A, pp. 388-389.

table conference in September 1931 as "sole representative of the Congress."

The London negotiations broke down over the question of Congress' role in India's Nationalist movement. Gandhi insisted that Congress represented India. The British, however, viewed Congress merely as one among many Indian parties, including the League, depressed classes, princes, and Liberals. No understanding could be reached, for as Gandhi put it, "Congress contemplates a partnership . . . a connection with the British people—but that connection to be such as can exist between two absolute equals." [19] He then articulated what was perhaps the first statement of the modern "Commonwealth" ideal, which could be acceptable to a free India, explaining, "I have aspired—I still aspire—to be a citizen, not in the Empire, but in a Commonwealth; in a partnership if possible . . . of mutual benefit." Returning to India "empty-handed," Gandhi was rearrested in January 1932. The following August, Britain announced its "Communal Award," consisting of no less than twelve separate electorates, as an integral part of the new constitution in the making. The pattern begun in 1909 was thus multiplied with a vengeance, and among the "separate" political groups added were Hindu untouchables. Gandhi interpreted this action as official treachery of the lowest sort, Britain's bid to divide and rule the Hindu majority. From his prison cell, The Mahatma announced his intention to "fast unto death" unless government agreed to retract its divisive offer. During his week-long fast in September 1932, Gandhi conferred daily with Dr. Bhimrao Ramji Ambedkar (1891-1956), the brilliant leader of India's fifty million untouchables, who was to become free India's first minister of law. The "Poona Pact" agreed upon by Gandhi and Ambedkar on September 26 ended the fast, and kept the untouchables within the general Hindu electorate by promising them far more representatives in all elected bodies than they would have received under Britain's separate electorate offer. Typical of his political "tactics," Gandhi had sacrificed the substance of power for the preservation of principle. Congress Brahmans shook their heads in disapprobation, but The Mahatma had proved himself a true champion of the untouchables, and at the same time a wiser politician than his tough-minded colleagues. Yet he placed little faith in purely political solutions for

[19] Gandhi on September 15, 1931, at the India Round Table Conference (second session), *Proceedings of Federal Structure Committee and Minorities Committee*, p. 17, quoted in *EI & P*, p. 243.

India's multitudinous problems. He knew too much of the real suffering and degradation of India's village masses to accept naïve pana-
ceas like the transfer of power from British to Indian agency. He was
drawn more and more to consideration of the still bewildering problems of rural economy, and a search for some real solution to the
primary problem of poverty. In August 1934 he finally terminated
the second *satyagraha* campaign and resolved to devote himself to
rural uplift work, especially the propagation of hand spinning and
weaving of home-spun cloth. He considered the spinning-wheel a
true symbol of Indian dignity and independence, and daily devoted
himself at least to one hour of this hand labor, insisting that all true
disciples of his must do the same. Though the economic value of this
program is highly dubious, there can be no argument about the psychological value of such labor to peasants who were otherwise obliged
to remain totally indigent each year between sowing and harvest.

The Government of India Act of 1935 was the fruit of many years
of earnest effort, Liberal Indian as well as English, and it became the
constitutional skeleton for both India and Pakistan one decade after
its implementation in 1937. Under this Act a "Federation" of Indian
provinces and princely states was to be established, and though the
latter never joined in the scheme, the "federal principle" was indeed
incorporated as the basis of Indian government. Provincial autonomy
was greatly increased, and instead of dyarchy, fully responsible cabinet government was introduced into all eleven provinces of British
India. There were now to be more than 1,500 elected members in
provincial councils, and the total enfranchised population of British
India was raised to some thirty millions. Dyarchy was extended to
the center, with only such crucial portfolios as revenue, defense, and
foreign affairs "reserved" to government appointees. The viceroy and
governors were still to have a veto over all legislation, but the latter
reached a "gentlemen's agreement" with Congress in 1937 promising
to refrain from resorting to this last vestige of despoitic rule. All legislative councils now had large elective majorities, though the extension of "separate electorates" was seen as a factor mitigating against
the overall power of the Congress representatives. As president of
Congress in 1936, Nehru initially denounced the Act as nothing but a
"new charter of slavery to strengthen the bonds of imperialist domination," [20] but less than a year later he stumped the country as the

[20] Nehru's presidential address at the Lucknow Congress, April 12, 1936, *EI &
P*, p. 248.

foremost campaigner for Congress in the great election of 1937. Congress won majorities in five provinces, and was able to dominate coalition cabinets in two more. The Muslim League, however, amassed less than 5 per cent of the total vote, and no clear majority in any one of four Muslim-majority provinces. With so apparent a repudiation of Muslim communalism by the population at large, it is hardly surprising that Nehru refused absolutely to consider forming coalition cabinets with the League in any province. He failed to take the League seriously as a vital political factor in 1937, thereby commiting what was perhaps the worst political blunder of his career. He had grossly underestimated the power and singular capacity of the League's new leader, Muhammad Ali Jinnah (1876-1949), who after 1937 became the foremost adversary of Nehru and Congress.

Jinnah, who came to be revered as the *Qaid-i-azam* (Supreme Leader) of Pakistan, started his political career as a member of Congress. He had studied law in England as a young man, and was one of the most brilliant barristers of Bombay in the early years of the twentieth century. Urbane and liberal in thought and manner, he was perhaps the last person one might have believed capable of directing a mass political movement destined to partition India. Yet, like Gandhi, he was gifted with charismatic qualities that defy definition. Though he joined the League in 1913, it was more than two decades before he attained a position of dominance within that party. Indeed, after 1921, when he quit Congress in disgust at the multitude of ill-clad, pan-chewing, Hindi-speaking peoples lured into its fold by The Mahatma, Jinnah seemed to have abandoned India entirely for his new home in England, where he lived with his English wife and practiced law. After his wife's death, however, he returned to India in 1934, and dedicated himself heart, soul, and mind to the Muslim League. Perhaps strangest of all was the predominantly cerebral character of Jinnah's mass leadership. His cold, trenchant, arrogant manner was extreme enough to be remarkably attractive. He had no intimates, only dedicated followers and equally dedicated enemies. He had no vices, no petty or selfish ambitions, no point of personal vulnerability whatsoever. Every leader of Congress underestimated him in this regard, for most of them thought he was merely bargaining for position, seeking a ministry in their cabinet, agitating for demands he never truly expected to have fulfilled. They underestimated his drive and singleminded dedication to the cause he made his own. By refusing to negotiate with him in 1937, Nehru drove Jinnah to resort to different means to attain the end that had become the one all-consuming purpose of his life, the creation of Pakistan.

The idea of Pakistan ("Land of the Pure") is of amazingly recent vintage. The name itself was never used before the early 1930s, and though Muslims like Sir Sayyid Ahmad Khan had warned the British as early as 1883 that India's diversity of races and religions would make any simple system of representative government impossible, few Muslims seriously advocated political partition as a necessary corollary of independence more than a decade before 1947. Jinnah's precursor as president of the League, however, Muhammad Iqbal (1873-1938), has justly been honored as the "spiritual father" of Muslim India's new nation. The greatest Urdu-Persian poet of his time, Iqbal was a many-faceted genius—philosopher, lawyer, teacher, and politician—who was educated in Germany, England, and India. In his 1930 presidential address to the League, Iqbal announced that he would "like to see the Punjab, North-West Frontier Province, Sind and Baluchistan amalgamated into a single State. Self-government within the British empire or without the British empire, the formation of a consolidated North-West Muslim State appears to me to be the final destiny of the Muslims, at least of North-West India."[21] Jinnah inherited the task of fulfilling this dream, adding in the process the Muslim-majority half of Bengal.

The years 1937-39, during which Congress enjoyed its first taste of real political power, at least within the seven provinces its ministries controlled, became concomitantly the seed-time for Pakistan. While Hindu ministers acquired invaluable training and experience in the practical direction of public affairs, Jinnah toured the land collecting the grievances (whether legitimate or imagined) of Muslims everywhere, and daily announced from platform and press that under the "Hindu Congress *Raj*" Islam was "in danger." Muslims, who had ignored the communal arguments of the League as long as British officers continued to hold the reins of power, suddenly sensed the validity of Jinnah's warnings as a result of accidental or conscious discrimination or ineptitude on the part of the new rulers in several provinces. The Congress flag now flew from government buildings. The Congress anthem, Bankimchandra Chatterji's (1838-94) *Bande Mataram* ("Hail to thee, Mother"), a poem derived from a novel about Hindu Bengal's fight for freedom from Muslim tyranny, was

[21] From Iqbal, *Speeches and Statements* . . . , pp. 34-36, quoted in de Bary et al, *op. cit.*, p. 767.

now sung on all public occasions. Hindi (not Urdu) became the official language in most provinces. Nepotism, which had always been considered more of a virtue than vice in Indian society, naturally induced Hindu officials to hire more Hindus than Muslims for public positions. Jinnah's "list" of grievances became a powerful indictment against Hindu-Muslim unity.

With the outbreak of World War II a new opportunity arose to help bolster the League's position. On September 3, 1939, Lord Linlithgow (viceroy from 1936-43) declared British India to be at war with the Axis Powers, without bothering first to consult the Congress high command. Though Nehru and other internationally conscious progressive leaders of India personally sympathized with the Allied Powers, Congress considered the viceroy's action so grossly insulting to Indian opinion that the high command ordered all Congress ministers to resign their posts in October 1939. Jinnah himself could hardly have suggested a more beneficial act from the League's point of view. He called upon Muslims throughout the subcontinent to celebrate the abdication of Congress provincial governments as a "Day of Deliverance." He offered, moreover, his full cooperation to the *raj* in its hour of crisis, and the Muslim League was thus able to reap a harvest of natural British gratitude after the war. At the Lahore meeting of the League in March 1940, Jinnah declared that India's Hindu-Muslim problem was "not of an inter-communal character but manifestly of an international one, and it must be treated as such." He called for Partition of India into "autonomous national states" after the war was over, insisting that "any repetition" of the Congress provincial government era of 1937-39 "must lead to civil war." The league then passed its historic Resolution embodying the formula used to partition the subcontinent and create Pakistan, namely:

> that geographically contiguous units are demarcated into regions which should be so constituted with such territorial readjustments as may be necessary that the areas in which the Muslims are numerically in a majority, as in the north-western and eastern zones of India, should be grouped to constitute "independent States" in which the constituent units shall be autonomous and sovereign.[22]

[22] *Parlimentary Papers*, X, *India and the War (1939-40)*, Cmd. 6196, quoted in *El & P*, pp. 354-355.

The viceroy responded cordially to this resolution, and promised that the interests of loyal Muslims would not be ignored by any future British proposals for India.

Congress, on the other hand, returned to the wilderness of non-cooperation, remembering now the bitter aftermath of an earlier World War in which India had given its all to save an ungrateful Empire. In October 1940 Gandhi launched an "individual" *satyagraha* campaign, choosing his most trusted followers to offer symbolic opposition to British martial law. The first of these *satyagrahis* was the saintly Vinoba Bhave, the second Jawaharlal Nehru. By mid-1941 almost 15,000 Congressmen were behind bars. Many members of Congress and more militant Hindu parties, however, were not content with nonviolent opposition, and incendiary underground activity flared throughout India during these war years. The leader of India's pro-Axis faction at this time was Subhas Bose, a militant Bengali patriot twice elected president of Congress (in 1938 and 1939), though because of his open split with Gandhi and the high command he was forced to resign his post in 1939. Bose then organized a party of his own, the Forward Bloc, which became a powerful political force in Bengal. An outspoken advocate of violence against British rule, Bose was arrested in 1940 and kept under house detention until he managed to disguise himself and effect a dramatic escape from India in 1941, fleeing to Berlin via Moscow. Insisting that "Britain's enemy is India's friend," Bose joined the Axis whole-heartedly, beaming daily broadcasts from Berlin to India during 1942-43 in which he called upon his countrymen to join in open revolt against British tyranny. He even organized a "Free Indian Legion" in Nazi Germany, which became a regular part of the Wehrmacht, but there were so few Indians in Europe at this time that Bose was soon obliged to look elsewhere for the manpower of his "Liberation Army." After she captured Singapore in February 1942 and proceeded to overrun all of Southeast Asia, Japan offered far richer opportunities. Some 60,000 Indians among the British garrison on Singapore Island had been surrendered to the Japanese, and over two million Indian civilians were residents, mostly of Burma and Malaya when the Japanese took control of those countries. In 1943 Bose was carried in a German submarine around the tip of Africa and across the Indian ocean to Singapore, reaching his new headquarters in July. He then organized the Indian prisoners of war into an Indian National Army, and in October 1943 announced the creation of a provisional government of "Free India," of which he became head of state, prime minister, minister of war, and minister of foreign affairs. This puppet government of Japan's Greater East Asia Co-prosperity Sphere directly declared war upon Great Britain and the United States, and Bose led his army up the Malay archipelago to Burma and across the Indian border into Manipur state with the battle-cries of "Let's go to Delhi!" and "Victory to India!" By May 1944 the I.N.A. had advanced to Manipur's capital, Imphal, which had it fallen would have opened the road to Assam and Bengal, where Bose was awaited by millions as a liberator. But Imphal held till the monsoon made further action impossible for some crucial three months, after which the tide turned dramatically. By May 1945 the I.N.A. had surrendered at Rangoon. Bose himself escaped on the last Japanese plane to leave Saigon, but it crashed on landing on Formosa, where he died in August 1945.

The fall of Singapore in 1942 and the unexpected swiftness of Japan's advance alerted Churchill's war cabinet to initiate new efforts at winning the active support of Congress. In March Sir Stafford Cripps, leader of the House of Commons and a personal friend of Gandhi and Nehru, was sent to India with Britain's offer, the promise of dominion status for an "Indian Union" to be established immediately after the war. Cripps discussed his proposal with Congress leaders, explaining that a constituent assembly would be elected by provincial legislatures to draft the constitution of the new Commonwealth dominion, but that any province which preferred to do so could "opt out" of the union. Gandhi and Nehru considered this offer of provincial free choice direct encouragement to the League's demand for Pakistan, and absolutely refused to accept. His mission a failure, Cripps returned to London, and shortly after his departure Gandhi coined the slogan "Quit India!" which for British soldiers and officials was the unpleasant equivalent of "Yank, go home!" The "Quit India" campaign mounted in momentum by the end of 1942 and more than 60,000 Congressmen, including the high command, were thrown into jail, where they remained for the rest of the war.

Though politically India's response to the Second World War was far different from what it had been to the First, the economic stimulus provided by wartime demands was much the same. Industry boomed, and inflation brought fortunes to some and hardships to others, hitting Bengal hardest in 1943, where soaring prices of rice intensified the worst famine to plague that region in almost a century. Despite *satyagraha*, the British army was able to recruit some two million Indians by the height of the wartime effort, and a navy and air force were developed in India as well. Britain's financial debt to India mounted to the equivalent of above four billion dollars in sterling balances, thanks to the sudden rise in British demand for Indian imports. Terrorist activity, including the blowing up of railroad tracks, detonation of buildings, and assassination of British soldiers, made the continued retention of India expensive in ways other than purely financial. By 1945 there was growing conviction in England that India had become more of a liability than an asset. With the war's end most Britons were too weary and were confronted with too many burdens of their own to worry about the manifold problems of Empire. The victory of Clement Attlee's Labor Party in July 1945 reflected in good measure Britain's abandoment of the imperial dream. Though Churchill may never have agreed to preside over the "dissolution" of the Crown's overseas domain, Attlee was equally unwilling to preside over its resurrection as a viable reality. In 1946, therefore, the burning question about India for Great Britain was no longer how best to retain her, but rather what was the simplest, fairest, and quickest way to leave.

Elections held in the winter of 1945 under the Act of 1935 revealed the impressive growth of Muslim League power, for League candidates swept the votes of some 90 per cent of the Muslim quarter of India's population. Jinnah rightly interpreted this vote as a popular mandate for his "two-nation policy," and was able now to press more vigorously than ever for partition. In the spring of 1946 Attlee sent a three-man cabinet mission to India to set up machinery for the transition in government, which was by then imminent. The mission, dominated by Cripps, was determined to establish an interim government and secure agreement on the convening of a constituent assembly. The scheme it presented to Congress and the League called for a federal union government compromised of provincial groups, predominantly Hindu and Muslim in population, with the groups of provinces retaining full autonomy except in such matters as defense and foreign affairs. Nehru and Jinnah met at Simla with the viceroy, Lord Wavell (viceroy from 1943-47), but were unable to agree on whether priority should be given to the drafting of the group or union part of the constitution, and whether taxation should be included among the union's powers. Finally, the cabinet mission proposed a settlement whereby three groups would be created out of British India, essentially the two parts of present-day Pakistan and the Indian Union, with princely states allowed to join whichever contiguous group they wished, and provinces given the right to shift from one group to another if their legislatures so voted after the first elections were held. Jinnah accepted the proposal, but Congress hesitated. With each passing hour the British became more impatient with Indian vacillation and division. Nehru was also impatient. Jinnah remained adamant in demanding League parity with Congress on any interim government created to inaugurate the new system. Tempers flared and ego asserted itself on all sides as the moment of freedom drew closer. The basic Hindu-Muslim mistrust remained an unspoken factor at every conference table. Then in August 1946 Nehru informed the press that Congress could not, in fact, accept the cabinet mission's proposals, though many members of the Working Committee had already agreed to do so. Jinnah reacted with cold passion, bidding farewell to constitutional negotiation, and calling upon Muslims everywhere to resort to "direct action" on August 16. During the next three days some 6,000 Indians were killed in Calcutta alone. The year of communal slaughter that rose to crescendo pitch in August 1947 had begun. India's darkest hour was to coincide with the dawn of her freedom.

Lord Louis Mountbatten, Britain's last viceroy and dominion India's first governor-general, was sent out by Attlee to replace Wavell in April 1947. Mountbatten's assignment was to effect the final transfer of power from British to Indian rule by no later than June 1948. After spending more than a century in consolidating their grip over the subcontinent, the British were determined to pull out of India within one year. From their viewpoint, of course, India had become a mental and material drain on British resources, an ungrateful land of sullen and contentious people, who could not agree upon how to rule themselves and were unwilling to accept the aid or advice of others. The haste with which the British withdrew served only to stimulate chaos and facilitate the tragic slaughter that came with the migration of millions from one dominion to the other due to partition. An extra year, even an added few months of careful planning and firm policing of the newly defined borders, might have saved hundreds of thousands of lives, alleviating much of the bitterness which clouded the two new nations' relations from their inception.

By mid-1947, however, everyone but Gandhi was in a desperate hurry. Politicians who had spent much of their lives behind prison bars were eager for the spoils of real power. Officials who had watched their old world crumble were anxious to return home to a land of stability and security. Parliament wanted to be rid of the eternally tangled knots of Indian affairs. On July 18, 1947, the Indian Independence Act was passed at Westminster, ordering the creation of independent dominions of India and Pakistan on August 15, 1947, to be governed by the Act of 1935 until such time as each would decide upon a constitution of its own. A partition commission set to work for a month to divide the homeland and public assets of one-fifth of mankind into three sections. The Northwest, consisting of divided Punjab, Sind, the northwest provinces, and British Baluchistan, was to become West Pakistan. The Northeast, with the eastern half of Bengal, became East Pakistan. The truncated remainder of the subcontinent emerged as independent India.

At midnight on August 14-15, 1947, Prime Minister Jawaharlal Nehru informed his new nation that:

> The task of wresting freedom and ousting the foreign government has been before us till now and that task is now accomplished. But uprooting the foreign domination is not all. Unless and until each and every Indian breathes the air of freedom and his miseries are banished and his hard lot is improved, our task remains unfinished.

The Union Jack was hauled down from Delhi's Red Fort, and India's tricolor raised aloft. The epoch of British rule was over, and that of independent India begun.

SIX

THE NEHRU ERA

Just as Gandhi personified India's Nationalist movement after 1921, Nehru,[1] India's first prime minister, symbolized his nation during its first fifteen years of independent rule. The symbol was often misleading, for Nehru was in many respects atypical of India, and what he represented in word and deed was the ideal, the loftiest aspiration of his countrymen, rather than the reality of their condition. Yet his popularity and power from 1947 through 1962 were unique, and few monarchs or dictators of world history have so affected their governments' world images and policies as did this democratically elected, responsible leader of modern India. The reasons for Nehru's success seem more obvious to Western observers than did Gandhi's. Jawaharlal was, after all, the typical hero-figure of modern times: high-born, wealthy, handsome, brilliant, yet idealistic, self-sacrificing, dedicated to national service rather than individual pleasure; dreamer and doer; the artist with a touch of the poet in his soul, yet a practical man of the world.

A Kashmiri Brahman of Allahabad, the only son of Motilal Nehru, young Jawaharlal, born on November 14, 1889, was enrolled at Harrow in 1905, and two years later at Trinity College, Cambridge, where he took his degree in 1910. In 1912 he became a barrister of the Inner Temple, returning to Allahabad to practice law for some eight years. He joined Congress in 1913, and became a disciple of Gandhi in 1920, following his father as president of Congress in 1929. Intellectually and temperamentally Nehru was more Western than Indian; his mental makeup was a unique mixture of Liberalism, Fabian Socialism, and Marxism, and his personality was dynamic, impulsive, passionate. In some respects he was the antithesis of

[1] See Nehru, *Toward Freedom;* and Michael Brecher, *Nehru. A Political Biography* (London: Oxford University Press, 1959).

148

Gandhi, yet he recognized The Mahatma as the heart of India, and always remained a loyal son of his spiritual father. By the time India attained independence Nehru was fifty-eight, yet his freshness of mind and amazing physical vitality made him seem young. Youthfulness was part of the secret of his appeal and political success. He captured the imagination of India's new generation of intellectuals. He was an inexhaustible political campaigner in a country so vast and so poorly equipped with rapid transport that few men could match his pace. His writings, his speeches, his mere presence, all exuded vigor and fresh life. He cared as intensely about minute details as he did about matters of momentous import. He went everywhere, spoke to everyone, concerned himself with everything. He was one of the great stylists of the English language in modern times, a brilliant public speaker and charming conversationalist. All Indians could identify with Gandhi; most wished they could be like Nehru.

From August 15, 1947 until January 26, 1950, India was a dominion; thereafter she became a totally independent republic. The first months of freedom were darkened by mass migrations to and from Pakistan, economic dislocation, war in Kashmir, and the murder of Mahatma Gandhi on January 30, 1948.[2] Never was so new a nation so quickly burdened with such tragic and weighty problems. An estmiated ten million Hindus, Muslims, and Sikhs crossed the borders of the Punjab and Bengal in a matter of months, with somewhere between one-half and one million killed in the bloody process. The resettlement of immigrants from Pakistan still remained unfinished, especially in Calcutta, after eighteen years of independence. In addition, personal property, public monetary, and natural resource (primarily Indus water) disputes plagued India for more than a decade after partition. The integrated economy of British India was shattered overnight by political fiat. West Pakistan, the bread-basket of the subcontinent, was suddenly divorced from the coal and iron-producing India it had long helped to feed. East Pakistan, the jute plantation for Hughli factories, was arbitrarily severed from the major industrial market for its major product. Landowners in Calcutta were stripped of their property across the newly delineated border. Bombay mill-owners lost their raw cotton supply from Sind. Trade collapsed as tarriff barriers rose like forbidding walls to seal off the new neighboring states from economic intercourse.

[2] For a fictional account of the assassination see Stanley Wolpert, *Nine Hours to Rama* (New York: Random House, 1962).

Internally, India was faced with integrating over 500 princely states into the new dominion. Sardar Patel and his gifted assistant, V. P. Menon,[3] successfully cajoled, convinced, and coerced a multitude of maharajas into joining the new union. Hyderabad and Kashmir, the two largest states, presented the only serious obstacles to this process of peaceful integration. Hyderabad, most populous of the Indian states with over sixteen million subjects, less than 15 per cent of whom were Muslim, was still ruled by the Muslim *nizam* and his noble courtiers. The *nizam* hoped to retain internal autonomy, and refused to sign an "Instrument of Accession" to India for more than a year. Finally, in September 1948, Indian troops invaded the *nizam's* territory to "restore order" there, and in less than a week all armed resistance collapsed. As noted in chapter one, Kashmir proved a thornier problem.

Politically, India's first major objective was to draft a constitution. The Constituent Assembly, convened in December 1946, labored almost three years at this monumental assignment. Nehru himself delineated his nation's constitutional "objectives" in a Resolution presented to the newly formed Assembly on December 13, 1946, affirming that India was to become "an Independent Sovereign Republic"[4] and "Union" of British India and surrounding states, in which "all power and authority" would be "derived from the people." Within that republic everyone would be guaranteed "justice, social, economic and political: equality of status, of opportunity, and before the law; freedom of thought, expression, belief, faith, worship, vocation, association and action, subject to law and public morality." Dr. B. R. Ambedkar, leader of the untouchables, was elected chairman of the drafting committee as proof of Congress' intention to implement fully these democratic and egalitarian objectives. The constitution was approved by the Assembly in November 1949, to be effective from January 26, 1950. A year later India held its first national election, with some 173 millions enfranchised by universal adult suffrage, the largest electorate in world history. Nearly 4,000 seats for elective office were contested by more than 17,000 Indian candidates, representing some sixty different political parties. Though

[3] V. P. Menon, *The Story of the Integration of the Indian States* (New York: Macmillan, 1956).

[4] Speech: Pandit Nehru (extract), December 13, 1946, in *India, 1947-50. Internal Affairs*, ed. S. L. Poplai (London: Oxford University Press, 1959), I, pp. 85ff.

approximately 80 per cent of the enfranchised population was totally illiterate, more than one hundred million Indians took the trouble to vote for their official representatives in an impressive display of national consciousness; for most voters this was the first lesson in democratic process.

With Nehru as its leading campaigner (he personally reached an estimated thirty million people, traveling over 30,000 miles in little more than forty days), Congress won a popular plurality (some 45 per cent of the total votes cast), and impressive majority (362 out of 489 seats) in the ruling lower house of Parliament. As president of its dominant party and prime minister of the republic, Nehru held the reins of power firmly. Determined to use his five-year mandate to good advantage, Nehru led his government in a program of energetic reform, economic and social as well as political.

As an intellectual Socialist, Nehru had stressed the need for governmental direction in economic planning as early as 1931, when he moved the Karachi Congress to pass a resolution calling for nationalization of key Indian industries. Since then Congress was committed to the development of a "Socialist democracy" in India, and in January 1948 Nehru became chairman of the economic program committee of Congress, which laid down the broad policy lines for future planning. In March 1950 a national Planning Commission was created, with Nehru at its head, to draw up a master plan for the "most effective and balanced utilization of the country's resources." During his entire tenure as prime minister, Nehru remained chairman of this Planning Commission. The first Five Year Plan, inaugurated in April 1951, was a fairly modest proposal, calling for an 11 per cent growth in national income by 1956, or an overall increase of from about eighteen to twenty million dollars worth of goods and services. Transportation and communications, especially the grossly depleted rolling stock of India's railroads (heavily overworked during the war), received the largest single share of planned expenditure, though agricultural development was also stressed, above all the need for irrigation through multipurpose dam, irrigation, and hydrolectric projects. For lack of resources, government almost entirely ignored heavy industry until the inauguration of the second Plan. Economic planning was the Indian government's official attack upon the devastating problem of poverty, which at the start of the first Plan kept India's predominantly peasant population of some 360 millions hovering on the brink of starvation. The estimated per capita annual income in

1951 was less than sixty dollars, and for approximately fifty million untouchables and another forty million landless laborers it was far less. Despite concerted national effort, insufficient capital, inadequate concentration of savings, lack of technical skills, mass illiteracy, endemic diseases of every kind and the grinding inertia of poverty all conspired, together with the inexorable growth in population, to hinder any dramatic improvement in the economic situation as a whole. Therefore, though the goals of the first Plan were achieved, Nehru and Congress agreed that the pace was not swift enough. At its Avadi session in 1955, Congress resolved to plan in the future "with a view to the establishment of a socialistic pattern of society, where the principle means of production are under social ownership of control, production is progressively speeded up and there is equitable distribution of the national wealth."

The second Plan (1956-61), therefore, allotted a much larger share (about 20 per cent) of total expenditure to the development of heavy industry and mineral extraction. Nehru never favored sweeping nationalization of existing industry, but rather a "socialization of the vacuum" approach, which in view of India's industrial underdevelopment was, of course, potentially most significant. Private enterprise in India, however, recognized that the Congress government was highly flexible in interpreting the "socialistic pattern" it was resolved to develop, and India's economy, like Hinduism itself, remained singularly tolerant and eclectic. The second Plan's expenditure was to be almost three times that of the first, an estimated ten billion dollars, about half of which was, it was hoped, to come from private investment. The major goals were: an 18 per cent increase in per capita income, to somewhere around seventy dollars per annum; a 150 per cent boost in heavy industrial production; about a 25 per cent rise in agricultural output; and the creation of some ten million new jobs to absorb the equivalent expansion in the labor market during this period. By 1961 the Planning Commission hoped "to rebuild rural India, to lay the foundations of industrial progress, and to secure to the greatest extent feasible opportunities for weaker and under-privileged sections of our people and the balanced development of all parts of the country." Lack of capital and several years of poor rain obliged the government to cut back expenditure in 1958, and the Plan fell short of its anticipated goals. Population pressure proved to be far more serious a drain on Indian resources than anyone in the cabinet seems to have anticipated. V. K. Krishna Menon, for example, a close friend and trusted adviser of Nehru's, who served as ambassador to the United Nations and minister of defense (1957-62) as well as a member of the Planning Commission after 1957, used to counter advise on India's urgent need for more family planning and population control by saying that new Indians were born with two hands capable of work and only one mouth to feed. By 1961 India's population had jumped to about 440 millions; what would have been a 42 per cent per capita income increase for the population of 1951 became only 16 per cent for the new total. Added population meant that the level of Indian unemloyment, perhaps the greatest in the world today, actually increased rather than diminished despite protracted and concerted national economic effort.

By the end of the second Plan India's national income had been raised to the equivalent of about thirty billion dollars. India was able to produce about three and one-half million tons of steel ingots, and fifty-five million tons of coal, but the value of her exports remained little more than about one billion dollars, and without continuing and substantial foreign aid even modest planning on a national scale would have been almost impossible. Congress and Nehru, however, had made the Plans and continued dynamic economic growth under government stimulus the key plank in their platform, and all nations of the world concerned with the preservation of democratic self-government in India, as well as the plight of her vast population, took a vital interest in helping India to help itself. It was generally realized that, although the urgent and compelling problem of Indian poverty is as much an international as an internal Indian problem, its resolution must ultimately be worked out by Indians themselves and that aid must be given freely. Suspicions, doubts, and anxieties are as real a legacy of Western intrusion and British rule for millions of Indian minds as the English language itself. National pride, self-determination, and the importance of self-help are in turn vital and valuable legacies of the Nationalist struggle. Nehru fully appreciated all of these forces in the mental makeup of modern India, and his power within India was based in good measure upon his unique capacity for articulating the "Indian position" to the world at large.

Throughout his premiership, Nehru served as his own foreign minister. Indeed, until 1962 India's foreign policy was primarily Nehru's. He tried to make India a "third force" of nonalignment in a world polarized by the cold war. The pillars of Indian foreign policy in the Nehru era were naturally based on national self-interest, but because of the peculiar nature of recent Indian and indeed world history, they acquired a highly moralistic and often broadly attractive tone. Anticolonialism and antiracism dominated most of Prime Minister Nehru's pronouncements on foreign affairs, and his genuine concern and sensitivity about both were shared by India's intellectual elite. The positive side of these reactions against British autocracy and prejudice was expressed in terms of India's pro-Asian and -African position in world councils, and though Nehru denied any ambitions of ever becoming the head of an Afro-Asian power bloc, he was in fact looked to by leaders in many emerging nations of both continents as their natural spokesman. Even before independence, in March and April 1947, India sponsored an Asian Relations Conference in Delhi, attended by representatives of some twenty-eight African and Asian countries. Early in 1949 India convened a second conference of fifteen African and Asian powers to consider the Dutch "police action" in Indonesia. The following year, Nehru told India's *Lok Sabha* that "The biggest fact of the modern world is the resurgence of Asia." [5] Despite national disagreements and regional as well as cultural differences, there was, he insisted "such a thing as Asian sentiment." At the Afro-Asian Conference of twenty-nine states held at Bandung, Indonesia, in 1955, Nehru played a leading role, though the challenge for Afro-Asian leadership posed by China became more apparent during those sessions through the personal popularity and aggressiveness of Chou En-lai.

Sino-Indian relations became, in good measure, the practical testing ground for Nehru's policy after 1954. In April of that year a Sino-Indian trade treaty was concluded over Tibet which articulated the five principles that Nehru hoped might become the basis of all future agreements among major world powers. Those were: mutual respect for each other's territorial integrity and sovereignty; nonagression; noninterference in each other's internal affairs; equality and mutual benefit; and peaceful coexistence. Here was India's alternative to the martial confrontation and "mutual distrust" of the United States and the Soviet Union. If the two greatest powers of Asia, one governed by the principles of democratic liberalism, the other by communism, could arrive at so equable an international agreement and live up to it, why could not the nations of Europe and America do the same?

[5] Speech in Parliament, March 17, 1950, *Jawaharlal Nehru's Speeches, 1949-1953* (Delhi: Publications Division, Ministry of Information and Broadcasting, 1954), Second Impression, p. 144.

Nehru recognized, of course, that China not only shared much of India's great cultural heritage, but also had experienced a protracted recent period of Western imperial oppression, and hence felt the same revulsion for colonialism and racism. Yet, on the other hand, had not Russia and America, both offsprings of Western civilization, so recently fought as allies against Axis tyranny? Surely the same five principles might apply equally well, if only given a fair trial. From India's vantage point the sole alternative seemed mutual destruction and possible world annihilation. The era of *"Hindu-Chin Bhai Bhai"* ("Indians and Chinese are Brothers") was, however, short-lived, and as noted in Chapter One, Chinese "cartographic aggression" against India's northern tier became a massive military invasion in 1962. The Chinese action profoundly shocked Nehru personally, and was a tragic warning to India. She has since recognized that a treaty of nonaggression alone may not suffice to deter every international aggressive impulse.

Peace was one of the pillars of India's pre-1962 policy, and as the leading Asian power within the Commonwealth, India was able to play a unique mediating role in the settlement of several major world conflicts, including the Korean War, the war in French Indochina, and the conflict in the Congo. India has strongly supported United Nations efforts to secure world peace, and has served on U.N. commissions created for precisely that purpose. India's decision to remain in the Commonwealth has, moreover, helped that remarkable association of free nations to set an example for mankind of the potential for harmonious international intercourse among peoples of the most diverse racial, religious, and cultural backgrounds which may well prove to be the most important historical legacy of British imperial expansion. In view of the primary value Gandhi placed upon *ahimsa,* India's stress on nonviolence as part of her foreign policy is perhaps less surprising than the several instances in which she resorted instead to violent solutions. Though India initially brought the Kashmir conflict before the Security Council for peaceful resolution, recent Indian intransigence on the question of a plebiscite, despite insistence that the "Pakistani aggression" first be "vacated," has reduced that struggle to a stalemate based on military confrontation. Sporadic violence continues along the Kashmir "cease-fire" line, and it may at any time drag India and Pakistan into war. The December 1961 invasion of Goa by Indian troops was another instance in which the Nehru government abandoned its policy of striving to

seek peaceful solutions to international problems. Admittedly, India
had been impressively patient in her negotiations and entreaties to
Portugal for more than a decade preceding the military action. There
was, moreover, understandably strong feeling among India's population at large, as well as perhaps the majority of Goa's more than
600,000 residents, in favor of integrating Goa within the new Indian
Union. After the British withdrawal, lesser European powers, which
had obviously retained toeholds in India by British sufferance, were
expected to follow Britain's example and quit India as well. The
French did so in 1954, when they gave up Pondicherry, their last
and major remaining Indian enclave. The Portuguese, however, stub-
bornly insisted after 1950 that Goa, Diu, and Daman were "integral"
parts of their nation. Since under 2,000 residents of Goa were Portuguese by birth, over 60 per cent were Hindu by religion, and most of
the population spoke Konkani, a dialect of Marathi, as their native
language, Indians had little difficulty in refuting these claims. Within
Goa, moreover, a "liberation committee" led several *satyagraha* campaigns in 1954 and 1955. Portuguese troops were far less considerate
than the British had been, and many of these *satyagrahis* were killed
during their nonviolent demonstrations and marches. Nehru had been
almost alone for several years before 1961 in withstanding mounting
Indian pressure within his own country to move troops across the
hostile border and reclaim by force what had been taken by force
so many centuries ago. As the most outspoken advocate of peaceful
settlement of international disputes in the world at large, India's
prime minister was naturally aware of how damaging to India's
peacemaking prestige any forceable seizure of Goa was bound to
be. Why then did he finally capitulate? Perhaps he was simply
tired of saying no to those who so long urged him to say yes. Perhaps
he abandoned all hope of ever changing Portugal's "state of heart"
on this issue. Possibly he sensed that Congress desperately needed
the acclaim which so popular an action was bound to bring to a
Party that was often and openly criticized within India for having lost the "spirit of the Freedom Struggle" now that it had long
held political power. For whatever reasons, Nehru reversed himself.
India's army moved in and took full control, almost without fighting.
Goa, Diu, and Daman came under Delhi's central administration as
India's newest "Union territory."

Constitutionally committed to the development of a "secular and
welfare" state, the government of India embarked under Nehru's

direction upon a comprehensive program of social reform. Thanks to Gandhi's encouragement, millions of Hindu women had enlisted in the ranks of his *satyagraha* movements, many enduring long prison terms and violence. Nehru's elderly mother had been struck down in a police charge in 1932, only a few years before she died. In 1929 government had taken the first major step since 1891 against infant marriage, by passing the Child Marriage Restraint Act. This Act raised the minimum legal age of marriage to eighteen for males and fourteen for females. After independence, more vigorous legislation was proposed by Liberal leaders of Congress to reform the Hindu Code, and the Hindu Marriage Act of 1955 raised the age of marriageable females to fifteen, made bigamy and polygamy criminal offenses, and introduced divorce initiated by a wife into Hindu law. A year later the Hindu Succession Act gave females, including widows, claims to shares in property inheritance equal to those of their male siblings. The Hindu Adoption and Maintenance Act of 1956, moreover, gave women as well as men the power to adopt children, and called for maintenance of widows as well as separated wives as long as they did not convert to another faith. Orthodox Hindu opposition to these measures was strident, yet Nehru's popularity and the continued power of Congress made their enactment, if not rigid enforcement, possible. In the second national elections of 1957, Congress won a slightly larger percentage of the popular vote than it had amassed in 1951-52, receiving in all some fifty-one million out of 113 millon votes cast.

Partition of the subcontinent had removed one major source of disunity from the Indian scene, yet the linguistic provinces controversy, reflecting a deeper sort of cultural "communalism" within India, soon became a very urgent issue confronting Nehru's government. Viewed from the perspective of history, the concept of national unity for India may be recognized as a relatively recent growth, stimulated greatly by united opposition (predominantly Hindu) to the consolidation of British rule. By and large "Indian" history is the patchquilt product of numerous regional histories, with more of a continental than national character, at least until the nineteenth century. The substitution of English for Sanskrit and Persian as the official language of administration, law, and university education was one of the most important factors facilitating this growth of national awareness among Indians. Until 1920 all sessions of Congress were conducted in English, and even the most ardently anti-British leaders of Congress like Tilak were obliged to use English when they spoke at "Nationalist" meetings outside the linguistic borders of their own region. Gandhi, however, recognized that without a national language indigenous to India Congress would perforce remain the debating society of a minority intellectual elite. Though his own native tongue was Gujarati, The Mahatma sponsored Hindi, spoken by a plurality of Indians, as the national linguistic substitute for English. At the Nagpur Congress in 1920 thousands of Hindi-speaking members attended and listened to speeches in their own language. For every non-Hindi speaker (like Jinnah) who was thus alienated from Congress meetings, hundreds of hitherto apolitical Indians were lured into the arena of struggle. The Congress constitution was revised that same year with some twenty-one provincial committees established along regional linguistic lines rather than existing territorial divisions, thus committing Congress implicitly to the redrawing of India's provincial borders on a linguistic basis. While striving to develop an indigenous national language for India, Gandhi was at the same time eager to attract mass support in all non-Hindi speaking regions by popularizing the Congress program through the major regional languages. The program of national education stimulated substitution of regional languages and Hindi for English in secondary schools and colleges throughout the country. The Indian constitution designated Hindi in the Devanagri script the "official language of the Union," though English would "continue to be used" for all official purposes until 1965. (This time limit has subsequently been removed, and English remains in practice as "official" a national language of India as Hindi.) The constitution also provided for the creation of a special commission in 1955 to study the entire language problem of India.

Those agitating for the creation of new linguistic provinces refused, however, to wait for official action. The Telugu-speaking population of Madras, conscious of its glorious history under the ancient Andhra Empire (which flourished at about the dawn of the Christian era) and chafing under the provinical control of a predominantly Tamil-speaking bureaucracy, launched a vigorous campaign for the administrative separation of *Andhra Pradesh* (Andhra State) from Madras in 1952. Potti Sriramalu, the aged leader of this nonviolent struggle, emulated Gandhi by undertaking a fast-unto-death on behalf of this demand. Sriramalu's death in December 1952 brought a change of heart in Delhi, and within a year Andhra State was born. A "Pandora's box" [6] of regional linguistic demands for the geographical re-apportionment of India had been flung open. The States Reorgani-zation Commission, created in 1955, submitted its proposal for the redrawing of India's internal map in 1956, recommending the crea-tion of fourteen linguistic states. Instead of resolving the divisive regional agitation, however, this report served only to provoke violent agitation in Bombay, where Marathi- and Gujarati-speaking factions were irate at being left under one administrative unit. The Samyukta Maharastra Samiti (United Maharastra Party) and Maha Gujarat Parishad (Great Gujarat Party) launched mass demonstrations call-ing for Bombay's partition along linguistic lines. Political differences were subordinated to regional language loyalties by leaders through-out the state, and the 1957 elections were fought in this region on the overriding issue of linguistic regional loyalty versus national unity. The latter lost, and Congress candidates who called for cool heads in averting factional strife that could lead to India's fragmentation were defeated by a united front of Hindu Communalists, Socialists, and Communists, who made language and regional culture their political battlecry. Bombay was finally divided into Gujarat and Maharashtra in 1960. Similar agitation for the creation of a Punjabi-speaking prov-ince out of the predominantly Hindi-language state of India's Punjab continued unsuccessfully throughout the Nehru era. The central government resisted this demand, while yielding to others, on the grounds that religious communalism, rather than linguistic con-sciousness, primarily inspired the movement and so far has remained adamantly unyielding.

The centrifugal forces of language, religion, and caste, which have so long divided Indian society, were hardly eliminated by the end of the Nehru era. Nehru himself, of course, labored relentlessly to weld India into a unified nation capable of withstanding any and all divi-sive strain. He spoke tirelessly against "all disruptive and fissiparous tendencies," including provincialism and casteism, which he rightly recognized as the most dangerous legacy of India's lengthy evolution. The central Indian Administrative Service, military establishment, and transport and communications facilities under government con-trol were potent forces of unified order which, together with centrally directed economic planning, seemed capable of overcoming any tend-ency toward "Balkanization" of the subcontinent. Nonetheless, by

[6] See Selig S. Harrison, *India. The Most Dangerous Decades* (Princeton: Princeton University Press, 1960).

the closing years of Nehru's life Congress itself was becoming more provincial in character, and its leading lights were the heads of state governments rather than the Central Working Committee. Regional problems, regional languages, and intraregional rivalries had seriously undermined the spirit of national unity by 1962, and paradoxically enough it was China's aggression that reminded India of the importance of maintaining unified purpose and power.

Although he is deservedly called "Father of the Nation," Gandhi's social, political, and economic philosophy tended in the direction of decentralization rather than toward greater administrative unity. Stressing as they did the importance of village self-sufficiency and rural uplift, and advocating the liberation of peasant and rural society from urban industrial dependency, Gandhi's teachings logically implied village autonomy. Several months after his assassination, his leading disciple, Vinoba Bhave, embarked upon a scheme of rural economic reform, called *bhoodan* (gift of land). Vinoba appealed to large landholders for the gift of some portion of their land so that he might distribute it among the landless. His appeal was so simple and singularly Indian in character that he was able to persuade tens of thousands of owners to turn over millions of acres of land voluntarily within less than a decade. Actually, he had more trouble redistributing the land than receiving it, for he worked without an organized cadre of secretaries and accountants. Much of the land he received was, moreover, of marginal utility, hardly sufficing to support the landless laborers resettled upon it. After several years of experimentation with the *bhoodan* movement, Vinoba developed a broader plan, which called for the "gift of a village," so that he might in turn more equably distribute the entire village's lands among those residing within its boundaries. Simultaneously, he asked for the "gift of life" from anyone willing to devote his full time and labors to the Gandhian cause of *sarvodaya* (the uplift of all). Vinoba's saintly character and inspiring personal example (weighing less than one hundred pounds he walked from between five to fifteen miles each day on his foot-pilgrimage) stimulated many prominent public leaders to join his campaign, most famous of whom was one of the founders of India's Congress Socialist Party (and later the Praja Socialist Party), Jayaprakash Narayan. As Vinoba's disciple, Jayaprakash has devoted his life to the rebirth of India along "community" lines rather than those of caste, class, race, religion, or politics, all of which, he insists, "divide men into different, often conflicting, groups." [7] His new philosophy of a "co-operative society," a macro-cosmic extension of the interdependent yet self-sufficient village community, still remains to be tested. It might possibly offer India a unique alternative to industrialized centralization along Western lines or traditional sociopolitical fragmentation.

In 1958 Nehru sought to unburden himself of public responsibilities, hinting that he wished to retire from political life. The uproar of protests and pleas that followed from congressmen throughout India was, however, too great to ignore. Even at sixty-nine Nehru could not escape the yoke of duty which he had so willingly accepted for more than three decades. Who, after all, could fill the many posts he filled nearly so well? The favorite guessing game of Indian tea and cocktail parties—"After Nehru who?"—had been transformed in many circles to a querulous "After Nehru—what?" Like a vast banyan tree, the prime minister's overawing presence seemed by comparison to stunt the development of all those who hovered in the comforting shade of his official family. His vitality remained undiminished. He was reputed to exhaust three personal secretaries daily with his rigorous schedule. Free India was his child. How could he ever abandon it?

By 1962, however, rumors of Nehru's deteriorating health had begun to cause public anxiety. Colleagues closest to the prime minister recognized that their seventy-two-year-old leader's years of service to his country were numbered. Liver and prostate ailments had started taking their toll of the great man's time and energy. The most powerful cabinet ministers began lobbying, it seemed, for national support in their imminent bid for succession to the premiership. Then, in mid-1963, Nehru exploded the political bomb-shell which came to be known as the Kamarj Plan, after its author, Congress President Kumaraswami Kamaraj Nadar. That Plan, ostensibly designed to "revitalize" Congress at the grass roots of provincial organization, called for the resignation of six cabinet ministers of the central government and six chief ministers of state governments. Among those whom Nehru invited to resign were Congress leaders who until August 1963 had appeared most likely to inherit his mantle, especially Finance Minister Moraji Desai, Food and Agriculture Minister S. K. Patil, and Home Affairs Minister Lal Bahadur Shastri. At the state level, Chandra Bhanu Gupta, chief minister of Uttar Pradesh, and

[7] J. Narayan, "The True Community," *Bhoodan* (March 5, 1960), IV, 45, p. 1.

Baksi Gulam Muhammad, chief minister of Jammu and Kashmir, were also relegated to the obscurity of politicians without office. The shake-up in Indian leadership was unprecedented, and augured the meteoric rise in power of Kamaraj himself and Nehru's apparent determination personally to retain control of India's destiny as long as possible. The political demise a year earlier of Krishna Menon, forced to resign as defense minister in the wake of India's unpreparedness to resist Chinese aggression, had removed the leading "left-wing" contender for Nehru's position from power. The Kamaraj Plan removed the leading "right-wing" aspirants, Desai and Patil, and apparently the foremost "centrist" as well, Shastri. It was rumored that perhaps Nehru was grooming his brilliant daughter, Mrs. Indira Gandhi, leader of the Congress "ginger group" and former president of the party, for the coveted job of national leadership. For despite their competence and personal dedication to duty, none of the new leading lights in the late-1963 cabinet seemed capable of commanding the nationwide allegiance required of a prime minister. Indeed, by the end of 1963 all of Mr. Nehru's most probable successors were outside the cabinet.

In January 1964, while attending the Bhubaneshwar Congress, Nehru suffered a stroke from which he never fully recovered. In the immediate aftermath of this paralyzing illness, Nanda and Krishnamachari shared the bulk of the prime minister's duties, but within a fortnight Lal Bahadur Shastri had been recalled to the cabinet as minister without portfolio. Thereafter Shastri assumed a more and more commanding role, both in the cabinet and in *Lok Sabha*, and it was generally believed that Nehru called his then most trusted political lieutenant back into the government for the explicit purpose of preparing him for the work he took over after mid-1964.

Nehru, of whom Gandhi had said, "he is what his name signifies—a 'jawahar,' that is, a jewel," [8] died on May 27, 1964. He was cremated the following day at *Shanti Ghat* (The Steps of Peace) on the bank of the Yamuna at Delhi, some 300 yards from *Raj Ghat* (Royal Steps), where Gandhi's cremation had taken place. More than a million of the bereaved who watched shouted *"Panditji amar rahe"* ("Panditji has become immortal") as the sandlewood flames rose from his pyre. Twelve days of national mourning were officially declared, during which Gulzarilal Nanda served as prime minister of a caretaker

[8] *Times of India* (May 28, 1964), V. CXXVI, 149, p. 16.

government until Congress convened to choose Shastri as prime minister.

The Nehru era, the first seventeen years of free India's growing pains and idealistic adolescence, had come to an end. The legacy of "Panditji," however, remained immortalized in his prolific labors on behalf of India's unity, secularization, and progressive economic development, and in the stirring corpus of his writings as well. His life was something of a modern epic, a heroic human search for purer values, deeper meaning, and social identity. In many ways it was a love story of this man and his people, his nation. True lover that he was, Nehru taught India to see herself, her real and potential greatness and beauty and her faults and blemishes as well. He helped transform India into what she is today, but more important, he set a standard, projected a vision, of what she might one day achieve and become. Let us hope that the nation which has survived his passing might yet fulfill his vision.

The best guide to available studies on India in English is
J. Michael Mahar, *India: A Critical Bibliography* (Tucson, 1964), while
a useful introduction to Indian history for the student and secondary
school teacher is Robert I. Crane, *The History of India: Its Study and
Interpretation* (Washington, D.C., 1958). Comprehensive bibliographies
on India (and indeed all of Asia) are published annually as the fifth number of *The Journal of Asian Studies*.

General Surveys

The best introductory survey of Indian history is W. Norman Brown,
The United States and India & Pakistan, rev. and enlarged ed. (Cambridge, 1963). A more detailed history is T. G. P. Spear, *India: A Modern History* (Ann Arbor, 1962). The volume which long served as Britain's quasi-official primer on Indian history, V. A. Smith, *The Oxford
History of India* was edited by Spear in its revised third edition (Oxford,
1958). The Indian counterpart of Smith's turgid handbook is R. C. Majumdar, H. C. Raychaudhuri, and K. K. Datta, *An Advanced History of
India*, sec. ed. (London, 1950). An excellent supplement to Brown and
Spear is the primary source anthology, *Sources of Indian Tradition*, com-
piled by Wm. T. de Bary et al (New York, 1958). Though dated and
often grossly inaccurate, C. C. Davies, *An Historical Atlas of the Indian
Peninsula* (Oxford, 1954) is still the only available atlas on Indian his-
tory. Other useful surveys include: Jawaharlal Nehru, *The Discovery of
India* (New York, 1946, also ed. with a forward and comments by Robert
I. Crane in pocketbook, Anchor Books, 1960); and W. H. Moreland and
A. C. Chatterjee, *A Short History of India*, third ed. (London, 1953).

The Hindu Heritage

The best brief introduction to pre-Aryan Indus civilization is Stuart
Piggott, *Prehistoric India* (Penguin books, reprint, 1961). Another useful
study of India's early history in the light of archaeology is Mortimer
Wheeler, *Early India and Pakistan to Ashoka* (New York, 1959). There

are several excellent surveys of Indian art, including: Benjamin Rowland, *The Art and Architecture of India: Buddhist: Hindu: Jain*, second ed. (Penguin, 1956); Stella Kramrisch, *The Art of India Through the Ages* (New York, 1954); and Herman Goetz, *India: Five Thousand Years of Indian Art* (London, 1960). For a survey of Buddhism in India, see Edward Conze, *Buddhist Thought in India* (London, 1962). For a brief introduction to the primary sources of Buddhism see *Buddhist Scriptures*, trans. by Edward Conze (Penguin, 1959). Among the richest legacies of ancient India are the delightful animal fables, Sanskrit epics, and classical stories now easily available in fine translations in: *The Panchatantra*, tr. by Arthur W. Ryder (Chicago, 1962); *Tales of Ancient India*, tr. by J. A. B. van Buitenen (New York, 1961); and *Gods, Demons, and Others*, tr. by R. K. Narayan (New York, 1964).

The Impact of Islam

The best brief analysis of Islam in general is H. A. R. Gibb, *Mohammedanism: An Historical Survey*, second edition (New York, 1953). For surveys of Islam in India, see: S. R. Sharma, *The Crescent in India: A Study in Medieval History*, rev. ed. (Bombay, 1954); S. M. Ikram, *Muslim Civilization in India*, ed. A. T. Embree (New York, 1964); Murray T. Titus, *Islam in India and Pakistan*, rev. ed. (Calcutta, 1959); and Wilfred C. Smith, *Modern Islam in India; A Social Analysis*, rev. ed. (London, 1946). Unlike Hindus, Muslims early developed a strong tradition of historical scholarship, and have thus left their own detailed account of the Muslim epoch in India, recently republished in thirty-one volumes as *A History of India as Told by Its Own Historians*, eds. Henry M. Elliot and John Dowson (Calcutta, 1952-59). William H. Moreland has published three excellent studies of Muslim India's economic history: *India at the Death of Akbar* (London, 1920); *From Akbar to Aurangzeb* (London, 1923); and *The Agrarian System of Moslem India* (Cambridge, 1929). The more advanced student of Mughal India should consult S. R. Sharma. *A Bibliography of Mughal India* (1526-1707 A.D.) (Bombay, 1942) for further sources.

British Conquest and Rule

The best history of the early centuries of European expansion in India is W. W. Hunter, *A History of British India* (London, 1899 and 1912), 2 Vols. Among the best surveys of British rule in India are: P. E. Roberts, *History of British India under the Company and the Crown*, third rev. ed. (London, 1952); Edward Thompson and G. T. Garratt, *Rise and Fulfillment of British Rule in India* (London, 1934); and for a briefer survey, C. H. Philips, *India* (New York, 1949). A most useful source book covering the first century of the British epoch is Ramsay Muir, *The Making of British India, 1756-1858* (Manchester, 1923). A provocative anthology of various appraisals of British rule by Indian as well as British authors is *The British in India: Imperialism or Trusteeship?*, ed. with an introduction by Martin D. Lewis (Boston, 1962). In the same series on "Problems in European Civilization" is another excellent work on India, *1857: Mutiny or Revolt?*, ed. with an introduction by A. T. Embree (Boston, 1963). The best introduction to the interrelated economic and political activities of the British East India Company during its early years of power is Holden Furber, *John Company at Work* (Cambridge, 1948). For the intricate operations of the Company at home, see: C. H. Philips, *The East India Company, 1784-1834*, second ed. (Manchester, 1961); and B. B. Misra, *The Central Administration of the East Indian Company, 1773-1834* (Manchester, 1960). There are many biographies and historical monographs of Britain's early rulers in India, including such illuminating studies as: A. M. Davies, *Clive of Plassey* (New York, 1939); Keith G. Feiling, *Warren Hastings* (London, 1954); Penderel Moon, *Warren Hastings and British India* (London, 1947); A. M. Davies, *Strange Destiny: A Biography of Warren Hastings* (New York, 1935); A. Aspinall, *Cornwallis in Bengal* (Manchester, 1931); P. E. Roberts, *India Under Wellesley* (London, 1929); A. T. Embree, *Charles Grant and British Rule in India* (New York, 1962); E. J. Thompson, *Life of Charles, Lord Metcalfe* (London, 1937); W. W. Hunter, *The Marquess of Dalhousie* (London, 1905); D. C. Boulger, *Lord William Bentinck* (Oxford, 1897); and Holden Furber, *Henry Dundas: First Viscount Melville* (Oxford, 1931). Recently a number of excellent monographs on British Indian Intellectual history have been published, especially: Eric Stokes, *The English Utilitarians and India* (Oxford, 1959); George D. Bearce, *British Attitudes Towards India, 1784-1858* (Oxford, 1961); and N. S. Bose, *The Indian Awakening and Bengal* (Calcutta, 1960). The historiography on the Indian War of 1857-58 is legion, but the best histories of this era are among the earliest and latest to be written, one by a British, the other by an Indian, scholar: John W. Kaye, *A History of the Sepoy War in India, 1857-1858*, 8th ed. (London, 1877-1880), 3 Vols.; and S. N. Sen, *Eighteen Fifty-Seven* (New Delhi, 1957).

Crown Raj, Nationalism, and Partition

There is as yet no adequate single history of the last century of British India, though we now have an excellent volume of primary sources covering this era in *The Evolution of India & Pakistan, 1858-1947*, ed. C. H. Philips (London, 1962). There are many useful monographs dealing with special aspects or limited periods of the era such as: T. R. Metcalf, *The Aftermath of Revolt: India, 1857-1870* (Princeton, 1964); S. Gopal, *The Viceroyalty of Lord Ripon, 1880-1884* (London, 1953); and H. Tinker, *The Foundations of Local Self-Government in India, Pakistan and Burma* (London, 1954).

So many books have been written on India's Nationalist movement that a special bibliography of them has been published by J. S. Sharma, *Indian National Congress: A Descriptive Bibliography of India's Struggle for Freedom* (Delhi, 1959). An official history of the Congress was written by B. Pattabhi Sitaramayya, *The History of the Indian National Congress* (Madras, 1935, and 1947), 2 Vols. The government of India has projected a new three-volume history of this movement, but as yet only the first volume is in print, Tara Chand, *History of the Freedom Movement in India* (New Delhi, 1961). A good general survey of Indian nationalism is W. R. Smith, *Nationalism and Reform in India* (New Haven, 1938). The pre-Gandhi era of Indian nationalism is treated in Stanley Wolpert, *Tilak and Gokhale: Revolution and Reform in the Making of Modern India* (Berkeley and Los Angeles, 1962). To date the best post–World War I studies of nationalism are the works of leaders active in the struggle, especially: Jawaharlal Nehru, *Toward Freedom* (New York, 1941); and S. C. Bose, *The Indian Struggle, 1920-34* (London, 1935), and *The Indian Struggle, 1935-42* (Calcutta, 1952). Gandhi's autobiography, *The Story of My Experiments with Truth* (Washington, D.C., 1948) is, of course, an invaluable primary source. The most complete biography of Gandhi is D. G. Tendulkar, *Mahatma*, rev. ed. (Delhi, 1960-63), 8 Vols. A good brief introduction to Gandhi's life is Louis Fischer, *Gandhi: His Life and Message for the World* (Signet paperback, 1954). A most useful anthology of primary source materials from the writings and speeches of leading Nationalists is *The Nationalist Movement: Indian Political Thought from Ranade to Bhave*, ed. D. Mackenzie Brown (Berkeley and Los Angeles, 1961).

The History of Muslim India's Nationalist movement, which led to the birth of Pakistan, is explored in Ram Gopal, *Indian Muslims: A Political History, 1858-1947* (Bombay, 1959); Richard Symonds, *The Making of Pakistan*, third ed. (London, 1951); and K. K. Aziz, *Britain and Muslim India* (London, 1963).

Independent India

The best study of Nehru and his era to date is Michael Brecher, *Nehru: A Political Biography* (London, 1959). Nehru's autobiography, *op. cit.*, is invaluable for Panditji's early years and involvement in the Nationalist movement, and several volumes of Nehru's post-independence speeches are also excellent primary sources for his era, especially: *Independence and After* (Delhi, 1949); *Jawaharlal Nehru's Speeches, 1949-1953* (Delhi, 1954); and *Jawaharlal Nehru's Speeches, 1953-1957* (Delhi, 1958). A useful collection of primary sources dealing with the first three formative years of Indian independence is: *India, 1947-50*, ed. S. L. Poplai (Oxford, 1959), 2 Vols., the first volume treating *Internal Affairs*, the second,

External Affairs. For the story of Princely states' integration into the Indian Union, see V. P. Menon, *The Story of the Integration of the Indian States* (New York, 1956). There are several very good surveys of the government and politics of independent India, particularly: Norman D. Palmer, *The Indian Political System* (Boston, 1962); and H. Tinker, *India and Pakistan: A Political Analysis* (New York, 1962). A number of excellent monographs have recently been published on special aspects of the administrative and political system, including: Myron Weiner, *Party Politics in India: The Development of a Multi-Party System* (Princeton, 1957), and *Political Change in South Asia* (Calcutta, 1963); W. H. Morris-Jones, *Parliament in India* (London, 1957); and Gene D. Overstreet and Marshall Windmiller, *Communism in India* (Berkeley and Los Angeles, 1959). The impact of administration on economic planning is explored in an excellent anthology of articles, *Administration and Economic Development in India*, eds. Ralph Braibanti and Joseph J. Spengler (Durham, 1963); while the interrelationships of political and social forces in modern India are examined in another fine anthology, *Politics and Society in India*, ed. C. H. Philips (London, 1963). A most useful anthology on the varieties of political leadership in India is *Leadership and Political Institutions in India*, eds. Richard L. Park and Irene Tinker (Princeton, 1959).

Of the numerous excellent studies on caste and village India, only a few may be mentioned, especially; John Hutton, *Caste in India*, third ed. (Bombay, 1961); G. S. Ghurye, *Caste and Class in India*, second ed. (Bombay, 1957); Taya Zinkin, *Caste Today* (London, 1962); S. C. Dube, *Indian Village* (Ithaca, 1955); *Village India: Studies in the Little Community*, ed. McKim Marriott (Chicago, 1955); Adrian C. Mayer, *Caste and Kinship in Central India* (Berkeley and Los Angeles, 1960); and William H. Wiser and C. V. Wiser, *Behind Mud Walls, 1930-1960*, second rev. ed. (Berkeley and Los Angeles, 1963). The best study of Indian economic development is Wilfred Malenbaum, *Prospects for Indian Development* (New York, 1962). An excellent analysis of the traditional obstacles to economic progress in rural India is Kusum Nair, *Blossoms in the Dust: The Human Factor in Indian Development* (New York, 1962). The continuing problems associated with linguistic diversity in India and their implications are astutely considered in Selig S. Harrison, *India: The Most Dangerous Decades* (Princeton, 1960). The factor of urban growth and its implications for India's future are dealt with in the anthology *India's Urban Future*, ed. Roy Turner (Berkeley and Los Angeles, 1962). Secularization and its inroads in a predominantly religious society is considered by D. E. Smith, *India as a Secular State* (Princeton, 1963). The impact of English education on India's intellectual elite is explored by E. Shils, *The Intellectual Between Tradition and Modernity: The Indian Situation* (The Hague, 1960). An attempt at historical psychoanalysis of "the Indian mind" is made by G. M. Carstairs, *The Twice-Born: A Study of a Community of High-Caste Hindus* (Bloomington, 1961).

INDEX

Abdullah, Shaikh Mohammed, 28-29
Act of August 1858, 101-102
Act of 1919, 127-128
Act of 1935, 139, 147
Afro-Asian conference, 25, 154
Agni (God of Fire), 32
Agra, 57, 61, 62, 69, 92
Agriculture, 2
Ahimsa, 19
Ahmadabad, 5, 19
Ahmadnagar, 62
Aix-la-Chapelle, treaty of, 74
Akbar ("The Great"), 57-59
Aksai Chin desert, 24
Alam, Shah, 77
Albuquerque, Alfonso d', 65
Alexander the Great, 40
Aliverdi Khan, 75
All-India Trade Union Congress, 136
Allah, laws of, 63
Ambedkar, Dr. Bhimrao Ranji, 138, 150
American Baptist Mission, 89
Amherst, Lord William, 84
Amritsar, 125-127
Andhra, 6
Anglo-French rivalry, 72-75
Anglo-Maratha war, 83
Anglo-Sikh war, 86
Antwerp, 67
Anwar-ud-din, 72
Appleby, Paul H., 13
Aravalli range of Rajasthan, 4, 6

Arthashastra, 40
Arts, 44-46; dance, 44-45; drama, 44; music, 44-45; textiles, 46
Arya-Varta, 6
Aryan conquest, 3-4, 6, 32
Aryan era, 32-33; society classes of, 32; Brahman, 32; Kshatriya, 32; Vaishya, 32
Aryan Society, 116
Ashoka, 40
Asian Relations Conference, 154
Asiatic Society of Bengal, 87-88
Assam, 115
Ataturk, Mustafa, 134
Attlee, Clement, 145
Aurangzeb, 59-60, 61-62, 72
Ava, Court of, 84
Awliya, Nizam-ud-din, 51
Ayub Khan, 28
Azad, 27
Azad, Abul Kalam, 121-122

Babur, Zehir-ed-Din Muhammed, 56-57
Bahadur Shah II, 96-97
Baji Rao II, 83
Baksar, 77
Baksi Gulam Muhammad, 162
Banaras, 4, 52, 97
Banerjea, Surendranath, 112
Baptist Missionary Society, 89
Bara Hoti, 24
Beck, Theodore, 122

171

Bengal, 58, 70, 72, 75-83, 106, 109; Asiatic Society of, 87-88; jute products of, 92; partition of, 115-116
Bengal, Bay of, 31, 69
Besant, Annie, 117
Bharat, 31
Bharatiya Jan Sangh (Indian Peoples') party, 14, 15-16
Bhave, Vinoba, 143, 160
Bhilai, 21
Bhutto, Z. A., 29
Bihar, 3, 11, 34, 70
Bijapur, 61
"Black Hole" prison, 75
Blavatsky, Madame Helena, 117
Bokharo, 21
Bombay, 1, 19, 65, 69, 71-72, 109; division along linguistic lines, 159
Bombay Spinning and Weaving Company, 92
Bose, Subhas, 115, 133, 135, 143-144; creation of "Free India," 144
Boughton, Dr. Gabriel, 70
Bourdonnais, Mahé de la, 73
Brahma Society, 89
Brahman, 32
Brahmaputra river, 3-4
British, *see* Great Britain
British India Association of Bengal, 110
British Indian Association of Oudh, 110
Buddhism, 34-35
Burke, Edmund, 79
Burma, 5, 84-85

Calcutta, 10, 28, 72, 73, 75-76, 84, 89, 92
Caliph, 54
Canning, Lord, 97, 107
Carey, William, 89
Caste Disabilities Act, 93
Central Legislative Council, 119-120
Chandarnagar, 73, 76
Chandragupta Maurya, 40
Charles I, 71
Charles II, 71
Charnock, Job, 72

Charter Act of 1833, 90, 91
Chauri Chaura, incident at, 135
Chenab river, 26
China, Republic of, 24-26; Indian dispute, 24-26; Pakistan treaty, 29
Chinggis Khan, 56-57
Chinsura, 70, 76
Chiplunkar, Vishnu Krishna, 111-112
Chota Nagpur, 5
Chou En-lai, 24
Church Missionary Society, 89
Clive, Robert, 74-75, 76
Coal mining, 21-22
Coen, Jan Pieterszoon, 67-68
Colombo, Ceylon, 25, 65, 68
Commonwealth Conference, 28
Commonwealth of Nations, 8
Communist party, 14, 136
Congress, 113-114; emergence of National Social Conference, 114; resolutions brought before, 113-114
Congress party, 8, 10, 14
Constitution, 11-12
Cornwallis, Charles, 81
Coromandel, 70
Cotton production, 104-105
Courten's Association, 71
Cripps, Sir Stafford, 144, 145
Cromwell, Oliver, 71
Curzon, George Nathanial, 115-116
Curzon, Lord, 114

Dalhousie, Lord James, 86-87, 92, 93; economic reforms of, 92; social reforms of, 93
Dar-al-Islam, 63
Dar-al-Ulum, 121
Das, Chitta Ranjan, 135
Deccan, 7, 58, 62, 106
Deccan Education Society, 111, 114
de Gama, Vasco, 64
Delhi, 19, 24, 50, 56, 57, 62, 76, 96-97
Desai, Moraji, 161
Dharma, 35
Diet, 2
Drake, Sir Francis, 66
Dravida Munnetra Kazhagan (DMK), party, 7

Dravidian language, 6-7
Dufferin, Lord, 113, 119
Dundas, Henry, 80
Dupleix, Joseph François, 73-75
Durgapur, 21
Durrani, Ahmad Shah, 63
Dutch: cartography school, 67; power in Indies, 66-68
Dyer, General Reginald E. H., 126-127

East India Company, 68-69, 71, 77-78, 80, 84, 88-90; dissolution of, 98
East India Railway, 92
Eastern Bengal, 115
Economy, 17-22; coal mining, 21-22; famine, 19; Five-year Plan, 21; religious beliefs affecting, 19-20; steel production, 21; textile production, 22; unemployment problems, 21
Eden, George, 85
Education, 22-23
Elections, national, 150-151, 157
Ellenborough, Earl of, 86
Elphinstone College, 111
England, see Great Britain
Exports, 22, 106
External affairs, 24-29; Kashmir dispute, 26-29; Sino-Indian dispute, 24-26

Famine, 19, 106
Fasting, 38
Fergusson College, 111
Five-year Plan, 21; first, 151-152; second, 152-153
Food and Agriculture Organization of the United Nations, 2
Freedom party, 14, 15
French East India Company, 72-73

Gandhi, Mrs. Indira, 10, 162
Gandhi, Mohandas Karamchand (Mahatma), 1, 10, 14, 35, 36, 105, 115, 123-124; murder of, 149; political rise of, 128-147
Ganga river, 3
Ganges Canal, 92
Gautama, Siddharta, 34

General Service Enlistment Act, 95
Geography, 3-8
Ghazni, 47, 49
Ghulam Mohammed Sadiq, 27, 28
Goa, 65, 66, 67, 69; union into India, 156
Gobind Singh, 52, 60
George III, 80
Gokhale, Gopal Krishna, 14, 111-112, 117-118, 119
Golconda, 61
Good Hope, Cape of, 66
Government, 8-17; Congress, 14; constitution, 11-12; independence from Great Britain, 8; judiciary, 11-12; legislature, 10, 92-93
Grain imports, 2
Gram panchayats (village councils), 13
Grant, Charles, 87
Great Britain: Anglo-French rivalry, 72-75; in Bengal, 75-83; conquest and rule, 64-98; consolidation of Raj, 84-87; legacy of 1857, 101-109; Government of India Act, 101-102; Victoria's Proclamation, 102-103; merchants in India, 68-72; ninety years of rule, 101-147; partition demands, 117-147; dominion status, 124; political communalism, 123; representative apportionment, 122-123; partition from, 117-147; power in Indies, 66-68; "Quit India" campaign, 144; reform and renaissance, 87-93; abolition of trade monopoly, 88; Charter Act of 1833, 90; educational allocations, 88; missionary activity, 88; Penal Code, 91; postal service, 92; public works department, 92; railroad construction, 92; telegraph system inauguration, 92; reforms for Indian autonomy, 135; war of 1857-1858, 93-98; withdrawal from India, 146-147
Gujarat, 5, 58, 62, 69
Gulab Singh, 86
Gupta, Chandra Bhanu, 161
Gupta dynasty, 40
Guptan era, 44-45

Harappan people, 3, 6
Harappan civilization, 30-32
Hardinge, Lord, 126
Hari Singh, 26
Harijans, 19
Harsha Vardhana, 46
Hastings, Warren, 78-80
Himalayas, 3
Hindi language, 4, 142
Hindu Adoption and Maintenance Act
   of 1956, 157
Hindu Khush, 3
Hindu Marriage Act of 1955, 157
Hindu Succession Act, 157
Hindu University, 117
Hindu Widows' Remarriage Act, 93
Hinduism, 35-39, 49-54
Hindus, 3, 17; the arts of, 44-46; Aryan
   era, 32-33; caste system, 6, 7, 16, 17;
   heritage of, 30-46; Buddhist and Jain
   revolt, 34-35; Upanishadic revolt, 33-
   34; polity, 40-42; pre-Aryan era, 30-
   32; society of, 42-44; castes within,
   42-44; female role, 42-43
History, 3-8, 30-46; Aryan conquest, 3-
   4, 6, 32
History of British India, 90
Home Rule League, 117
Hughli, 70, 72
Hume, Allan Octavian, 112-113
Hun invasions, 46
Hussain, Dr. Zakir, 11
Hyderabad, 150

Ibbetson, Sir Denzil, 125
Ilbert Bill of 1883, 108
Ilbert, Sir Courtney, 108
Imports, 22, 105-106
Independence Day (January 26), 137
India Act of 1784, 80
Indian Association, 112
Indian Councils Act of 1909, 118, 119
Indian Independence Act, 147; prob-
   lems attendant to independence,
   149-150
Indian National Army, 144
Indian National Conference, 112
Indian National Congress, 8, 109

Indian People's party, 14, 15-16
Indo-Aryan tribes, 3-4
Indonesia, 7
Indus river, 3-4, 26
Indus Valley, 6; archeology, 30-32; civ-
   ilization of, 30-32
Industry: coal mining, 21-22; steel pro-
   duction, 21; textile production, 22
"Infallibility Decree," 58
Influenza, epidemic of 1918, 124-125
International problems; Chinese fron-
   tier, 2; Kashmir dispute, 2, 26-29
Iqbal, Muhammad, 141
Irwin, Lord, 131, 137
Isaacs, Rufus, 134
Islams, 47-49; and Hinduism con-
   trasted, 49-54; impact of, 47-63; re-
   ligious doctrine, 47-49

Jafar, Mir, 76, 77
Jahan, Shah, 59
Jahangir, 59
Jai Singh, 61
Jainism, 34-35
Jana Gana Mana (anthem), 133
Java, 67
Jesuits, 66
Jhelum river, 26
Jihad (holy war), 28
Jinnah, Muhammad Ali, 140-142, 145-
   146
Jones, Sir William, 87
Judicial system, 11-12
Jute mill, 92

Kabul, 61, 85-86
Kailasantha, 44
Kamaraj, Kumaraswami Nadar, 9, 161
Kamarj Plan, 161-162
Kashmir, 16, 26-29, 58, 86, 150, 155
Kasim, Mir, 77
Kasimbazar, 75
Kerala, 5-6
Khilafat movement, 134
Khurshid, K. H., 28
Konkani, 5
Koran, the, 47-48

Krishna Menon, V. K., 152-153, 162; as ambassador to United Nations, 153
Kshatriya, 32
Kumaon Regiment, 25
Kutb Minar, 53

Ladakh, 24, 25, 26
Lamb, Alastair, 26
Lambert, Commodore, 85
Land, 2-8
Landsdowne, Lord, 119
Languages; Dravidian, 6; Hindi, 4 Marathi, 7
Lawrence, John, 97, 104
Lawrence, Henry, 97
Legacy of 1857: economic burden of, 104; famine, 106; racial antipathy, 106-107
Legislature, 10; lower house (Lok Sabha), 10; upper house (Rajya Sabha), 10
Lhasa, 24
"Liberal Charter," see Charter Act of 1833
Linlithgow, Lord, 142
Literature, 7
Lok Sabha (lower house), 10, 14, 15
London Missionary Society, 89
Longju, 24
Lucknow, 96-97
Lytton, Lord, 108, 111

Macaulay, Thomas Babington, 90, 91
McMahon Line, 24, 25
Madhya Pradesh, 4
Madras, 12, 70, 73, 74, 97
Madras Native Association, 110
Madrid, Treaty of, 69
Magadha, 34
Magellan, Straits of, 66
Mahabharata, 33
Maharashtra, 4-7
Mahasabha party, 136
Mahavira, Vardhamana, 34
Malabar, 5
Malaviya, Mohan, 117
Malenbaum, Wilfred, 21

Malnutrition, 3
Manchester School's free trade policy, 105
Mansabdari system, 58
Marathi language, 7
Martin, François, 73
Masani, 15
Mauritus Island, 73
Mauryan dynasty, 40
Mayo, Lord, 121
Mecca, 48, 49
Meerut, 96
Mehta, Pherozeshah, 112
Menon, V. P., 150
Mill, James, 90
Minto, Lord, 122-123
Mohenjo-daro, 31
Monsoons, 5
Montagu, Sir Edwin, 124
Morley, John, 102, 118
Mountbatten, Lord Louis, 146
Mughal Empire, 47
Mughal rule, 56-63; Akbar ("The Great"), 57-59; Aurangzeb, 59-60; Babur, Zehir-ed-Din Muhammed, 56-57; Jahan, Shah, 59; Jahangir, 59
Muhammadan Anglo-Oriental College, 122
Muhammadan Literary Society, 122
Munda linguists, 5
Murshidabrad, 76
Muslim League, 122-123, 136, 140
Muslims, 3, 47; administration during sultanate, 54-56; ruling dynasties during three centuries of sultanate, 54-55
Mysore, 6

Nadir Shah, 62
Nagaland, 12
Naidu, Sarojini, 132
Nair, Kusum, 19
Naoroji, Dadabhai, 112
Narayan, Jayaprakash, 160-161
National Cadet Corps (NCC), 25
National problems; poverty, 2; unity retention, 2

National Social Conference, 114

Nationalism, first phase, 109-117; Bengal partition, 115-116; economic exploitations, 112; emergence of National Congress, 113-114; restoration of ego, 117

Nehru, Jawaharlal, 1, 14, 24, 28, 40; foreign policies of, 153-154; as president of Congress, 136-137, 139-140, 145-146; as prime minister, 147-163

Nehru, Motilal, 127, 135

Nepali Gurkhas, 84

Netherlands Indies, 67

Nicholas I, Tsar, 85

Nicholson, John, 97

Nizam-ul-Mulk, 62

North, Lord, 78

North-East Frontier Agency (NEFA), 24, 25

Olcott, Henry Steel, 117

Ootacamund, 29

Ormuz, 69

Oudh, 79; annexation of, 94

Pakistan, 2, 3, 10, 47, 50, 86, 123, 149; creation of, 141-142; independence of, 147; and Kashmir, 16, 26-29; treaty with China, 29

Palmerston, Lord, 85

Panchayati raj, 12-13

Panipat, 62-63

Patel, Sardar Vallabhbhai, 134, 150

Paterfamilias, 18

Patil, S. K., 161

Patwari, 21

Penal Code, 91, 114

Peninsular India, 5-6

People, 2-8

Phadnis, Nana, 83

Philip II, 66

Pipal tree, 31

Planning Commission, 21, 151, 152

Plassey, battle of, 62, 76, 77

Politics, 8-17; Bharatiya Jan Sangh (Indian Peoples') party, 14, 15-16; Communist party, 14; Congress party, 8, 10, 14; Socialist party, 14, 15; Swatantra (Freedom) party, 14, 15

Pondicherry, 73-75, 156

Poona, 111

Poona Public Society, 110-111

Population, 2; expansion problems, 152-153

Portugal; occupation of Goa, 155-156; power in Asia, 64-66

Postal Service, 92

Prasad, Rajendra, 11

Pre-Aryan era, 30-32

Presidency College, 93

Presidential election, 11

Presidential powers, 11

Public Works Department, 92

Pulicat, 70

Punjab, 125-126; Colonization Act of 1907, 125

Radhakrishnan, Dr. Sarvepalli, 11

Rai, Lala Lajpat, 125

Raj consolidation, 84-87

Rajagopalachari, Chakravarti, 15

Rajasthan, 4, 12

Rajputana, 106

Rajya Sabha (upper house), 10

Ramadan fast, 49

Ramayana, 7

Ranade, Mahadev Govind, 111, 114

Rangoon, 84

Ranjit Singh, 84

Rashtriya Svayamsevak Sangh (National Self-service Society), 136

Ravi river, 26

Regulating Act of 1773, 78

Regulations of 1793, 81

Republic of India, 8

Rezang La, 25

Robinson, George Frederick, 108

Roe, Sir Thomas, 69

Rohilla Afghans, 79

Rourkela, 21

"Rowlatt Acts," 125

Roy, Manabendra Nath, 136

Roy, Ram Mohun, 89, 109

St. George fort, 70
St. Thomé, battle of, 73
Saltpetre, 70
San Filippe, 66
Sayyid, Ahmad Khan, 122
Scoble, Sir Andrew, 114
Sèvres, Treaty of, 133
Shaitan Singh, 25
Shamsuddin, Kwaja, 27, 28
Shanta-rasa, 4
Shastri, Lal Bahadur, 1, 10, 28, 161-162; political background, 8-9
Shivaji Maharaj, 61
Shudras, 6
Shuja-ud-daula, 77
Siberia, 3
Simla, 24
Sindhia, Mahadji, 83
Singapore, 65, 143-144
Sinkiang province, 24
Sino-Indian dispute, 24-26
Sino-Indian trade treaty, 154
Sino-Pakistan treaty, 29
Siraj-ud-daula, 75, 76
Smythe, Thomas, 66
Socialist party, 14, 15
Society, 17-22; caste system in, 17-18; female role in, 18; *harijans*, 19; Hindus, 17-18
Spanish Armada, 66
Spice Islands, 67-68
Srinagar, 26, 28
Sriramalu, Potti, 158
States' divisions, 12
States' jurisdiction, 12
States Reorganization Commission, 159
States, union of, 12; district councils, 13; division of, 12; jurisdiction, 12
Steel production, 21
Story of My Experiments with Truth, The (Gandhi), 129
Suez Canal, 106
Sufism, 48, 51
Sumeria, 31
Supreme Court, 11
Surat, 68, 69, 73
Swarajist Party, 135-136

Swaran Singh, 9-10, 29
Swatantra (Freedom) party, 14, 15

Tagore, Debendranath, 89
Tagore, Rabindranath, 133
Taj Mahal, 59
Tamil, 7
Tata Iron and Steel Company, 124
Tata, Sir Jamsetji, 15, 116
Tea industry, 92
Tegh Bahadur, 60
Telegraph system inauguration, 92
Textile production, 22
Thar Desert, 4
Theosophical Society, 117
Tibeto-Burmans, 84
Tilak, Bal Gangadhar, 14, 38-39, 61, 111-112, 114-115, 119
Todar Mal, 58
Tuberculosis, 3
Tungabhadra Project, 5
Tughluq, Firuz, 55
Turko-Afghan dynasties, 47

Unemployment problems, 21
United East India Company, 67
United Nations Food and Agriculture Organization of, 2; V. K. Krishna Menon as ambassador to, 153; Security Council of, 27, 155
Upanishadic revolt, 33-34
Urdu language, 53
Urheim, 4
Uttar Pradesh, 3-4, 24; Congress, 9

Vaishya, 32
Varna, 6
V*edas*, books of Aryan canon, 32; *Atharya*, 32; *Rig*, 32; *Sama*, 32; *Yajur*, 32
Vereenigde Oostindische Compagnie (V. O. C.), 67
Vernacular Press Act, 111
Victoria's Proclamation, 102-103, 107
Vidyasagar, Pandit Ishwara Chandra, 93
Vindhya-Satpura mountains, 5, 6
Vindhyas, 6

War of 1857-1858, 93-98; causes of: annexation of Oudh, 94; enactment of General Service Enlistment Act, 95; rebellion at use of greased cartridges, 95-96
Wavell, Lord, 145
Wellesley, Richard Colley, 82-83, 84
West Bengal, 3, 28
West Pakistan, 47

Western Ghats, 5
White, Jr., Lynn, 45
World War I, 123-125
World War II, 142

Yamuna-Ganga river, 3-4
Yoga, 51
Zamindars, 20
Zila parishads (district councils), 13

The Modern Nations in Historical Perspective Series

ARGENTINA, Arthur P. Whitaker—S-601

AUSTRALIA, Russel Ward—S-610

THE BALKANS, Charles Jelavich
and Barbara Jelavich—S-611

CENTRAL AMERICA, Mario Rodríguez—S-609

CEYLON, Sinnappah Arasaratnam—S-603

CHINA, Kenneth Scott Latourette—S-607

CUBA, HAITI, & THE DOMINICAN REPUBLIC,
John E. Fagg—S-615

FRANCE, John C. Cairns—S-617

INDIA, Stanley Wolpert—S-613

INDONESIA, J. D. Legge—S-606

ITALY, Massimo Salvadori—S-612

MOROCCO, ALGERIA, TUNISIA, Richard M. Brace—S-604

NEW ZEALAND, William J. Cameron—S-608

NIGERIA AND GHANA, John E. Flint—S-618

THE PHILIPPINES, Onofre D. Corpuz—S-616

RUSSIA, Robert V. Daniels—S-602

SCANDINAVIA, John H. Wuorinen—S-614

VENEZUELA AND COLOMBIA, Harry Bernstein—S-605